6 724 960 000

A Life
Without Limits

A Life
Without Limits

Chrissie Wellington
with Michael Aylwin

Constable • London

To my family. My foundation.
My victories are also yours.

Constable & Robinson Ltd
55–56 Russell Square
London WC1B 4HP
www.constablerobinson.com

First published in the UK by Constable,
an imprint of Constable & Robinson Ltd, 2012

A copy of the British Library Cataloguing in
Publication data is available from the British Library

ISBN: 978-1-84901-713-8 (HB)
ISBN: 978-1-78033-671-8 (TPB)

Printed and bound in the UK

1 3 5 7 9 10 8 6 4 2

Contents

Acknowledgments

My life has been shaped by so many amazing people. I have been able to include many of you in this book, but by no means all. I am indebted to each and every one of you for your unconditional friendship, advice, tough love, inspiration and guidance.

In particular, I want to give thanks to my wonderful mum and dad, my brother and sister-in-law, my grandparents, my aunt and uncle and cousins for providing me with a family cocoon of love, support and encouragement; to Tom for teaching me the meaning of true love; to my friends around the world, most of whom have known me long before triathlon, and whose support means more to me than they could ever know. To Brett for trusting in me and in himself when all around might have doubted, to Dave for refining me into the athlete I am today and to Frank Horwill, Don Feltwell and Jon Sadler who taught me always to try and never to stop believing in the power of my dreams. Since the writing of this book, Frank has sadly passed away. He was a true legend in British athletics, and his loss leaves a large hole in the sport, as well as in the lives of so many athletes, mine included.

To Paul Robertshaw and all at the BRAT Club, as well as my first triathlon coach, Tim Weeks, for introducing me to this wonderful sport and in so doing changing my life beyond recognition. And to my manager, Ben, for showing me that it can be 'show-friends', not simply 'show-business'. Of course, my incredible sponsors deserve a special mention. You know who you are, but, in particular, I'd like to thank Ryan and Matt at TYR, who have been there from the start, and Brooks, Cannondale and CytoSport – our long-term partnerships have powered me to heights I could never have imagined.

We are privileged in triathlon to have our sport driven by the most enthusiastic and inspiring participants, both the spectators and the competitors of any age or ability. I am constantly inspired by the time and energy people devote to the sport, as well as by the emails and tweets I receive in the way of personal support. On race day, sharing the highs and lows with so many thousands of age-groupers is always a joy. But a special thanks, too, to my professional competitors and training partners, whose talents have given me the kick up the butt to be the best I can be and whose generosity of spirit knows no bounds.

I would also like to thank the charities for which I am honoured to be a patron, including Jane's Appeal, The Blazeman Foundation for ALS, Challenged Athletes Foundation, Envision, Girls Education Nepal and GOTRibal. I am honoured to be involved with your wonderful work and will do what I can to support you in whatever ways I can.

For the production of this book, my deepest gratitude goes to Andreas Campomar and Nicola Jeanes of Constable & Robinson, Rolf Zettersten and Kate Hartson of Center Street, Jonathan Conway of Mulcahy Conway Associates, Jonny McWilliams of the Wasserman Media Group and to Michael Aylwin for enabling me to put my life into words.

Your support has enabled me to live a life without limits and for that I am so sincerely grateful.

Foreword

I'd been cycling at a steady pace for nearly a hundred miles. The barren road knifed through thick, black lava fields that tolerated little in the way of life among their rocks. Every now and then a bougainvillea bush would appear in splendid isolation on the roadside, but otherwise I had just the long white line I was following on the side of the road for company. The tropical sun was high overhead, so high that my bike and I cast barely any shadow. And the road stretched out ahead of me, now empty of cyclists. I was in the lead.

I took a moment to allow this to sink in. I wasn't sure who the two girls I'd just passed were, because I knew barely anyone in this race. It might have been the World Championships of the most gruelling single-day event in sport, but this was all new to me. The Pacific Ocean was royal blue to my right, and to my left rose the volcano of Hualalai, shrouded in cloud. If you're lucky, the cloud cover extends down to the coast, but we were having no such luck, and the heat hung over the tarmac like a wicked spirit distorting the way ahead.

It was just past midday. Five and a half hours earlier our race had begun in the waters of that ocean. If everything went well, I could expect another four until the finish line. Officially it was up past ninety in the shade, but out here on this stark naked road it was over 100. And the wind was ferocious. Coming down off the volcano, it had already forced me once onto the rumble strips at the side of the road. It was frightening to cycle in such a crosswind, but it stripped you bare as well. This was like racing in a blast furnace. In a couple of hours' time I would be back out here, this time on foot, well into the marathon that completes the day's activities. By then it would be even hotter. Would I still be in the lead?

This was an ironman triathlon, *the* Ironman Triathlon. Every October, the World Championships of the sport are held in Kona on the Island of Hawaii. An ironman is the longest distance of triathlon – a 2.4-mile swim, 112 miles on the bike, and then you run a marathon.

Unbeknown to me, four previous champions had by now dropped out of the race. In an ironman, even the world's best face a challenge just to finish. I was in pole position. This didn't seem real.

I don't think I'd ever struck anyone as obvious world-champion material. For a start, there's my nickname. It's Muppet. And, yes, it's for pretty much the reasons you would think. I have always been accident-prone and low on common sense. I was sports-mad as a kid, but there was no sign of any unusual talent.

But I've also been driven, for as long as I can remember, by a fierce determination to make the best of myself and to try to make the best of the world around me. Eight months earlier, I had given up my job in the Civil Service to become a professional triathlete. International development was my passion, but when bureaucracy and red tape started to get me down, sport offered itself as the perfect way to get things moving again – both in terms of my own development and my ambitions to help others. I have seen how sport can empower people and cross boundaries.

It has always empowered me, but only now, with that road stretching clear ahead of me, did I start to sense what a chance I had. The girl who had come from nowhere, the muppet who had taken the lead! I had to make sure that this was just the beginning. There was a hell of a long way still to go, so much more to overcome. But if I could do it . . .

1

The Ironman

The ironman. Just the name excites me. It is one of the most awe-inspiring events in sport. I fell in love with it the first time I attended one – and that was as a mere spectator, less than five months earlier.

It's a question of scale. Biggest is not necessarily best, they say, but it is when it comes to endurance sport. There is a special mystique about the marathon, for example, because of its length – but that's just the bit you do at the end of an ironman.

That first taste I had of an ironman was in June 2007, at Ironman Switzerland in Zurich. I was there because the day before I had competed in, and won, an Olympic-distance triathlon (in length, less than a quarter of an ironman). Immediately, I realised that the ironman was the main event. The sense of occasion had risen with the length of the race.

There is a special buzz that hangs in the air, like when the best team in the world comes to town. The occasion inspires extraordinary things in people – extraordinary excitement in those watching, extraordinary levels of performance from those competing.

But what raises ironman above other sports is the visceral nature of the contest against a fixed and unyielding foe: the contest against the race itself. You see humanity at its rawest, at its best and its worst.

The ironman brings that out in you. Finishing it is a victory. People vomit at the side of the road, they lose control of their basic functions, they collapse, they become delirious, desperate to reach the finish line, when sometimes that finish line is still miles away. It evokes such emotion and requires you to dig to the depths, physically and mentally. And then there is the euphoria and relief of making it to the end. Inspirational is the only word to describe it. You don't get that from a game of cricket or football.

The first ironman triathlon took place on my first birthday, 18 February 1978. It started life as an argument. Who were fitter, runners or swimmers? The debate raged around one table at an awards ceremony after a running race on Oahu, Hawaii. John Collins, a US Navy commander, threw cyclists into the mix, having read that Eddy Merckx, the Belgian cyclist, had the highest oxygen uptake of any athlete ever measured. There and then, it occurred to him that, if they combined the Waikiki Roughwater Swim, the Around Oahu Bike Race and the Honolulu Marathon, they would have the perfect test to settle the argument. The first to finish would be called the Ironman. He leaped onto the stage, grabbed the microphone and proclaimed his idea. They laughed at it.

Nevertheless, a year later the first 'Ironman' was contested by Collins and his friends. Fifteen competitors started; twelve finished. The winner was Gordon Haller, a taxi driver, completing the 140.6 miles in a little under twelve hours. Collins finished in seventeen hours.

The following year's race attracted the attention of a passing journalist, who wrote an article for *Sports Illustrated* describing what he saw. This inspired hundreds to compete in 1980. In 1981 the race was moved from Oahu to its current home, the less-populated Hawaii Island, or 'the Big Island', as it is fondly nicknamed. The US network ABC expressed an interest in covering the race. And in 1982, its legend was sealed.

That year, a young student called Julie Moss decided to compete in the Ironman as part of the thesis for her degree in physical education. Apart from a passion for surfing, she had little experience of competitive sport, but, incredibly, she found herself leading the women's race by mile eight of the marathon. The longer she held the lead, the more determined she became to win – and the less able to carry on. With each step she was reaching deeper and deeper inside herself.

She collapsed for the first time a few hundred yards from the finish. She managed to get back to her feet and carry on, with the nearest female competitor still a few minutes behind, but her body was shutting down. The crowd formed a tunnel, urging her on, while volunteers rushed to her aid. She fended them off, knowing that their support would disqualify her. Night had fallen, and the merciless lights of the ABC cameras captured her struggle. She collapsed again only twenty yards from the line. Volunteers tried to lift her to her feet, but she would not be helped. At that point, Kathleen McCartney, the second-placed female, ran past, oblivious, and trotted to the finish line where she was pronounced champion. Moss crawled the remaining yards to the line on her bloodied hands and knees, reaching it twenty-nine seconds later, after more than eleven hours of racing.

It was a drama that captured the imagination of millions of Americans and has become a part of the sport's folklore. Now ironman races proliferate around the world. The original race has turned into the annual World Championships, contested by 1,800 athletes, cheered on by thousands of spectators in Hawaii on the weekend of the first full moon in October. More than 50,000 hopefuls try to qualify for it each year.

The buzz at any ironman, let alone the World Championships, is palpable. Among the athletes it is born of a nervous excitement about what might lie ahead. For the elite the question might be, will I win today? But, even for them and certainly for everyone else, the main question is, will I finish and at what cost? Even if your body does not break down through sheer fatigue, there is ample scope for an unsuspected injury, be it in the mass brawl that is the swim, the high-speed road race on the bike, or the relentless pounding of the streets as you drag yourself through the marathon. The effects of any illness are magnified in bodies that are being pushed to their limit. And then there is the perennial threat of mechanical failure on the bike, gastro-intestinal dehydration or overheating.

As a result, the rituals of the ironman athlete are meticulous. From the pre-dawn breakfast, it is down to the start with hundreds of other athletes to begin the extensive application of Vaseline. It pays not to stand on ceremony. Chafing is one of the ironman athlete's worst enemies. It may not stop you, but it hurts like hell, mostly round the crotch, the underarms and the nipples. These areas need copious amounts of lubrication. The less shame you have about it the better for your race.

Ideally, you take to the water and warm up about fifteen minutes before the start. Ironman swims are almost always conducted in open water. The temperature determines whether you are allowed a wetsuit. As the start approaches, you scull in the water, lying on your front, staying afloat, waiting for the gun. At some races, as in the tropical waters off Hawaii, this can be one of the most beautiful, sublime moments of your year – certainly of your day.

Then the gun goes off, and all hell breaks loose. The idea is to get 'on the feet' of the fastest swimmers, in other words to move in behind them and take advantage of their slipstream. It is, effectively, a fight. Limbs flail and can catch you anywhere on your person. People might swim over the top of you. The water churns up, making it difficult to breathe. If the sea is choppy it is worse still. You are in a washing machine.

For the elite, this will go on for around an hour. For anyone who wants to continue beyond the swim, it must not go on for more than two hours and twenty minutes. Here is another cruelty to contend with – the cut-off times. If you do not complete the 2.4-mile swim in that time, you are not allowed to continue. The same applies to the other two disciplines. If you are still cycling ten and a half hours after the start, you must stop. And at midnight, seventeen hours after the start, the officials head out onto the course to round up those still pounding the streets to tell them they haven't made it.

The resultant scenes are heart-rending. You might think that people would feel relieved to be spared further punishment on a course that is so clearly beating them, but no, that is not the ironman way. They are distraught, inconsolable that they will not be allowed to finish what they had started, not just a few hours earlier when they began the race but years earlier when they began to dream. Everybody has their own reason for taking on an ironman; nobody enters into it with anything less than all their heart.

Once you've found your bike in the area known as 'transition' (this should take you around two minutes), it is out onto the open road, where the best will take the next four and a half to five hours to complete the 112-mile bike course. The sun rises ever higher during this stage. In hot countries, this is when the race becomes truly punishing. But rain brings its own problems too, and wind, particularly when combined with either of the above, can play havoc. A tailwind is all right, but riding into a headwind is much the same as riding up a hill. Crosswinds are even worse. If they are strong enough they are quite unnerving, making the bike difficult to control and sometimes blowing you off the road.

It is on the bike that you may first develop a need for the toilet. Again, it pays not to be squeamish. There is the occasional Portaloo on the course, but the most time-efficient solution, I find, is to go in my pants. If you're on the run, a quick crouch over a roadside ditch is acceptable. But on the bike, unless a flat tyre causes a natural break, going on the saddle is the best way. This is when the earlier application of Vaseline really comes into its own. And don't underestimate the use of urine as a weapon. On the bike it is forbidden to take advantage of someone's slipstream, even though it is allowed in the swim. We call it drafting. To get too close to the bike in front is not only dangerous but cheating. There are a series of official penalties for anyone caught doing it, but people still do. If anyone does it to me, I let off a warning shot, and they usually back off. It is yet another reason to keep yourself hydrated.

The final leg is when even the best start to wrestle with their demons. After 112 miles sitting on an unforgiving saddle, crouched low over the handlebars to maximise your aerodynamics and pumping your legs remorselessly, taking to your feet for the marathon can be a strange sensation. Your legs will feel like jelly for the first few minutes, but that will pass. Soon they will feel like lead.

It is impossible to swim, bike and run for the best part of a day and not experience bad times. Illness, dehydration and physical niggles, not to mention full-blown injuries, come and go throughout. There is also the mental anguish – that long road stretching out ahead of you, the landmarks that just won't come quickly enough. You can't listen to music; you have only the throb of blood through your head for company, and the screams of every unthinking fibre in your body that they want to stop. This is when the mind must take over. Ironman is as much a mental game as a physical one.

Everything is redeemed, though, by the sight of the finish line. The crowds, whose exhortations around the course lift many a flagging body and soul, focus all of their energy around the final few yards. Whether you finish first or 1,001st, they make you feel like a champion. Your body may be wrecked, muscles cramping, skin chafing, toenails falling off and feet blistering, but you have joined a special club. After all of my races, I stay at the finish line all night to welcome people home. I wouldn't want to be anywhere else. We professionals do nothing but eat, sleep and train for these events, but it's the thousands who take on an ironman for the love of it who inspire me the most.

Julie Moss was the first great hero of the sport, but there have been countless others since, and most of them get nowhere near the podium. People fighting old age, illness and disability, those recovering from horrific injury, others simply wrestling with the demands of a day job – these are the heroes of ironman.

Sport has a unique ability to inspire and empower. If used correctly, it can be such a force for good. Ironman is a relatively new pursuit and, although it grows exponentially each year, it is still a 'minority' sport. Maybe this freshness is what gives it its energy, but there is something about its gruelling nature, as well, that inspires people to find the best in themselves and in each other. Because, make no mistake – that is what it does. The ironman walked into my life quite suddenly, and changed it for ever.

2

Out of Norfolk

It's at this point in a sporting autobiography that the author traditionally launches into an account of the brilliant athletic achievements of their youth, of how they were always destined to become a professional athlete. Unfortunately, I have no such tale to tell.

I did play wing attack in the Downham Market High School netball team that won the Norfolk Schools Championship in 1993. And I wasn't a bad swimmer. I won the odd race at the Thetford Dolphins Swimming Club, although Julie Williams would usually beat me.

And that's about it in terms of sporting achievement for the first twenty-five years of my life. Mine really is the story of the accidental athlete. When your nickname is Muppet, the chances are you are not a child prodigy.

But if there was one thing that marked me out as unusual it was my drive. I would go so far as to describe it as obsessive-compulsive. I have, and always have had, the most powerful urge to make the best of myself. At times I have not been able to control it; at times it has taken me to some unpleasant places; but it is also an essential part of who I am, and I cannot make any apology for this.

My early sporting career might have been modest, but my academic career was more impressive. I attribute that to my determination, as I do the success I enjoyed as a civil servant in my career before triathlon. But, as a sensitive soul who has always worried – too much most of the time – about what other people think of her, this obsession with self-improvement has often spilled into other less positive preoccupations.

My relationship with my body has been a difficult one over the years. At times I have loved it, at times I have despaired of it, at times I have seen it as little more than a plaything to be bent to my will, as if it were somehow separate from me.

It's a control thing. I am a control freak, basically. Which is good and bad. If there is something you don't like about your life, then to me it is perfectly possible and logical to change it. That's the good side. The bad side is that hideous feeling of panic and anger when you come up against something you can't control. And then there is the danger that the idea of being in control itself gets out of control, so that it becomes an end in itself and causes you to lose sight of everything else. Addiction might be another way of putting that.

I have an addictive personality. Sport is my drug of choice these days. It's one of the best drugs there is. It keeps you fit and healthy, even if, in the case of ironman, it pushes your body to the limit. The word 'addiction' comes with negative connotations, but it doesn't have to be a damaging impulse. It's all about channelling your craving into something positive. Family, friends and coaches are invaluable sources of objectivity, able to know you in a way you can never know yourself – from the outside – and able to look out for signs of negative addiction that you may be unable to recognise. But in time you get to know yourself, and with a better understanding of yourself comes the ability to modulate the highs and lows. More of the control, less of the freak.

I love my body now, not because I like what I see in the mirror particularly, more because I no longer look in the mirror and see just contours of flesh and colour, there to be scrutinised and manipulated. Now I see my body as a holistic system that enables me to do what I do. More importantly, I see it as bound up intricately with *me*, enabling me to be who I am. That change has been a gradual one, but it is sport that helped me to initiate it and certainly to consolidate it. Which is strange – or maybe it's not – because, as much as I have always adored sport, it used to be the one area of my life where I'd let myself off the drive for self-improvement. It was simply a way of making friends, which is its beauty, no matter how good you are at it.

I have barely any sporting pedigree. My paternal grandfather, Harry, was a keen cricketer and cyclist. On a weekend he would think nothing of cycling from London to Southend. But neither of my parents, Lin and Steve, have ever shown any passion for competitive sport. They have always loved the outdoors – so much of our family life was spent in the fresh air – but I know of no sporting ambitions before or after my brother, Matty, and I came along. Even if they had harboured them, there would have been no time to indulge, what with all the ferrying around they had to do, taking Matty and me to this and that. Because I might not have shown any exceptional talent, but I was mad about sport. I was mad about everything.

My overwhelming memory of childhood is of a happy one. I was born in Bury St Edmunds Hospital in 1977 and brought up in the house where my parents live to this day, in the village of Feltwell in Norfolk. We were never rich, but neither did we want for anything, especially in the way of love and support. Dad worked as a printer and then, when I was a young girl, he became a sales rep, selling paper to the print trade. I remember the excitement when he was given a company car. It even had a cassette player! Mum used to work in the evenings at the US Air Force Base at Lakenheath. Dad would get home at 5.30 p.m., and she would leave at 6 p.m. It meant she was able to take us to and from school and be around during the school holidays, while she and Dad earned enough to keep us ticking over. They made huge sacrifices.

It all created a platform for me and Matty, and we ran around on it for all we were worth. Spirits were always high; mud, tears and injuries never far away. Feltwell was a small community, but we threw ourselves into it. Dad ran the local youth club; Mum helped out at the local playgroup. Our house was a constant hub of activity, with people coming and going. There were regular parties. The family barbecues were legendary. The snapshots I carry in my head of those times are idyllic – picnics, cycling down country lanes, Dad's bedtime stories (including the one about Mr Mole, who went out one morning and couldn't find his home when he returned because all these other molehills had sprung up in the meantime), the fancy-dress outfits that Mum made us for the Feltwell Fête each year, family holidays, Christmases at my aunt and uncle's with my cousins, Rob and Tim. And then there were the tears. I vividly recall the time I slipped on a friend's climbing frame and bit my tongue so deeply it was hanging off. There was blood everywhere. Not quite so idyllic, but all part of the tapestry. I was a ridiculously accident-prone child (and adult). Hence that nickname, courtesy of my cousin and one of my best friends, Tim.

It was a very stable upbringing that I enjoyed, rich and varied. I think my driven nature, or at least the young instinct it would develop from, was great for me as a child. I knew only that the world was full of so many wonderful things and that I must embrace as many of them as possible. It didn't matter what the pursuit – studies, art, sport, drama – I just had to be at the centre of it.

My brother, who is three years younger than me, is also driven, but not so obsessively. Growing up, ours was the classic sibling relationship, full of love and laughter, and littered with the obligatory fights. It's not clear where I get my obsessive nature from, or my fieriness. My mother used to be pretty feisty; my father was the mellow one.

Either way, this relentless determination to make the most of myself is something I was probably born with. It is also the 'brave face' syndrome, always wanting to appear strong and successful and, just as importantly, not wanting to show any weakness, for fear of people judging me negatively. I cannot remember a time when I haven't been compelled by it.

I was particularly driven at school. My first was Edmund de Moundeford Primary School, just around the corner from our house, where I was particularly inspired by the headmaster, the late Mr Feltwell. (That he and the village shared the same name was a coincidence.) From there through secondary school to university, I was focused and disciplined, with one goal in mind – to be the best in my class. My capacity for hard work knew no bounds.

Not that I'd want you to think I was a dull girl! All work and no play was definitely not my style. It was more like all work and all play. I suppose we might see in it the seeds of my aptitude for endurance sport – everything was a hundred miles an hour, and it was non-stop. Sometimes I was restless even when asleep. I used to sleepwalk as a child. I once walked into my brother's room and gave him a pillow, and on a few occasions I tried to get out of the house. But there were also moments of calm. I used to take myself off, for example, to paint the old church out at the back of our house. The impulse may have been to add another activity to my campaign of self-improvement (my grandfather Harry was very artistic), but I did also enjoy the chance to be on my own and to reflect. As long as I was doing something, I was happy.

Never was I happier than when playing sport. School was for achievement; sport was for recreation. It started off with swimming. I was dangled in water for the first time at three weeks old, and thereafter was taken every week. I never showed any signs of fear, and by the age of three I could swim. I had my first tricycle at around the same time. At primary school further sports were introduced – rounders, netball, cross-country, high jump and long jump. The egg-

and-spoon race, obviously. The school sports day was a huge event. I never shied away from racing. I loved the competition, but it was the social side of things that really appealed, the chance to spend time with friends in a loosely structured setting, to compete without the same pressure I seemed to put myself under in the classroom.

I learned to swim at Thetford swimming pool, and at the age of six earned my certificate for swimming a mile (still got it – I keep everything). The adjoining leisure centre hosted a gymnastics class, which I started to attend with a few of my friends from Feltwell. I was appalling. In my blue-and-pink leotard and with my hair in bunches, I had the balance and coordination of a baby giraffe. Far more appealing were the activities of the swimming club, the Thetford Dolphins, next door in that special pool where I'd learned to swim. My nose was practically pressed up against the window, looking in. I begged my parents to let me join, and at the age of eight I was a fully fledged Dolphin. So began one of the most important associations of my early life.

We trained three evenings a week, and at 7.30 a.m. on a Saturday morning. Then, every Saturday evening, there were the galas. It formed the hub of my social life, and soon became a big part of my parents' social life, too. My mum took an exam in judging and timekeeping so she could help out.

I loved it. I was able to give vent to all the normal childhood mischief I denied myself in the classroom – the luxury of being naughty, the thrill of being sent out (usually with Michaela Wilson) for talking too much! It meant my bond with the place and with my friends in it was really strong.

It didn't really bother me when I didn't win. I was good – I think I still hold one of the club records – but I wasn't the best. I won my fair share of races, but Julie Williams usually edged me, and I never threatened to beat the best boys. What did I care? This was more about being with my friends, meeting boys and prancing up and down the side of the pool in my swimwear. It was also about travelling to galas, even beyond the market towns of East Anglia. Thetford is twinned with Hürth in Germany and Spijkenisse in the Netherlands, and each year one of us would take a turn to host the other two. One year we would have German or Dutch swimmers staying at our house, the next we would pile onto a coach and catch the ferry to Europe. For a young teenager this was amazing, a huge highlight. We would be put up by a family, go on daytrips, experience a new country, new food . . . oh, and do a bit of swimming.

Despite my lack of application, I did show some potential in the pool. On the advice of my swim coach, my parents sat me down when I was fifteen and asked me if I wanted to join the Norwich Penguins. This represented a step up in class from the Thetford Dolphins. Knowing how ambitious I was in other pursuits they said they would drive me to Norwich, which was an hour away, if I wanted to take my swimming further. I said no. I felt it would detract from my studies and, besides, I was happy at our small club with my special network of friends.

Everyone is equal in the water. With our swimsuits, goggles and caps on, there wasn't much scope for expressing how cool we were. My swimming friends and I had all grown up together, and together we took on those early awkward teenage years. I was in my element, totally comfortable in an environment with no front to it.

Secondary school, though, was different. I chose Downham Market High School over the more local Methwold. It was a forty-five-minute bus ride away, but it enjoyed a better reputation at the time for academia and sport. It took me much longer to find my place there. I enjoyed my time at school, but I derived a lot of that enjoyment from working hard and achieving good grades. In my first and second years in particular, I just wasn't one of the in-crowd. I was a naive eleven-year-old when I arrived, sensible, studious and not very trendy. I didn't want to have to dry my hair after swimming, so I wore my hair short, like a boy's. Some of the other girls seemed impossibly cool. They were having sex – one even became pregnant, aged eleven. They were getting periods and growing breasts; their skirts were so short you could practically see their knickers; they wore loafers. I, on the other hand, was a late developer. With my flat chest, short hair, sensible skirt and heavy shoes, I suddenly became aware of the way I looked – and I didn't like it. For the first time in my life, I felt alienated. I was getting my first taste of the world as an unaccommodating place, and it bothered me. I am a sensitive soul, and I've always wanted to be liked.

Those first two years at school were awkward in that respect, but I've never been one to sit around feeling sorry for myself, so in time, I did something about it. One of the first measures I took was to grow my hair into a big curly mane. It took an age to style each morning. Sometimes it wouldn't sit in the particular way I wanted it to, and I would throw a tantrum at my poor mum. That control thing again.

Another example of my obsession with control was my attitude towards smoking. To me, every person who smoked was voluntarily killing themselves, and doing it quite openly. My greatest fear was that my parents would take it up. The knowledge that I wouldn't be able to stop them tore at me. So I loathed the habit from an early age. I was terrified, too, of becoming a drug addict, and my attitude towards alcohol was unforgiving. I didn't drink until I was twenty, and I hated it when my dad got drunk. Not that he did to any significant degree, but the mere possibility of a loss of control alarmed me.

By the age of thirteen or fourteen, I had found my feet at school. I was never totally in my element, as I was at the swimming club, but I made a couple of new friends in the third year and started to dress a bit more fashionably. Boys began to notice me. Sport also helped, to a degree. I played hockey and netball for the school. We were a successful netball team, becoming county champions. The team comprised the in-crowd, so I had a foot in the trendy camp, but I was still not one of them. I remember being the victim of teasing on the way back from one tournament.

Being a part of that set would have been nice, but it was nowhere near as important to me as excelling in my studies. Thankfully, the hard work paid off. My lower-school career ended with straight As at GCSE. It stunned me at the time. Straight As was something that happened to other people. Not to me. When it happened, I was overjoyed. I had my first taste of defying what I had thought possible. It endorsed my policy of working flat out to make the most of myself, so I cranked that up even further for my A-levels.

Needless to say, that didn't open any doors into the trendy club. In the sixth form I suffered hostility from one boy in particular. To this day I don't know what I did to upset him. We were in our mid-teens, so the merry-go-round of boys and girls was well under way. Even I had shed enough of my naivety to have developed an appetite for the opposite sex. I used to work it in my funky little crop tops on a Friday night down at Rollerbury, the roller-skating rink in Bury St Edmunds. I'd had my first kiss at fourteen (Gareth Whisson at the Thetford Dolphins Christmas disco), and from then on the usual awkward fumblings took place on a reasonably regular basis at Rollerbury and beyond. So it's possible I once kissed the wrong person, or something, but I'm not convinced that would explain what happened next.

One day I walked into the common room at school, and there, scrawled on the wall in angry letters were the words, 'Christine Wellington is a slag'. I was devastated. Even now as I think about it, I can feel the hot flush that surged through me then, of embarrassment and anger. I've got a pretty good idea who it was. Why he did it I have no idea. Of course, such stunts reveal far more about the people who perpetrate them than they reveal about the victims, which is precisely nothing. Still, the hostility of it caught me unawares. That someone should feel so ill of me that he be moved to write it up like that for all to see.

I'm not the sort of person to rise to that sort of thing. On those occasions in my life when I have encountered hostility like that, I have tended to internalise it and to withdraw into myself. It doesn't happen very often, but this was the most damaging instance, because it changed me for a while.

I was going out with my first boyfriend at the time, Matty Knight. He was in the year below and a lovely, gentle-hearted soul. Over the next year or so I did something that was very unlike me. I fell into a low-key, introverted existence with him. The sixth form became a subdued phase of my life, dominated by A-levels (biology, geography and English), babysitting and hanging out with Matty.

This was when concerns about my body image really started to kick in. It was the early 1990s, and we were being bombarded with images of waiflike supermodels. *Just 17* was my girly magazine of choice at the time, and you couldn't turn a page without Kate Moss or some other delicate sprite teasing you with her perfection. The yearning to look like these apparent goddesses was strong, and came with the equally compelling terror of ever turning fat. I was lucky in that I had never been one to put on weight. I have always adored food of every kind. It took me a while to come to terms with baked beans, but I love them now, which means there is no food left that I would not happily devour. In those days, I used to eat pizza and chips by the bucketload after swimming and when we stopped on the way back from netball tournaments. I never seemed to pile on the pounds.

But the nagging fear remained that one day I might. Coupled with my lust for control, it made me fertile ground for an eating disorder. I had a friend at the time who told me once that she had been experimenting with bulimia. When she explained it to me, it planted a seed in my mind. It sounded pretty disgusting, but here was a way

17

of controlling what you could and couldn't eat. If ever I felt a pang of guilt over something I had eaten, which was beginning to happen more and more as I reached the age of seventeen, all I had to do was to bring it up again. I tried to think of a downside.

The first time you make yourself sick, you imagine that through this you can have the best of both worlds. No longer do you have to watch how many chocolate bars you eat, or even feel guilty when you do. But the more you make yourself sick, the more it takes its toll. It sounded pretty disgusting because it was. I spent more moments over the following few years than I would care to count doubled up over a toilet bowl, trying to spit the cloying bile and acid from my mouth before it rotted my teeth. My throat would grow hoarse and sore. I quickly realised that I shouldn't be doing it, that it was an unnatural thing to do, but I persevered because it satisfied my craving for control.

It was a secret. Only my friend knew. Matty would have been horrified, I think. It made no sense. I had a boyfriend I cared about who loved me as I was, but, perversely, that made me even more concerned about keeping a certain kind of figure. He would never have put any pressure on me over the shape of my body. It was all down to the pressure I put on myself. I wasn't happy about it and I did it despite myself, but there has always been that little voice in my head urging me on to some notion of perfection, urging me to retain control over myself.

It was the same impulse that drove me on at school and that drives me on now as a triathlete. I have to give it everything, to do the best I can. In this case it started out both as a desire to look like Kate Moss and as a fear of becoming fat, the carrot and stick, which are one and the same. Being so competitive and so sensitive to the views of others, I was bound to internalise the images we were being bombarded with. I have always been my own worst critic. People might say to me, 'You've got an amazing figure,' but I would strive for more. Soon you lose sight of the original object of the exercise – to achieve and maintain a certain look.

Bulimia never worked in that sense, anyway. First, I wasn't very good at it. Sometimes I would fail to bring anything up, and a crashing sense of disappointment would come over me. Second, the theory of it is flawed – once you've eaten something, you don't just magic it out of your system by throwing it up. I never lost any weight as a result. Yet I continued with it, off and on, until well into my time at university. It didn't matter that it wasn't working. It was the illusion of control that had me.

My social life in the sixth form suffered from a combination of the writing on the wall, and the importance I attached to my studies and my relationship with Matty. I did go out. De Niro's nightclub in Newmarket was a regular haunt on Friday or Saturday nights, but I didn't drink and so I was the designated driver. I was, and still am, an appalling driver. My accident-prone nature extended to that as well. The very day I passed my test I went round to Matty's house in Mum's car. I drove into a ditch. Hadn't quite worked out how the headlights worked. A bit later I wrote off Mum's car altogether by driving into a butcher's van.

I left school with three As at A-level and an A* (they had just introduced the star system) for the geology GCSE I had taken as an extra subject. I'd applied to Oxford, but they put me in St Hilda's, an all girls' college, and I knew even before the interview that I didn't want to go there. I walked in and this woman with glasses on the end of her nose asked, 'Christine, what is science?' I wasn't very good at thinking on my feet back then. Everything I had achieved had been through hard graft; I was uncomfortable having questions fired at me that I couldn't prepare for.

They didn't accept me, but I can't say I was disappointed about not going. The rejection certainly hurt, though. Other than the first time I tried to qualify as a lifeguard at Bury St Edmunds pool when I was sixteen, I had never failed anything.

My dad drove me to all the universities I'd applied to, and I chose Birmingham. We used to go on canal holidays as a family – Dad is passionate about them – and I remember one that took us through Birmingham when I was fourteen or fifteen. The canal goes right through the university grounds, and my mum and I were walking along the towpath at one point. Through the trees I could see this beautiful courtyard of red-brick buildings, dominated by a huge clock tower, which turned out to be 'Old Joe', the tallest free-standing clock tower in the world.

'That looks amazing,' I said to Mum.

Dad told me it was the campus of Birmingham University.

'I want to go there one day,' I said.

When the day came, my dad dropped me off. Neither of my parents had been to university, so this was a poignant watershed for me and, in a strange way, for my family. I will always remember my dad's parting advice: 'Just seize every opportunity you have, embrace every experience. Make a mark, for all the right reasons.'

I threw myself into it from the start, and I thrived. I was a rare example of an eighteen year old who didn't drink, but you would never have known it if you hadn't watched carefully. University was a chance to snap out of the lull that I had fallen into over the past year or so. I was at the forefront of all the usual student antics. Wednesday night was Sports Night at the student union. Having joined the swimming club, it was one of the highlights of my week. I may not have been drunk like everyone else, but it's amazing how high you can get on those other types of spirit – exuberance, joy and a love of friendship. And lashings of Red Bull and Coke.

As ever, studies took precedence over everything else. My geography degree inspired and enthralled me in equal measure. I was privileged to be placed in a tutor group led by the wonderful Dr Jon Sadler, who remains a friend to this day. The biogeography of small invertebrates was his bag. Mine was economic geography, so there was not much of an overlap there, but he proved a wonderful support and sounding board. I was on a mission, and he provided me with all the encouragement I needed. The dash between lecture theatre and library was one of my chief sporting endeavours at university. As soon as the lecturer had said his bit I was out of there, straight to the library to be the first to check out the journals and photocopy the articles. I was quite selfish in that regard – not that there was ever much competition to be the first to lay hands on the relevant edition of the *Journal of Economic Geography*. As always, the competition came from within. Something inside me was constantly driving and driving and driving. I had to make the most of it; I had to make the most of me. There could be no slack, anywhere, not in my time, not in my head, not across my skin. If there were any, the guilt wouldn't bear thinking about.

The policy of making the most of things applied just as much to socialising. After that subdued period in the sixth form, the sparkle was back. I found a great network of friends in Birmingham. My relationship with Matty didn't last very long into my time there. We intended to keep it going, but deep down I think I knew that it wasn't going to last. This was a new adventure. I wanted to make a clean break, I wanted to fly. Even my name was up for reinvention. Until that point, I had always been known as Chris or Christine. At university I decided that I would introduce myself as Chrissie. I wanted it to be the start of a new me, or at least the rediscovery of an old one. I have been Chrissie ever since.

I joined the university swimming team, more for the social side than any sporting ambitions. It was the one area where I let myself off the hook in terms of pressure. With the rest of my life stretched to capacity, the swimming team formed a vital outlet for recreation and socialising, rather than achievement. I swam twice a week and then played a full part in the usual student japes – blow-up sheep, traffic cones, that kind of thing – despite, for the first year at any rate,

21

remaining sober. I don't know what it says about me that I could have been one of the leading protagonists without the excuse of inebriation! We used to play 'drinking golf' round the pubs of Edgbaston, where you drink your pint in as few gulps as possible. I drank Coke. Nobody seemed to mind, and after a few 'holes' I was as crazy as the rest of them.

By Christmas, I had a new boyfriend, James Alback. He was charismatic, lively and enthusiastic. There was no danger of retreating into a shell with him around. Our relationship was to last for two years, and there was never a dull moment. We argued ferociously on occasion. Our political views were opposed, and he was very into his clothes and his labels. At the end of our first summer holiday, we went on a ramshackle old tour bus across America from Boston. It was a spectacular two weeks, but James, or Jay as we knew him, wasn't so keen on slumming it. For me, spending the night under the stars in a sleeping bag was a magical experience; Jay was more bothered about keeping the dirt off his Ralph Lauren shirts! He couldn't wait to get to San Francisco and a proper shower. Differences aside, though, he represented the kind of spirit I was hoping to embrace. I hadn't liked the introverted person I had become. I wanted to exude energy and confidence, to be the kind of person to light up a room when I walked into it. You can never know whether you're managing that, but you do know when you're not – and I hadn't been.

My policy was to embrace everything. I wrote for the student paper, *Redbrick*, on current affairs in and around the university. I was selected for the university council. I was the geography representative to the board. I became captain of the swimming team.

And I became chair of BUNAC, the British Universities North America Club. Through BUNAC I spent most of my first two summer holidays teaching swimming at Beaver Country Day School in a suburb of Boston. They were wonderful times in a wonderful city. I adored teaching the kids and watching them overcome their fear of the water.

At weekends we went to Cape Cod or to watch the Red Sox. I made some great friends. As the only foreigner, I was like a kind of mascot to them. They loved my British accent and were fascinated by my experimentation with sit-ups, which my friend Gabriel and I used to indulge in at the poolside. I was known as Chrissie Abs of Steel.

When you're in America, it's virtually impossible to avoid those local specialities – Fourth of July cakes with thick frosting, bagels, jelly, peanut butter – and I didn't. I was still making myself sick, but it had long been clear to me that that tactic did not work. If I wanted to look good in my swimwear, I needed more, and it was sit-ups that satisfied my lust for self-improvement in Boston. Gabriel was the perfect training partner. She was a co-teacher on that camp. Beneath the laughter and socialising I think we both recognised in each other, even in that first year, a preoccupation with body image. She became a great friend, and is to this day.

Things started to change in my second year at university. First of all, I finally embraced alcohol. I had never found it difficult to resist. Not drinking had made me feel good about myself. I felt healthy and in control. But, of course, at that age, wherever you are, but particularly when you're at university, you are constantly surrounded by the stuff, and I was intrigued. I just wanted to try it. I literally never had.

I don't remember when I started, or what my first alcoholic drink was. I suspect it was vodka with a fruit-juice mixer at Old Joe's, the bar on campus. I liked it. Before long, I was swigging Malibu from a bottle at Frenzy on a Friday night, or buying a bottle of Lambrini with the girls for £1.99 from the local corner shop. I used to go to Cocksoc (the less than salubrious cocktail night at a local club), where for a £5 entry fee you could drink as much as you wanted from dustbins filled with cocktails.

What alcohol did for me, of course, was to make me even more outgoing than I already was. My friends were surprised when I suddenly started drinking. My parents couldn't believe it. We drank quite a lot. Very occasionally I lost control, which terrified me. Early on, I got too drunk on wine and was sick everywhere, but on the whole I knew when to stop.

Compared to that other type of vomiting that had been a feature of my life, it was nothing. The friend from home who had first told me about bulimia was now at university herself. She had come across an article on eating disorders as part of her degree. She knew I was still bulimic and she was concerned, so she sent me the article. In it she had underlined key sentences, warning of the short- and long-term effects – insomnia, psychological problems, digestive problems, dental, cardiac, dermatological and hormonal problems. It was a full-on illness. I was shaken by that, but also strangely reassured to know that it was a recognised condition that so many others suffered from. It raised big questions. In the same way as her own experimentation had first sown the seed in my mind, now my friend's concern was bringing about the beginning of the end.

But it was the second summer in Boston that proved the watershed for my bulimia. Gabriel and I came clean to each other over our obsessions and concerns about body image. I have no doubt that such conditions are so much more widespread than any of those sufferers realise, as they fight their own private battles. The truth is, you only really feel able to talk about it after you have been through it, never while it is actually happening. I have talked to so many friends since who have revealed that they suffered from the same thing.

That summer of 1997, Gabriel and I had some very open and frank discussions about the pressures we were feeling, about the tyranny of body image. Talking to somebody about it proved a great relief, and gave me the confidence to find other ways of tackling my obsession. Thanks to the article my friend had sent me, I was now far less bulimic anyway, but in America I was eating more than I should, or at least more than I thought I should. This precipitated my going for a few runs in Boston. At the swimming pool, I was soon back into the sit-ups. The desire to make the most of my body was still driving me, but at least it was in healthier directions for now. It struck me suddenly and quite forcefully that bulimia was not only irrational and dangerous, it was also disgusting. The sore throats were debilitating, and my teeth were not benefiting at all.

In my third year at university there was no bulimia. The rational side of me took over, as I realised what damage I was doing to myself. I started to put on a bit of weight, but most of all, emotionally I felt a huge weight lift. I was no longer constrained by this mental chokehold.

Pressure is a necessary evil if you want to achieve. It brings with it great stress, but you deal with it, and the redemption comes when you achieve things as a result. It can also be debilitating though, on a day-to-day level, especially if its benefits are illusory. The trick is to understand which pressures are necessary and which ones are the dangerous decoys, the ones that suck the life out of you for no reward. In ridding myself of bulimia, I had identified one of those and cut it out. I wish I could say that I had beaten the emotional urge to push my body to extremes in search of some self-devised notion of perfection. That was to lie dormant for the time being. But, physically, I had beaten bulimia.

The alleviation of the mental pressure was similar to when Brett Sutton started to coach me as a triathlete, nearly ten years later. He lobbied me incessantly to stop thinking and just to follow his orders without question, to trust that he knew what was best and to channel all my energies into the programme he had devised. Surrendering control like that was incredibly difficult for me to do, but when I did let go it felt the same way – like a weight being lifted.

Mentally it is hard coping with the weight of expectation I put on myself. Mentally it is hard trying to be the best the whole time. And I don't know who I'm trying to prove myself to. There is something inside me – not a voice exactly, but a deep-seated compulsion – that strives for perfection. But it's my own version of perfection, not to be perfect per se but just to be the best that I can be. That can lead to unnatural and excessive pressure. Sometimes I have difficulty being in the now, being present. I constantly worry, am I making the most out of this, am I making the most out of this, instead of just accepting and enjoying what *is*.

It does, though, make the pride and euphoria all the more intense when you do achieve something special. For me, that achievement came in the shape of a first-class degree in geography. I achieved the highest grade ever recorded in the department, and was awarded the title of University Scholar, 1998. My dissertation was published in a journal. When my family came to the graduation ceremony, I felt confident that I had followed my father's advice to make the most of every opportunity. With so many good friends graduating the same day, it was a very special occasion.

But the passing-out ceremony that stands out in my mind was the girls' trip to Magaluf that I went on that summer with three of my best friends from university. It was the apotheosis of my fledgling drinking career, and remains so to this day. Certainly, it bore precious little resemblance to the life I lead now, or indeed did then, even after I had embraced drinking as a pastime. My friend Emily broke her leg on the first night going up the steps to a nightclub, and spent the rest of the week in plaster. Not that it stopped her, or the rest of us. It was a week of the purest debauchery – drinking, sunbathing, drinking, meeting boys, drinking and drinking. Self-control was abandoned for the week, and I have to say it felt good. I had just achieved more than I could ever have imagined at university, so I had earned this time off the leash. I think of that week with a special fondness, maybe because I have never, before or since, just let myself go in such a gratuitous fashion. I did enjoy it, but it could never have lasted.

3

In Search of Myself

My initial plan after university was to become a lawyer. At the time, that was what I thought I wanted.

Lovell White Durrant accepted me on a week-long work placement in their London offices that summer. I found the work interesting and challenging, and I enjoyed the social side. Working in the City was novel. I had never lived in London before. As always, I was hugely enthusiastic and determined to make the most of this opportunity.

But I would be lying if I said I was particularly enthralled by corporate law. And during that week I found myself working on cases in defence of big companies whose causes I wouldn't have chosen – mobile phone companies, for example, who were contesting claims about the health effects of their devices. That did sow a seed of doubt, but generally I was happy with the path I had chosen. I am analytical and thorough and I love meeting people, so the law seemed to be a good fit. I have a high boredom threshold, too. All of which pointed towards a potentially successful career.

Lovells offered me a two-year training contract. First, though, I would have to take a law conversion course, so I applied to Nottingham University and was accepted for the start of the following academic year. I had a good twelve months to fill, so I decided to go travelling.

All summer, I had worked as a lifeguard at Centre Parcs and Thetford Sports Centre – not exactly *Baywatch*, but it was a wage. I was saving money more than I was saving lives, put it that way. After I'd cashed in a few Premium Bonds, and with some money Mum and Dad had given me for my eighteenth birthday, I managed to gather together about £3,000 for my trip.

My preparations didn't stop at that, though. I had a friend at Birmingham called Nick Wellings, who also happened to be a fellow native of Norfolk, hailing from Norwich. He had taken a gap year before university and travelled round the world. I was always intrigued by his stories, and his adventurous spirit and experiences inspired me. He was also a very keen cyclist and thought nothing of building a bike from scratch and heading off on 100km rides. Having no knowledge of, or interest in, bikes at the time, I was flabbergasted and intrigued.

As an outdoor enthusiast, Nick took himself off camping before our final year at university. He went to sleep in his tent one night and never woke up. We still don't know why. It was like a cot death but in an adult. I helped to organise a memorial service for him at the university, and got to know his parents well. They very kindly gave me his travel diaries before I went travelling. These formed an invaluable source of information and inspiration – I copied out the list of equipment he had taken with him. He had been on just the kind of adventures I wanted to go on.

With Nick's words in my head and a poem written by my mum pasted in my diary, I set off in November 1998 to Kenya, and from there joined a two-month truck expedition to South Africa. It was the start of a journey that changed the direction my life would take. I would return to the UK not after nine months, as planned, but almost two years later.

These trips are often defining passages in a person's life, and mine was no different. I became much more rounded as a person, including physically. It also catalysed the passion I had always had for international development. Not that I had grown up knowing it as that, but as a young child crying over the footage from Ethiopia, I had always been driven by a strong sense of the world's problems and a desire to do something about them. I organised bring-and-buy sales in Feltwell to raise money for Africa. Now this trip would harden that youthful instinct into something more clearly defined. It did much the same for my love of the outdoors and the natural world. And I met with the concomitant realisation that I was not passionate about commercial law. All in all, it was a journey of self-discovery, and it began, appropriately enough, in Africa.

The person who played the biggest part in it was a South African girl called Judy, or Jude, as we called her, who was my tent partner on the expedition. She was a couple of years older than me and deeply religious, but what struck me so powerfully was how self-assured she was, comfortable in her own skin and unconcerned with what the rest of us thought of her.

To begin with I looked askance at her, in the same way everyone else did. She was a pretty girl and knew how to enjoy herself, so she didn't wear her spirituality in a particularly obvious way, but her views on the world were unlike any I had ever known, and they cut across even those of a thrown-together group of travellers journeying through Africa.

June's confidence seemed rock solid, and yet there was not so much as a hint of arrogance. She was a lot of the things that I wasn't, certainly in terms of knowing who she was and where she sat in the world. She would say things like, 'I'm not here to make friends – I've got enough of those already.' Her complete indifference to what the others thought of her made a big impression on me. She didn't care that they laughed when she hugged a tree, which was one of her favourite pastimes. Her view of the natural world was a revelation. To me a tree was just a tree, but she would say, 'Trees are so old. They are like wise grandfathers and have seen so much. You can feel the life flowing through them.' We spent New Year at Victoria Falls, and I fell under the spell of a huge, 1,500-year-old baobab tree by the Zambezi river. I sat there painting it for about half an hour. Jude's love of the natural world reawakened mine.

But it was that poise of hers that struck me most. She encountered other people on her own terms, and would not be influenced by them. She would never, for example, have succumbed to an eating disorder. Her sympathy for anyone who did would have known no bounds, but to go down that road herself would never have occurred to her. That serenity rubbed off on me. By then I was well into my 'grungy' stage, having moved on from the short skirts and crop tops of my first two years at university, so I was receptive to her relaxed outlook on life. And throughout my time away I never felt at all threatened by my own affinity for eating disorders. I put on weight in Africa. There wasn't much physical activity, but there were a lot of the local Eat-Sum-More biscuits. And we did. In my combat trousers and trainers, I felt fine about gaining weight.

When we reached Cape Town, I spent three weeks travelling in South Africa with Jude and two other close friends I had made, Aline and Luanne. From there I flew to Auckland, where I rediscovered my love for trekking (I was an enthusiastic participant in the Duke of Edinburgh Award Scheme at school) and met one of the loves of my life, Steve. Sadly, we weren't together very long, but we packed a lot into it.

After two months in New Zealand I flew to Sydney. I had a work visa, so I was always going to base myself there for a while, although four months turned into eleven. I ended up in a three-bedroom flat in Bondi, which I shared with eleven others, including my cousin Tim and our mate Ian, or Easy, as he is known. It probably wasn't a lifestyle conducive to a legal career, but I managed to wangle my way into a law firm in Sydney, Heidtman and Co., where I worked as a paralegal and secretary. My boss was a wonderful woman called Penny Cable. She was a partner, and very sophisticated and glamorous, always immaculately turned out. We hit it off from the start, but, as much as I enjoyed working for her, I was increasingly plagued by doubt about law as a career. I'd written to Lovells, asking to defer the start of my contract – and hence my course in Nottingham – by a year. They'd agreed, and so I had a bit of time to enjoy Sydney, procrastinate and continue to mull things over.

It dawned on me that one of the reasons I had chosen law was just to be able to tell people that I was a solicitor. It was a way of channelling my academic qualifications into a suitably respectable vocation. All that work I had put in at school and university would be vindicated by a high-flying job that labelled me as being somebody.

Now I was perceiving the folly of such reasoning. 'I need to address some of the flaws in my personality,' I wrote in my diary. 'One of them is my tendency always to try to gain the approval and appreciation of others. I guess it's a reflection of my lack of self-confidence – needing constant reassurance. Strange, because I am sure that that's not the perception most people actually have of me.'

A year on from the completion of my degree, I was starting to miss the sense of achievement that comes from working hard. I was missing the creativity and the learning. I missed using my mind. About that time, my grandfather Harry, aged ninety-three, published his memoirs, *The End is My Beginning*. Would I ever feel inclined to do the same if I pursued a career that I'd chosen as a means of validating myself in the eyes of other people? 'When you are lying on your deathbed,' I wrote, 'you don't wish for more time in front of a computer.'

I sought advice from various friends – Penny, Jude, Jon Sadler. Jude sent me an email from South Africa, in which she wrote: 'You are changing and becoming a different person to the one you were when you left home. I think you should keep on travelling until you find your *passion* in this world. Don't panic about the time you are using now, it is all necessary for you to grow as a person and to get to know yourself in different circumstances. There are so many opportunities! Decide where you want to go and just do it.'

She signed off, 'Love, Mum', as she always did, and still does.

I wondered whether I should abandon law altogether. The victory that my heart was winning over my head (which still maintained I should secure my qualification and keep my options open) was the main reason, but I don't deny that the lifestyle in Sydney was also encouraging me away from the conservative option.

Those eleven months were a very special time for me. I tuned myself into the vibrant social scene. I was heavily into alternative music, particularly punk rock, and I went to countless gigs and open-air festivals. I drank and I ate as much as I ever had done.

I was putting on more and more weight, though, and unlike in Africa, it was starting to play on my mind. For the first couple of months in Sydney, Steve was off on his travels. While he was away I resolved to stop eating junk, lose a bit of weight and look good for him when he came back in June. When he did, we headed off up the east coast in a clapped-out old car we called Ballarat. Then, at the end of July, Steve left Sydney for good. We broke up, and I was devastated. I started running, just to take my mind off it.

There are a lot of beautiful people in Bondi, and they all seem to be thin and fit. It wasn't long before I felt the return of familiar twitches of anxiety over my body image. Just as powerfully, though, I also felt the pull of the beaches and the ocean. The upshot of it all was that I soon rediscovered my love of sport. If you love sport, Australia is a wonderful place to be.

In August, on a whim, I entered the City2Surf, a 14km run from the Central Business District to Bondi. 'It's a suicide mission!' I wrote in my diary. 'I'm sure there's no way I can run it all, but I will give it a shot!'

What a fuss I made! It seems laughable to me now. The race itself was so uplifting. I was swept along by the atmosphere and the 50,000 other competitors. It was a thrilling experience. 'In the end I worried about nothing,' I wrote. 'The race went brilliantly – better than I ever could have hoped. In fact, really, really good. I just got into a rhythm and kept going.' Inspired, I started running along the beach and cliff tops, although my idea of a long run then was half an hour.

I learned to surf, even if it took me months just to be able to stand on the board. I never gave up, practising every day, despite the indignity and pain of the thrashing the ocean gave me. It was just such a joy to be out on the waves. I was also swimming again, and took part in the 2km North Bondi Roughwater Ocean Swim in January 2000. It was much easier than I thought it would be, and I came fourth or fifth in my age group. I started to think it might be time to train a little more seriously.

Sydney was buzzing with millennial energy and I felt that changes were also taking place inside me. I wrote down my dreams for 2000: 'To be happy with myself and always make others happy. To be confident and give others confidence in themselves. To smile, to surf, to laugh and make others laugh. To read more widely. To try to be more tolerant of my weaknesses and of others, and not be so hard on myself all the time. To make people happy is the main one, I think. Biting my nails has to be in there somewhere too.'

I am pleased to say that I have more or less kicked the habit of biting my nails, although it does return sometimes if I'm anxious. It wasn't until I was cycle-touring in the Andes at the end of 2008 that I really cracked it. But I feel I've almost ticked that one off the list.

The other resolutions are more like ongoing guidelines to live my life by, particularly the one about the happiness of others. There's a crucial distinction between that and seeking the approval of others, which I sometimes confuse it with. I have received so much from people in my life and have always felt a strong desire to make others happy in return. It was a mantra of mine then, and it still is now. As much as anything, that was what drew me away from my path into law. I couldn't reconcile it with the practice of representing companies whose policies or products you might not agree with, or with charging two or three hundred pounds an hour while you did it.

Instead, I was hit by the revelation that I should take a master's in international development. I was almost certain I wanted to go into aid work, and this was one of the established ways in. Even thinking about it made me excited. It was what I was interested in, and something I felt that I would be good at. On 17 January 2000, after taking the advice of, among others, Jon Sadler, I resolved to pursue it. From Sydney I applied for courses in the UK and was accepted on one at the University of Manchester. The main problem was that I had no money, but I managed to secure a scholarship of £10,000 from the Economic and Social Research Council.

I left Sydney in March and travelled on my own through Asia for six months. That was an amazing time; I met so many fascinating people. By now I was really tackling one of those other resolutions of mine – to be more tolerant of others. When you're growing up, especially in Norfolk, your friends are very similar to you. But as I saw more of the world I met people from different walks of life, who wore different clothes and believed in different things. I might not have agreed with them all, but I learned to be much more accepting. I am now proud to number among my friends just such a wide variety of people. I am still not that tolerant of smokers, I have to admit, but I am working on that.

In Asia I travelled through Indonesia (a country I loved so much I was to write my master's thesis on it), Malaysia, Thailand, Laos, Burma and India. In Laos, I became a vegetarian. The screaming of the pigs as they were slaughtered in front of us, then roasted, is what finally did it for me. But, even before that, healthy eating had become more of a preoccupation than it had been in Australia. It wasn't so much a weight thing, more a question of what was available. Fresh fruit and vegetable stir fries were abundant, so they naturally became the bedrock of my diet. Just as naturally, I started to lose weight, and I liked that.

A storm was brewing.

I returned from Asia eleven days before the start of my master's, full of the virtues of healthy eating and so excited about resuming academic life. My dad drove me up to Manchester at the beginning of September 2000.

But it was now that the idea of healthy eating started to make a plaything of me. It began with the incessant reading of labels. Now that I was back in the West, I had to be careful if I wanted to maintain the healthy lifestyle I'd adopted in Asia. I had already re-established that I liked looking slim. I didn't want to return to the more decadent path I had followed in Australia. I didn't want anyone to say to me even something as innocuous as, 'You look well', because we all knew what that was a euphemism for. I continued with my new-found enthusiasm for fitness and started running with a vengeance. I was obsessive about it, in my crappy old trainers and second-hand running clothes, pounding through the fog in Victoria Park at six in the morning. Needless to say, the weight continued to fall off me.

I was back into my relentlessly driven mode, but this time it was eating me up more than ever. My best friend on the course was Naomi Humphries, who had a first-class degree from Oxford in Philosophy, Politics and Economics. I didn't know it at the time, but she tells me she found it hilarious how competitive I was over every piece of work we did. We were the strongest students on the course, but she was far more naturally intelligent than I was. In Naomi I was confronted with something I hadn't come across before – a rival in the classroom. It fuelled my competitiveness so that it burned even more ferociously. I had to beat her, and every time I didn't it made me seethe. Naomi was very driven too, but for her it was about improving herself; for me, it was about improving myself *and* beating everyone else.

Naomi was a very good cook, and she knew I wasn't eating enough. She would prepare me meals and slip added fat into them. Once she made me a pea and potato soup, swearing blind that that was all it was. Unbeknown to me, she had slipped in dollops of extra cream and olive oil. She told me that the hot chocolate she had made contained just one spoon of Options low-fat drinking chocolate, but really it had ladlefuls of the full fat stuff.

Nobody liked broaching the subject with me, and when they did I would pass off my skinniness as the result of a tropical disease I had picked up in Asia. I could see people were concerned, but the need to control my eating overrode everything. I started swimming, and then took up water polo. I was awful – couldn't catch, couldn't throw – but there was no hiding my weight loss in the pool. It made me even worse at water polo, because I was easily brushed aside. I was also getting very cold in the water. I played because it was an excuse to swim around like a lunatic and because there was a great social scene. I wasn't drinking much, but I would always go to the pub to meet people. And when I didn't I worked flat out on my master's, well into the night, before getting up at the crack of dawn to go running.

It was an unhealthy lifestyle, but I couldn't stop. Working relentlessly is an addiction; anorexia is an addiction. It had started off in the usual way – with the question of body image. But when you're so driven and compulsive, it turns into a competition within yourself. Each day, I would try to eat just a little less than the last. If I succeeded, that was a good thing. To do the reverse would be to give in to temptation, which was weakness. Occasionally, I would have a binge on crisps and chips at a party and I would berate myself for it. I had lost control. That meant punishment would follow.

But I was already punishing myself. My body was feeling the strain. I used to wake up in the night with an aching jaw, because I was grinding my teeth. That was partly through the stress I was putting myself under on the course, but anorexia affects your sleep patterns. Nowadays, my teeth are almost non-existent at the back, and I wear a gumshield in bed.

My hair grew dry and then started to fall out. I smothered it with conditioner. Downy hair, meanwhile, started to grow on my body. My periods stopped. I knew I was too thin, but I couldn't escape from what I was doing. I wanted to be rid of the chokehold it had on me. It's so mentally draining. Eating less may start as a means to an end, but in an anorexic it soon takes over as the end itself. You lose perspective. Yes, on some level I knew I was too thin, but you don't realise just how bad you look. In a mirror, you don't see what everyone else sees. Concerned friends might tell you you're looking thin, but that's exactly what an anorexic wants to hear. When people said it to me, I just thought, 'Great!'

My friends from water polo, Tamsin and Gemma, wanted me to see a doctor (in response to my insistence that I was suffering from a rare tropical disease). I lied and told them I was seeing one. I did, however, go once to see a counsellor at the university, but I didn't like it and never went back.

In the end, it was my family who snapped me out of it – that, and a photo.

My parents knew I had changed my eating patterns by becoming a vegetarian (always eager to accommodate everyone, Mum cooked me a nut roast that Christmas). By the summer of 2001, though, it was clear to them that I had a problem. They came up to visit me one weekend, and we went for a walk in the Peak District. I could tell by the look in their eyes that they were desperately worried, and it tweaked something deep inside me. A few days later, I developed some photos we had taken on the walk. One of them was of me. I was shocked. Somehow, seeing me there, frozen and isolated in a photo, taken out of that symbiotic relationship you have with the person in the mirror, brought home to me with devastating force how skinny and ill I had become. I looked awful.

I rang my parents and burst into tears, telling them everything.

'I'm coming to get you,' said Dad.

He drove up to Manchester and took me home to Norfolk. Term-time was over for the summer, so I was working under my own steam on my thesis, which had to be in by October. Dad took time off work, and I stayed at home for about a week.

'You don't have to say anything,' he said. 'I just want to be with you.'

I explained everything to him as best I could. He just couldn't comprehend it, but he was super-supportive. It was such an alien thing for him to have to deal with. He had no experience of it. Not being able to help was agonising for him.

'Chrissie, you've got so much going for you,' he said. 'You're beautiful, you've got a great mind, a great body. I just don't understand why you're doing this to yourself.'

He was at a loss. But, for me, just his being there and my being able to talk to him about it was enough.

We went for a walk and ended up in a coffee shop. He ordered a cake and tried to get me to eat some.

'I can't, Dad,' I said. 'I can't.'

'Chrissie, I don't know what to do for you. I don't know how to help.' And he broke down.

I'd never seen my dad cry. It tore at my soul. The fact that I'd caused him and Mum so much distress rocked me.

But it was my brother who delivered the killer blow. I went to stay with him in Greenwich, where he was studying. We had talked at length about my problem before, and he had always been sympathetic and supportive, but this time he showed me the toughest love he possibly could. It was what I needed. Our relationship has at times been feisty, and that feistiness helped to complete the turnaround.

'You're so selfish,' he said. 'Look at what you're doing. You're tearing Dad apart. And Mum. You think this is just an eating disorder, that it's just affecting you. Well, it's not. It's affecting our whole family. You don't care what you're doing to everyone else.'

He gave me both barrels. This was not the first time that had happened, but for the first time I didn't give him both barrels back. I took it in silence, because I knew he was right. Matty helped me then more than he could know. He woke me up to what was happening. I might not have shown it at the time, but my gratitude for what he did for me that day knew no bounds.

And maybe being with my brother brought home to me another realisation, which helped me then to learn to appreciate my body and continues to help me now. I am a combination of my mum and dad. If I hate what I see in the mirror, then indirectly I am being critical of them. And to be critical of them is the most absurd idea, since they are the two people I love and respect most in the world. Or, to approach it from the other way, if I love my mum and dad so much, which is a given, then it follows I should love, or at the very least appreciate, my body. I should appreciate me.

Which brings me back to those millennial resolutions, and the one I have tackled least successfully – to be tolerant of my weaknesses. I still have to learn to be kinder to myself. Those days at the end of my master's were a watershed for me in that respect, as in many others, but I have never quite shaken off that tendency to be self-critical. Indeed, it is less that I need to tolerate my weaknesses, and more that I need to realise that what I'm berating myself for isn't actually weakness at all. I have an illogical conception of what weakness is. If I lose a race, that is weakness; if I have a bad day's training, that is weakness. For me, anything short of perfection is weakness.

At least now I understand the problem. Learning to see my body less as an object to be manipulated and more as an integral part of me was a crucial step. And in even more simplistic terms, I saw all of a sudden the damage I was doing to it by not eating properly. I am not sure you are ever cured of the illness that is an eating disorder but the key for me was to have developed a healthier perspective about my body. Whereas I used to see it as no more than contours of skin and colour, now I see it as a holistic system that I respect and love for what it enables me to do.

Uneasily, I started eating more healthily. From the end of term in June until I handed in my thesis ('The Changing Form of the Indonesian State') at the end of September, I moved into digs with a guy called Rich, another great friend. He was a vegetarian and superb in the kitchen, and his cooking helped me back onto a more even keel.

One thing I didn't let up on, though, was my work. I think Rich, who was also completing a master's, raised an eyebrow over how hard – and late into the night – I was working and how stressed it made me. But that was an example of energy directed towards a positive goal, and I graduated with a distinction. Naomi was awarded a distinction as well. I don't know which of us got the higher mark. It didn't seem to matter so much any more, and that in itself was a sign of progress.

4

Development

It is interesting for me to look back through the diaries I kept during my travels. In June 1999 I was bemoaning my tendency to 'always try to please people'; five months later, as the millennium approached, I was renewing my lifelong vow to 'make people happy'. They may sound contradictory statements of intent, but I don't think pleasing people and making them happy are quite the same thing, even if they are two sides of the same coin. The first is akin to the impulse to worry about what other people think of you; the second is more about the desire to give to other people.

I would say my life has been dominated by two dynamics: an obsessive lust for control and self-improvement on the one hand, and concern about people and their situations on the other. From the latter has grown, perhaps fuelled by the former, my passion for development. I call it development these days, because that is the name they give it in politics and in higher education, but really it is just the desire to help people and to try to make the world a better place. It played a big part in my life when I was growing up.

It was the era of Band Aid and Live Aid. The footage from Africa reduced me to tears, and I remember vowing to do something to help. I was an avid fan of *Blue Peter*, and one episode in 1986 made a

41

particular impression on me. It concerned the famine in Ethiopia and the cataracts that were rendering so many of the Ethiopians blind. I went through to the kitchen and asked Mum if we could arrange a bring-and-buy sale in the village. I wrote a letter to *Blue Peter*, explaining how distraught I was and how much I wanted to help. They sent posters and an information pack, and we set about planning and promoting the event. It was a success, and we raised £173, which wasn't bad in the mid-1980s. I was overjoyed to be awarded my first Blue Peter badge. Still got it. Still got them all (I didn't stop there).

The television reports gave me my first inkling of a world beyond my own, a world that wasn't fair or equal, a world of poverty, war, disease and famine. But I also realised that this state of affairs wasn't necessarily a given, and that we have it in our power to make a difference, to make the world a better place for all. We have that choice. One thing's for sure, though – if we do nothing, it *will* be a given.

Buoyed by the success of the bring-and-buy sale, I set up further projects to raise money. I organised a litter-pick in the village (I hated litter). Then I wrote a version of *Aladdin* for the stage, which was put on at the primary school, complete with costumes and songs.

As I went through my teens and early adulthood, other pre-occupations took over, such as studying and socialising, but that passion for helping others has never left me. It was a big reason for spending those two summers of my university years in Boston, teaching children to swim. They ranged in age from three to ten, and seeing them grow in confidence and enthusiasm was so uplifting.

I remember one boy called Welcome Bender. He was four years old and didn't really interact with the other kids, although he was exceptionally bright. He was borderline genius when it came to discussing the solar system. He was also afraid of the water. But in time I gained his trust, he slowly grew in confidence and finally he learned to swim.

His is the case that sticks in my mind most poignantly, because of his fear of the water and the catharsis of his eventual victory over it, but this sort of journey was repeated over and over again in all the children on that camp. Watching them discover something of themselves brought home to me what a wonderful tool sport is in the making of people.

To oversee that process and help it along, meanwhile, reminded me of the joy of making a difference to other people's lives. It was an incredibly rewarding experience. When you receive letters and artwork from these kids and from their parents thanking you for helping them, it is pretty special. Still got them all.

However much your youth may be characterised by these passions and urges, they tend to burst out of you in a blur of unfocused activity. If they are to shape your life as an adult, they need time to come together and settle into something more coherent. That process happened for me during my travels.

Africa is where it started, encouraged by Jude and her unique perspective. To see how poor the locals were in economic terms, yet how rich in culture and emotion, made a deep impression on me.

As did the history. I was blown away, for example, by the rock art in the Rhodes Matopos National Park in Zimbabwe, painted by bushmen tens of thousands of years ago with hematite and animal bile. I was in tears as I listened to our guide recount how the bushmen's way of life has become eroded by the advance of modern 'civilisation', even more than their art has been. I felt an emotional connection with the natural world, and an anger rose deep inside me at the destruction of an entire way of life, precious in ways 'civilisation' could never conceive.

Early on in our journey through Africa, I got into the habit of giving out pens to the locals, before realising that this in no way benefits them in a long-term, sustainable way. It's not as if pens are growing on the trees out there. They will run out sooner or later. Handing them round willy-nilly would just breed dependency, even greed. Then I saw a child in Zanzibar wearing a McKids t-shirt from McDonald's. It started me thinking about the concept of 'development' and the underlying causes of poverty, including the West's role in perpetuating it. 'We give presents to the locals,' I wrote in my diary, 'perhaps as a means of alleviating our own guilt and making ourselves feel better, when really it does nothing to help people help themselves. In the longer term it actually has a negative impact on their development.'

It was the six months travelling through Asia, though, that had the biggest effect on me. By then I had decided to take the MA in development studies. To go from arriving at that decision to arriving in Indonesia so soon afterwards was a powerful progression. I immediately fell in love with the country – the lush green scenery, the terraced paddy fields, the ornate temples, the arts and crafts, the local food stalls, the volcanic peaks and shimmering turquoise lakes, the offerings of banana-leaf bowls everywhere I turned, filled with incense and flowers. I was seduced. My love affair with Indonesia was intense, and introduced me to the unfamiliar and the terrifying.

We visited the island of Siberut, off the west coast of Java, where we walked for hours to visit villages virtually untouched by Western civilisation, surrounded by the dense, vivid green jungle, where handmade wooden canoes are the only means of transport. We stayed in their 'longhouses' on stilts. The locals wore loincloths made of bark, and their bodies were covered in tattoos, rendered with a mixture of ash and sugar-cane juice hammered into the skin with a fine nail. On one hike through the jungle my walking boots broke and I had to spend the day walking barefoot through thick mud, rivers and foliage that seemed to consist primarily of sharp things. This is what the locals have to endure every day.

It was easy to feel completely immersed in another way of life, except, of course, that you were not and never could be. I suffered from the classic traveller's dilemma. It made me ask questions of the voyeuristic, selfish and contrived nature of travelling, as practised by Westerners. I felt very uncomfortable about what I was doing, but equally, how could I turn down the opportunity to visit these societies?

Another salutary experience came during a forty-hour bus ride with my Danish friend Pernille through Sulawesi, a large island to the north of Indonesia, more populous than Siberut but still largely untouched by tourism. Our journey to the north of the island coincided with an outbreak of violence in and around the town of Poso, a flare-up of the ongoing troubles between Christians and Muslims. Buildings were being burned, people murdered, and protagonists on both sides patrolled the area with guns and machetes. The streets were full of cars, as people tried to escape the violence. There were roadblocks every couple of hundred yards. We were travelling on a local bus, which was hijacked by Muslim fighters. They climbed aboard wearing masks like ninjas, their mouths set in grim, determined lines as they waved their machetes and ordered the driver to take them across town. They walked through the bus looking for Indonesian Christians, coming so close to me that I'm sure they must have heard the blood pounding in my ears.

After they had been driven where they wanted to go, they left the bus without touching us. The relief was, of course, overwhelming, but it came with more guilt – guilt that we were only passing through, that we had escaped because we were Western tourists. Who knows what would have happened to us if we hadn't been?

Elsewhere on my travels through Asia, Burma was under military dictatorship, and in Laos I saw first-hand the toll that the production and smoking of opium had taken on the local population, particularly among the men. None of it did anything to dampen the sense in me of a troubled, unfair world, or the desire to try to do something about it, however small. When I returned to the UK and went up to Manchester, I hoped my MA could be the start of my own contribution, but I also wanted some hands-on experience.

I signed up as a volunteer at the Salford Cathedral Homeless Centre. It was a drop-in centre rather than a residential one, but I went there twice a week. I served the homeless food, played cards and pool with them and simply listened to what they had to say. It was a real eye-opener. It's all too easy to see a homeless person on the street almost as a non-person. It doesn't really occur to you that they have a life and a family and have often been in so-called 'normal' jobs. But at some point, or points, along the way they have encountered adversity and have been unable to cope. A lot of them were ex-Forces. They had become institutionalised, and had left the system without any support.

Some of the things I saw were awful. Their shoes, for example, were almost welded to their feet so that you couldn't get them off. The socks had become a part of their feet, too, the skin growing into the fabric.

But, generally, I was struck by the generosity, openness and good humour of the people I met there. Some were happier to talk about their issues and where they had come from than others, but whenever you went there in a bad mood, or in my case with the tribulations of an eating disorder, it was all put into perspective. Your own problems paled into insignificance. I got so much from the experience. It was so gratifying and fulfilling, and it reconfirmed that I had made the right move by pursuing my MA in development. Even if I was concerned more with the international angle, I could see that the same principles applied closer to home.

When my MA was finished, they offered me a paid position at the centre. I decided not to take it, because I wanted to head back south. But my lifelong passion for development (I had a name for it now!) was stronger than ever, and I had some qualifications and experience to back it up. Now I needed to embark on a career.

5

Summits and Volcanoes

On Christmas Day 2001 I went out for a run. Training on Christmas Day is a landmark for any athlete. Considering I wasn't even an athlete to any serious degree at that point, I had to accept that running was now another addiction to add to my list.

I have trained every Christmas Day since then. But when I pounded the streets in 2001 on so holy a day, I did so with a particular goal in mind. I had entered the 2002 London Marathon.

It was my friend Amy who inspired me to do it. She had grown up with a heart defect and had never been a runner, and yet in 2001 she completed the race. I took the decision to enter while I was still in Manchester. I approached a charity, Hope for Children, who agreed to let me run under their banner if I raised £600. Then, when I moved to London that winter, I threw myself into the most unstructured yet obsessive training regime.

I simply ran. Once or twice a day, up and down the Thames path for an hour, the same route, rain or shine. I was living with Tim and Easy in Putney – or rather sleeping on some cushions on their floor – and was on an internship with Card Aid (i.e. selling Christmas cards). All of it was fun, like being back at uni. None of it really encouraged the sort of training values that a credible athlete might adopt. I was eating properly by now. Not necessarily a balanced diet, but it was a lot healthier, as was my perspective on it. That might have been because I justified it with all the running I was doing.

Running was now my primary addiction. I had handed in my thesis, and the London Marathon had replaced academia as the big goal in my life. I ran every day, and it was always for a certain amount of time, never a certain distance. One Sunday I ran for four hours, which I would never do now. It is quite likely that I actually ran more than a marathon without realising it.

I love maps. I've been known to lie in bed and just look at the A–Z. I enjoy seeing how places are connected. My dad had this tiny little measuring device that you could wheel across a map, and it would tell you – via the scale – the distance from A to B. I remember using that in the first few months of training, just to get a rough idea of how far I was running, but it wasn't very accurate. I vaguely plotted my routes on the A–Z – across Clapham Common (I had moved to Clapham North by then), up St John's Hill, through Wandsworth, around Richmond Park, down along the river . . . I just ran and ran. I had no clue about eating or drinking on my runs – so I didn't. And my clothes were decidedly suboptimal – beaten-up trainers, second-hand shorts and a t-shirt I used to wear travelling.

You couldn't beat me for enthusiasm, though. I was passionate about my new pastime/addiction. I ran the Reading Half-Marathon in March, and was astonished at my time. You get put in different starting pens at the London Marathon, based on your expected finish time, and after Reading I asked to be moved into a faster group.

By the time the day arrived, my excitement was soaring. My chief worry was having my photo taken. I've never liked the way I look with my hair pulled back. I have inherited an ear from my dad and an ear from my mum, such that one is significantly larger than the other. So whenever I'm in a photo I like to shake my hair out a bit and cover them up. My favoured hairstyle while running, however, is to have it starkly pulled back in a ponytail. It troubled me that there would likely be photos taken of me on Marathon day with my ears on show. I have never found a solution to this problem.

I spent the night before at my friend Emily's house in Greenwich, where I ate a meal of tuna and pasta, a pre-race convention I observe to this day. I slept fitfully and woke early, but down at the start I was very relaxed, if excited. I don't remember any nerves. My primary concern had morphed from photos to peeing. I have a relatively weak bladder, and the facilities were few and far between and very crowded. So I went behind the nearest bush, which is definitely a convention that I observe to this day.

I felt really good from the start. You always have people passing you at these things, but I was overtaking much more than I was being overtaken. Maybe I am remembering too fondly, but I don't recall ever being in any particular pain. Obviously, you get tired, but I just ran. And ran. The Isle of Dogs is quite tough mentally, because there are fewer people around, but, even then, it wasn't as bad as I'd thought it was going to be.

London looks different on Marathon day. It's a sensational feeling, running by those historic landmarks, cheered on by tens of thousands of well-wishers. It was a beautiful day, and my family had grabbed a position on Tower Bridge, displaying a knack for securing the best spots on the course that has served them well in the intervening years. I had a lot of support, as well, from friends and work colleagues.

And random members of the public. 'Go, girl!' was shouted frequently, because I seemed to be surrounded by men. This was when it dawned on me that I was running pretty fast. I had a watch on, but maths has always been my weakest subject, so I rarely ever calculate my expected finish time even now, and certainly didn't then. I knew from the Reading Half-Marathon that I was capable of running fast, but I was thinking along the lines of 3hr 45min, maybe 3hr 30min. As the end approached, though, I started to overtake a lot of the men who had overtaken me earlier in the day. As the cries of 'Go, girl' attested, I was a rarity as a woman this far advanced in the field. A couple of miles from the end, I thought, 'Shit, I'm going to come in under 3hr 15min!'

I saw my parents and brother as I rounded the corner at Buckingham Palace and headed for the finish line. The euphoria was indescribable. And the sheer surprise. I could not believe my eyes. The clock seemed to be reading 3hr 08min! This couldn't be right. I had annihilated all of my expectations!

At the finish line, I didn't fall over or collapse in a heap. I was too energised, too overjoyed for any of that. They put some foil round me (still got it), but that was surely just to stop me bursting with pride. I had come 1,838th out of 32,889, and eighty-third out of 7,956 women. Paula Radcliffe had won the women's race in 2hr 18min 56sec, so there may still have been a bit for me to work on, but I was blown away by the whole experience.

There must, though, have been more pain than I remember, because one memory I do have is of not being able to get up from the toilet in the Portaloo at the finish. I don't normally sit on a toilet seat – I sort of hover above it but here I had no choice, and fell onto it upon arrival. That was when my quads cramped up, leaving me stuck on the seat. I had to call out for my mum, who came in and pulled me off.

That 'moment' aside, it was wonderful to share the whole experience with my parents and brother. That day, I put to bed many demons as far as my eating was concerned. It corroborated the practice of channelling so much energy into running, and from then on, I turned from being a recreational athlete into one who took sport a lot more seriously. That might have meant even less down-time in a schedule that was becoming increasingly packed as my professional life grew busier and busier, but I'd always been a perpetual-motion kind of girl. And I just loved running.

A month before I ran the Marathon, I had joined the Department for Environment, Food and Rural Affairs (Defra), as a civil servant, executive-officer grade. This was my dream job, and it was my third, barely six months after I had moved to London from Manchester.

Initially, as I've mentioned, I had worked for Card Aid, selling charity Christmas cards at various shops around London. Trade had been quiet one day in their shop in Hampstead, so I looked up the details of other local charities in the *Yellow Pages*, with a view to finding a longer-term job. There weren't many, but one of them called itself the Gaia Foundation. Why not drop in on them during my lunch hour?

I was far from convinced I had come to the right place – it was a terraced house with a bright yellow door almost concealed by a bushy creeper – but I knocked anyway. A girl answered, and I was swept in and enveloped by an amazing little team of people. I spent the next two months working with them. They were helping communities and groups across the world feed into the preparations for the UN's World Summit on Sustainable Development, which was taking place later that year (2002) in Johannesburg. There was a special feel about the place. The vibe established at the front door by that overflowing creeper was carried on throughout the house. There were plants and bits of paper everywhere. It was all very organic and chaotic. And then, in a shed out the back, four of them spent what extra time they could find setting up their own youth-empowerment charity, called Envision. It is now a national organisation, and I am proud to be an ambassador for it.

The team were incredibly friendly, knowledgeable and passionate about grassroots development. We became close friends very quickly, and they did so much to inspire and enthuse me.

As much as I loved the personality of the Gaia Foundation, though, their slightly disorganised, fire-fighting style didn't suit my organised nature, so it was never going to be a job for life. I kept applying for other things and was accepted by Defra, who were initiating a recruitment drive. You didn't know which division of the department you would be based in, and they asked you for your preferences. I could think of nothing worse than working in pig-farming or swine flu or waste management. The only thing I wanted to do at Defra was to work in the international environmental division, or Environment Protection International (EPINT), to give it its official name. And that was what I got – a dream come true. I was to work on the team that was coordinating the whole of the UK Government's input into the World Summit on Sustainable Development.

It was a baptism of fire; I was flying by the seat of my pants. I'd never been in an office job before; I'd never even really worn a suit. But I threw my heart and soul into it. When I didn't know the answer to something, which was often, I made it up or found it out. I did a lot of extra work bringing myself up to speed. Before I knew it, I found myself in a position of some responsibility, because it was all hands on deck. Very soon I was attending meetings, then writing minutes of meetings, then representing the Government at meetings.

I loved it. It was a high-profile position with responsibility and credibility – and it was in a field I was passionate about. I learned a lot about government processes, and enjoyed a close working relationship with Margaret Beckett, who was the Secretary of State for Defra. She's into her caravanning and, what with my dad being obsessed with canals, we had many conversations in praise of the Great British Holiday. She is very sharp and knowledgeable, with a good command of her brief. You didn't have to spoon-feed her the policy lines. We worked some very late nights, particularly as the Summit, which was to be held in September, approached. And it was during the preparations that I met a girl called Georgina Ayre, who is now one of my best friends. She was a representative for Stakeholder Forum, an NGO, and a fellow runner, whose appetite for whirlwind activity may have exceeded even my own.

In September, we set off for the Summit in Johannesburg. All the great and the good were there, with the notable exception of George Bush, whose representatives did their level best to throw a spanner in the works at every turn. I met Tony Blair, who was surprisingly tanned and very charismatic. This was pre-Iraq, so I let him have his picture taken with me.

The timing of it all was wonderful for my career prospects. I was gaining first-hand experience of a high-level UN conference that took place only once every ten years. At one point, I found myself leading for the Government in a meeting with some Nigerian ministers. My superior, Andrew Randall, couldn't go, so I was sent instead. Everyone was so busy that opportunities like that would often come up. If anything needed to be done, my hand was the first in the air.

So there I was, with five Nigerian men of high standing, imparting the UK lines to take, finding common ground, trying to sway them towards our position wherever I could. There were quid pro quos, fall-back positions, bargaining chips. I was negotiating with international statesmen on behalf of my country. Nine months earlier I had been selling Christmas cards. Surreal isn't the word. I felt much the same as I was going to feel five years later when I took the lead in Hawaii for the first time, a few months after turning pro: a bit of a fraud. As if I were looking down on someone else doing it. Surely somebody would overtake me . . .

But it wasn't all negotiating with statesmen. I had an awful lot of photocopying to do as well, not to mention collating papers for ministers to take into negotiations. All of this gave me an intimate knowledge of the brief. There was no cutting and pasting; I knew it all off by heart, which meant I could walk into a room and fill in for someone higher up the pecking order.

Overall, the conference was deemed a success for the UK Government. All of the relevant departments were out there, but as the team leading the delegation it was also deemed a success for EPINT. From my own point of view the agreements established did not go nearly far enough, but there were 190-odd countries present, so a radical consensus was never going to be reached and probably never will be. The fact that one was reached at all was an achievement. The agreements were on too many aspects of development to go into here – they were on every issue you could possibly think of. But the key was always going to be the implementation. If the agreements are not integrated into government policies and action, it just becomes rhetoric. At EPINT, our job was to make sure they were.

On a personal level, the Summit was a great success for me. I was one of a few who were awarded bonuses by Margaret Beckett afterwards. All the ministers have an apartment in Whitehall, and she held a party for us at hers, above Horse Guards Parade, as a thank-you for our efforts.

Over the next couple of years I got to know her quite well. I wrote speeches for her and for the Environment Minister, Michael Meacher. I recall one particular instance at a UN conference in New York in 2004, when I was called to her hotel room to brief her in person. Unfortunately, my computer had just crashed, and I'd lost the document. I was absolutely terrified, and had to brief her from memory. But it all went really well, and we went out afterwards and got drunk on margaritas. My dad had told me never to mix work and alcohol, especially around your superiors. You had to pretend you were drinking, or at least drink some water as well. But these cocktails were just too good. So I ended up getting very drunk with Margaret Beckett. She drank more than me, mind you, but she can handle it. She loves a glass of wine. And a margarita.

After that whirlwind start in 2002, my career at Defra went from strength to strength. In 2003, my life was wonderful. Beyond work and running, I used to pore over *Time Out* and circle things to go to – museums, theatre, shows. My social life was buzzing. There was no man in my life, but there wouldn't have been time, even if I'd been looking for one.

I took some holiday over the New Year, leading into 2003, and visited Nepal, as I had always wanted to. I befriended three amazing Aussie guys, and we trekked to Annapurna Base Camp. I was blown away by the country and resolved to return. Then, towards the end of the year, I visited Tammy, a friend from Card Aid, in Tanzania, where she was working as a teacher at a local school. That, too, was an eye-opener. I saw things in a very different light from the last time I'd been to the country, as a fresh-faced graduate embarking on her first travels.

When you've studied and worked in development, you bring more of a problem-solving attitude to new places. Previously, my heart would bleed at some of the things I saw on my journeys through Africa and Asia, but I wouldn't think much about the causes or the possible solutions. Visiting, or revisiting, the actual places whose problems were held forth upon by dazzling delegates from around the world and ambitious civil servants in Westminster further fuelled doubts that were percolating in my mind. How much of an impact was our work having on the ground? Or, worse still, were our policies actually harming those we were purporting to help? My passion had always been for grassroots development work, and these trips reminded me of that. I loved my job, and the opportunity it brought to work with ministers and within the UN machinery, to meet statesmen such as Kofi Annan. But I was starting to question whether my ultimate intentions were being met.

Nevertheless, I was granted a temporary promotion, which lasted a year and a half, to the grade of higher executive officer. Towards the end of 2003, I started to work on post-conflict environmental reconstruction policy, particularly for Iraq, leading for Defra in negotiations with the United Nations Environment Programme (UNEP). I drafted the UK Government's policy and had it agreed at ministerial level, which was one of the most satisfying moments of my career.

One day, I represented Defra in an intergovernmental meeting on Iraq at the Locarno Suite in the Foreign and Commonwealth Office. I don't think I am breaking the Official Secrets Act by discussing what it's like in there. It's breathtaking just to go into that room. We took our seats at the table that Churchill and his team sat around during the Second World War. And a lot of politically sensitive information was exchanged around it when I was in there with officials from the MoD and the Foreign Office. A few years later, in 2009, my superior from that time asked for my files to help with the Chilcot Enquiry into the UK's role in the war.

I even made it into 10 Downing Street. With no knickers on. At that time, I was swimming before work every day. On this particular day, I cycled to the pool in my cycling gear, changed into my swimwear, swam, then cycled to Defra. When I changed into my work clothes, I discovered I had left my pants at home. Muppet. So I cycled from Defra to Downing Street with only my skirt between me and the saddle. They wouldn't let me leave my bike outside Number Ten, so I left it tied to a railing on Whitehall with a special plea not to have it blown up by security. Then I went inside for my meeting with Tony Blair's private secretary. I was especially careful not to do a Sharon Stone.

To my delight, it turns out that the inside of Number Ten is a very faithful reproduction of the set for *Love Actually*, one of my favourite films. Not that I got to explore much. I walked in through the front door and was taken up a flight of stairs to quite an austere, oak-panelled room. In between regular bouts of skirt-straightening, I looked around the place with awe. But I was also careful to appear nonchalant, as if I came in here every day. It's the Daley Thompson method, and something I follow meticulously as an athlete. However exhausted he might have felt at the end of an event, Daley always walked away nonchalantly, as if it hadn't hurt him at all. Never give your opponents anything.

Just as my career was taking off, so was my passion for competitive sport. No longer was it only a social pursuit (although it was still that), a mere distraction from the business of achievement elsewhere. Now it was an outlet for achievement in itself.

After the Marathon in 2002, I joined the Serpentine Running Club. I trained with them on Wednesday evenings after work, joining the group on the Three Parks loop, starting at Serpie's HQ by Marble Arch and running the 7.2 miles round Hyde Park, St James's Park and Green Park, back to Marble Arch. I held my own and started to get quite competitive with the boys. I ran a few times for the club, and that summer won the women's events in the club championships over one mile, 3km and 5km.

On Thursday evenings, the club trained at Battersea Park. I went along a couple of times that summer, where Frank Horwill, the legendary coach of British middle-distance runners, held his sessions. They looked a bit more serious than the Serpentine's, so I went over and got talking to him. I told him of my new ambition, which was to finish in under three hours at the 2003 London Marathon, and he said he could help.

He was in his mid-seventies at the time, a sprightly man, small of stature but huge of personality. Tuesdays and Thursdays we were down at the track, but it was his Saturday sessions I loved the most. We would start at the track, then go off on a 5km loop. Then he would have us running up and down banks carrying each other. There would be hopping races, press-ups, sit-ups. It was like being on an army camp. And he was very much the sergeant major, barking out orders and reprimands in his clipped Empire accent, never once losing the mischievous glint in his eye.

'You're all a bunch of pussies!' was a favourite of his.

He called the women 'wenches' and, even though he knew full well what my name was, he always called me 'Sissy'. We spent a lot of those sessions doubled up – and not just because we were knackered.

'Sissy!' he would shout at me as I ran past. 'How's your sex life? Have you got a man yet?'

'No, Frank.'

'Why not? What's wrong with you?'

He was very open about sex. He felt we should all be having it. No one could be a successful athlete, it seemed, unless they were having sex at least five times a week. He was constantly trying to pair us off with each other, and boasting about how many women he had on the go. 'Not dead yet, am I?' he would cry. And then he would drop and do a press-up.

Most of all, though, he was a wonderful man, and the first proper running coach I ever had. He gave me such confidence, and immediately I could see improvements. At last, there was some structure and variety to my training, which I found so enjoyable in a team environment. Frank had around a hundred articles on the Serpentine website, offering advice on every aspect of an athlete's regime. I printed them all off, kept them in a folder and studied them assiduously. I learned about nutrition, which meant another step away from anorexia. I was eating to run now, rather than running to justify my eating. My diet was balanced and tailored towards my sport. Running had replaced anorexia, and I felt and looked a lot healthier for it.

All of these things, though, are obsessive. Nothing had changed in my personality with regard to that lust for control, but now it had found a healthier outlet. I had put on weight since Manchester, but I was generally happy with how I looked. Or, maybe I should say that I was happy with my body, because it was no longer so much about how it looked, about that image in the mirror, but more about how it functioned, about how effectively it enabled me to pursue my new passion for running. Those years, 2002 and 2003, were wonderful times for me. I'd never been happier. Attaining a distinction for my MA had helped boost my confidence, but it was the London Marathon that really clinched it. And the way things took off so quickly at Defra further consolidated things.

But it was intense. I was fitting my running around my work, which was relentless as it was. I ran to work. Lunch hours were spent pounding the streets. 'Mate, does it look as if I've been running?' I would say to Georgie, before staggering into the office after lunch, red of face, in different clothes from the ones I'd been wearing in the morning, sweat trickling down my brow.

Two evenings a week, work permitting, I was training with Frank and his group, known as the Horwill Harriers. One Harrier was also a colleague of mine at Defra, Dorothea 'Dorchie' Lee. She is now Dorothea Cockerell because, to Frank's unbridled delight, she did get together with another in his group, Will Cockerell, a talented British marathon runner. Dorchie was an excellent athlete too – much better than I was. The two of us went over to Amsterdam one weekend in 2002 to run the Amsterdam Half-Marathon.

During the build-up to the 2003 London Marathon, I was so excited. I ran the Reading Half-Marathon and improved on the year before. I was on course for a sub-three-hour showing in London. I had my eyes on 2hr 57min.

My impatience with our capital's public transport meant I had bought a £50 second-hand mountain bike for commuting around town. A couple of weeks before the big day, I was cycling from my cousin Tim's house to mine in Clapham on a Sunday afternoon. The traffic was heavy on the north side of Clapham Common, so I was taking my time in the cycle lane. Suddenly, a car pulled into a petrol station and I had no time to stop. I hit the side of the car, flew over my handlebars and crashed onto the pavement, cutting open my chin. The bike followed me over, and some part of it – I think it must have been the end of a handlebar – thumped into my thigh. I was fine, but the blood from my chin was enough to involve an ambulance. Tim accompanied me to hospital, where I picked up four stitches.

Even as I was in mid-air, flying over the handlebars, I was thinking, 'Will I be able to run the Marathon?' I kept asking the paramedics the same question in the ambulance, even though my wounds seemed superficial. They released me that night, but the next time I tried to run it was clear something was not right with my left thigh. I ran on anyway, but within a couple of days I could no longer do that. I couldn't even stretch off my quad properly. I saw a doctor, and he diagnosed a haematoma. There was no way I could run the Marathon.

That was the year Paula Radcliffe broke the world record. It was the first time I had ever watched a marathon live. I was amazed at the sheer speed of the woman as she flew by. The atmosphere in the crowd was electrifying that year, as Britain's darling romped home. How I longed to be taking part. I was devastated.

My injury turned into quite a problem over the following months. Running so soon on my haematoma had exacerbated it, such that, after scans a few months later, they found a 5cm spur of bone growing from my femur. Myositis ossificans, they call it. Sometimes your body reacts to a haematoma by calcifying. If you then run on it, the muscle around it will tear, causing further bleeding and further calcification. I had stopped running quite soon after the injury, but I used the opportunity to start swimming again (initially with a float between my legs, on doctor's orders, so I didn't have to kick). I continued cycling to work. None of it seemed to bother my leg. But there it was, this bony spur. The specialist told me I just had to be patient and wait for the injury to heal and the bony spur to mature, that is, to stop growing. This it did by the end of 2003. It's still there now, though. I can actually feel it in my thigh.

Something else had been growing inside me in 2003, and that was the sense that my work at Defra was not making the difference to the world that I had hoped it might. I was becoming disillusioned with all the bureaucracy and red tape.

The breaking point came on a trip to the island of Jeju, in South Korea, at the end of March 2004. There was a forum being held there by the governing council of the United Nations Environment Programme (UNEP). We flew out business class on KLM and stayed in the five-star Lotte Hotel with its vast gilt foyer. Outside, the grounds were immaculately manicured. There was a massive replica of a Dutch windmill and an artificial volcano that went off at night every hour, on the hour. We spent a certain amount of time milling around beneath it, drinking wine and eating canapés.

I sat there one evening with Georgie, looking out at the scene. Suddenly, my quietly building doubts over the work we were doing came crashing in on me. For the first time, I felt naked revulsion for the hypocrisy of it all.

'What is this?' Georgie and I said to each other. 'We've flown business class, we're eating canapés, sipping champagne, staying at a five-star hotel with erupting volcanoes – and we're talking about eradicating poverty and delivering water and sanitation to the millions of people who don't have it.'

For so many people out there that week, what they were doing was a job, not a passion. They get so caught up in the minutiae of the text – where does this comma go, what does this word say? They don't take a step back and think about whether it is going to effect change.

Why are we negotiating a quantifiable target for the improvement of infrastructure? The fact that there is no demand for the infrastructure is what we need to be addressing, or that people do not have the capacity to use or maintain it.

A lot of the people I worked with were there for the crack of the negotiation. There was one guy in my team in particular, who thrived on it. It was his drug; it was a game. He wasn't passionate about international development. He was passionate about winning the argument, negotiating over the text. I'm sure he didn't worry too much about whether any of it trickled down to those living in poverty. A brief survey of the scene under the erupting volcano told you all you needed to know about how much some of these senior civil servants and diplomats valued their five-star lifestyle.

I won't act the innocent too much, though, when it comes to playing the game. Jeju was a great success for me. I was very confident in my job by now, building relationships with people that would benefit the UK. Occasionally I led for the Government in negotiating new text for water and sanitation, but usually I was sitting at the right hand of my boss, Roy Hathaway, who is a fantastic guy, feeding him information. A lot of negotiation takes place in smoky back rooms, and I played a part in that with the heads of delegation of the countries present. I ended up writing the paper that formed the EU's position on water and sanitation. What happens is that you draft the paper, incorporating all of the UK's priorities, get it rubber-stamped, whoop and cheer and, before you know it, it has become EU policy.

It was a busy week, but Georgie and I spent a fair amount of it going on runs. One evening we returned to the hotel to find that we were late for the big dinner that was being attended by all the heads and secretaries of state. We couldn't very well walk in through the foyer in our sweaty gear while the high-ranking dignitaries gathered in their penguin suits. Nor could we approach from the erupting volcano end, where the champagne was already being sipped. After a quick reconnoitre of which a double-0 agent might have been proud, we found a way into the hotel through the spa, shot up to our rooms and were soon chomping on canapés as if nothing had happened.

It was a familiar scenario. A few weeks later we went to the twelfth session of the UN Commission on Sustainable Development in New York, where I was to swig margaritas with Margaret Beckett. Georgie and I had both entered the Brooklyn Half-Marathon during the two-week stay. We got up at 5.30 a.m. every morning to run before our sixteen-hour day started, the UN negotiations stretching into the night. We would turn up at the 7.30 a.m. UK delegation meeting with red faces, freshly showered hair and a large bagel in our hands.

Running day in, day out with somebody is the quickest way to forge a friendship. For a start you're talking together for an hour or two each time. You see each other at your rawest, with no make-up or fancy clothes, just Lycra, sweat and sometimes tears. There is no façade to hide behind. You're running, it hurts and by the end of it you're feeling fairly broken and laid out bare. In New York that year I suffered some gastro distress and fertilised Central Park as we went round, just to add extra spice to the mix. How could Georgie and I not become the best of friends after that?

We had a wonderful day at the Brooklyn Half-Marathon. I came second out of around 1,200 women (and sixty-seventh out of 3,000 overall). Georgie came twenty-fifth, and I screamed, 'Go, girl!' from the sidelines as she approached the end. She later bought me a pair of knickers (still got them) with the words GO GIRL emblazoned across the bum. Before every race since, she has texted me the same message. It has become a kind of mantra for us.

After my epiphany in Jeju, I decided once and for all that it was time to look for new work at grassroots level. It was also around then that I happened upon triathlon. I was visiting my friends Pete and Rachel in Birmingham. Rachel was a member of the Birmingham Running and Triathlon (BRAT) Club, so I went with her to their Sunday swim session. There I met Paul Robertshaw, a man always on the lookout for fresh talent, as chairman of the BRAT club and as a single man with a glint in his eye! Either way, I credit him with the direction my life was about to take.

'Have you ever tried triathlon?' he asked me at the poolside.

'No.'

'You should give it a shot.'

Rachel told him about my recent achievements as a runner, and the three of us talked about triathlon. His enthusiasm and offers of support were infectious, and I left for London that night determined to buy myself a road bike and to find out more about this new sport.

It wasn't the first time I'd heard of it. At the Serpentine Running Club I had met a girl called Elinor Rest who competed for Great Britain at the Age Group World Championships in Cancún, Mexico in 2002. This achievement had made an impression on me, but it had also brought home the fact that I was rubbing shoulders with proper athletes. Now, eighteen months later, I rang Ellie to pick her brains further. She ended up selling me her third-hand, yellow-and-black Peugeot. It looked like a bumble bee. Still got it.

I didn't have a clue. It cost £300, which was a lot for me, and I just rode it as it was. No clip-in shoes, no bike fitting; I sat on it and pedalled.

My first race was the Eton Super Sprint on 16 May 2004, a short, sharp free-for-all in the shadow of Windsor Castle for enthusiasts of all standards. I came third in that first one, but won the next two I entered in June and July. My lace got caught round the crank of my bike in one of them, and I fell off; then I ran down the finish chute without realising there was another lap to go. So Muppet was still very much stalking my every move. But I was also getting pretty good at this swimming, biking, running lark, and these mishaps did not prevent me from winning. I was so happy – as proud as I'd ever been. I was awarded a Timex watch for each win, a little glass thingummy and a voucher for £40 (although entry was around £50).

Paul came to watch, and invited me to compete for the BRAT club. It didn't matter, apparently, that I lived in London, and he put me in touch with another club member, Matt Hawcroft, who lived nearby. Suddenly, I couldn't get enough of the training, especially the cycling. I would cycle home from work, head to Richmond Park and flog myself for three laps. But, as ever, there was no programme or structure. I just rode.

Under BRAT colours I entered the Milton Keynes Triathlon in July and the Bedford Triathlon in August. Both were Olympic distance, which is a 1.5km swim, a 40km bike ride and a 10km run. I came fourth at Milton Keynes and third at Bedford. I won a silver plate. The two girls who had beaten me had represented Great Britain at the Age Group World Championships. I knew then that I had a talent for triathlon. By that stage, though, developments on the work front were about to take me away on another adventure altogether.

6

Nepal

After the erupting volcano experience in Jeju, I started looking for some hands-on development work, and found myself drawn towards Nepal. On my travels through Asia in 2000, it was one country I hadn't visited, bar a brief stop in transit at Kathmandu airport, where I'd met the most engaging Nepali. I'd made a decision then to revisit the country properly, which I did over New Year 2003. After that three-week stay, during which I trekked to Annapurna Base Camp, I fell in love with the place.

After investigating options on the internet, I was offered a job by a local Nepali NGO called Rural Reconstruction Nepal (RRN), run by a well-known political activist called Dr Arjun Karki. The salary was $80 a month.

My heart screamed yes, but when it came to the crunch the decision was difficult. For all of my frustrations with it, my job at Defra was a good one and I did enjoy it. What was more, the following year (2005) would see the UK hold the presidency of the G8 and the EU. This meant my job would be invested with an increased level of responsibility. No longer would we be feeding into EU documents, we would actually be drafting them. The hours would be long, but the career progression rapid, as Georgie was to find out because she took my job when I left, and thrived.

It was always at the back of my mind, even after I decided to go to Nepal. Should I have stayed? Later it occurred to me that if I had stayed and made a success of it, would I ever have become a professional triathlete? On these decisions hang more than you can ever know at the time.

In the end, I applied for a sabbatical and my request was accepted. On 9 September 2004, I headed to Nepal.

It's easy to see why anyone would fall in love with Nepal, especially if they had a passion for the outdoors. It has some of the most awe-inspiring scenery in the world, and against the backdrop of the world's highest mountains the local culture of temples, festivals and free-ranging animals is vivid in colour and personality.

There is a lot wrong as well, though. The country was in the midst of a civil war when I arrived. The Communist Party of Nepal (Maoist) was intent on overthrowing the corrupt ruling monarchy and turning the country into a republic. They would eventually succeed, but when I arrived the conflict was well into its ninth year. The atmosphere was fraught. The Maoists drew their strength from the vast constituency of poor in Nepal who had nothing to lose. They destroyed police stations, army barracks and the local infrastructure, extorting money from tourists and calling frequent strikes or *bandhs*, which brought cities and towns to a halt. The monarchical government, through the Nepalese Army, responded with intimidatory tactics. More than 10,000 people died during the course of the ten-year civil war. It was a dangerous place to be, particularly at RRN. Arjun, our boss, was on a list of political dissidents wanted by the government. While I was there he was put under house arrest for antagonising them, and towards the end of my stay, in 2005, we had to smuggle him out of the country.

RRN operated out of a ramshackle building with wires everywhere, much like all of the buildings in Kathmandu, other than those owned by the government and the embassies. It turned out RRN was the largest local NGO in Nepal. Apart from me, a British woman called Ruth and an Austrian called Bernard, all of the employees were Nepali. Everyone was incredibly welcoming, and threw myself into the work as a jack of all trades, overhauling the website, editing documents, writing policy proposals and chapters for books, applying for funding and, in time, managing my own project, which was called the Community Water, Sanitation and Health (CWASH) project.

I loved my job, particularly the first-hand project management experience with CWASH. During the UN conference in New York in 2004, I had attended a lecture from a man called Dr Kamal Kar, who challenged the traditional concept of development through his Community-Led Total Sanitation scheme. The scheme did away with grand projects of investment and modernisation in poverty-stricken regions, and concentrated on education and empowerment at grassroots level. It was aimed at helping people to help themselves. He made a huge impression on me, and I enjoyed some lengthy discussions with him afterwards. I set about trying to pilot his scheme through CWASH.

The project was focused on the remote, conflict-ridden district of Salyan, a few hundred miles west of Kathmandu. It was not uncommon for a village of a hundred people to share one or two toilets. Men thought nothing of defecating in the open. Women would do the same, although custom allowed them to do so only before dawn or after dark.

Everyone in a community was encouraged to go on transect walks, or 'walks of shame', in which they identified how the waste was finding its way into rivers, livestock, crops, hands and feet. It led to the calculation that each person was ingesting between ten and twenty grams of faeces every day. Feelings of shame and disgust would trigger a desire for change and discussions about how the situation might be improved. It was a process of empowerment from ground level up. It was the very opposite of what we were doing beneath the erupting volcano.

CWASH took me deep into the Nepali countryside. We would drive for ten hours in a jeep along rocky roads to visit communities in the direst poverty, torn apart by the civil war. It was painful to witness, but so invigorating to empower them to improve their lives.

Immediately on arrival in Kathmandu I started investigating the prospects of pursuing triathlon. Not good. The only pool in the city was a 50m cesspit, so swimming was out of the question. I ran every morning when I first arrived, but you were taking your life in your hands among the Wacky Races traffic, smog and rabid dogs. So I soon bought myself a mountain bike and I christened him Prem (*premi* is Nepalese for boyfriend). Around that trusty steed, who had already traversed the Himalaya with his previous owner, my social life took off.

The first person I met was this wonderful, very married German guy, Cornelius. We soon forged a deep, platonic relationship that involved cycling off through the forests of Shivapuri National Park, to the north of the city, being eaten by leeches and carrying our bikes along what was left of trails washed away by the monsoon season.

I also joined a group of cyclists – six or seven local guys and anyone else who fancied coming along – organised by a Nepali called Sonam. He is a biking institution in Kathmandu, and owns the best bike shop in the city, Dusk Till Dawn. Through that group I met three *didis* ('sisters' in Nepali), an Argentinian called Agustina (or Tina), an Australian called Helen and a German called Billi. Tina is one of the kindest and calmest people I have ever met. Even now, if I get stressed about something, I ask myself what Tina would do. Billi, meanwhile, is my soulmate. We could have been separated at birth, our attitudes and characters are so similar. She was out there as a freelance journalist and translator.

Billi and Tina are mountaineers (Billi has since summited three mountains higher than 8,000m, including Everest), and they invited me on an expedition during Dashain, which is a two-week festival in celebration of the family. The Nepalese calendar is full of festivals. They seem to have more holidays than work days. Teej was my favourite – the festival for women, where every married woman wears the scarlet sari she wore on her wedding day. All the festivals are dazzling spectacles of colour and vivacity. People dance in their jewellery and throw coloured paint and water over each other. The cows, which wander where they please throughout the city, are bedecked with garlands, and each wears a crimson *tikka*, or painted dot, on its forehead.

But for my first Dashain in Nepal, I went with Tina and Billi to Langtang, a region in the north of Nepal that borders Tibet. We took the rickety 'bus' from Kathmandu and, as usual, chose to sit on the top most of the way, rather than be stuck inside with vomiting children, chickens, goats and mountains of luggage. This particular journey was about twelve hours, though, which was a bit hard on the bum. We were aiming to summit an unconquered 6,000m peak. There were harnesses, ropes and crampons involved. Tina and Billi were fine, but I hadn't got a clue. We were accompanied by our friend Namgya, who is a Sherpa. Unfortunately, an avalanche meant we didn't make it to the top, but we were the first to try. A couple of years later the mountain was renamed Baden-Powell Scout Peak, and now they lead expeditions up it.

It was on that trip that I had my first brush with altitude sickness. We had reached 4,500m when we decided we should climb what looked from where we were standing like a nearby hill. But because we were already standing at 4,500m, it was a hill whose summit was

5,300m above sea level. Me being me, I decided to see how fast I could get up it. Sure enough, I beat Billi and Tina to the top and celebrated among the coloured prayer flags on the summit. Well done me.

On the way down, though, things turned nasty. My head felt as if it were in a vice; the blood started to pound against the inside of my constricting skull. By the time I got back to the trekking lodge, I couldn't lift my head at all. I sat for hours slumped over my haunches, a broken woman. I thought I was going to die, which is far from an unreasonable fear with altitude sickness. I was afraid to go to sleep the pain was so intense, but Billi and Tina looked after me.

A day later, we went up to 5,000m and camped, and I was fine. The problem was not that I couldn't adapt to altitude; it was that I had gone up too quickly. I may have reached the top first, but Billi and Tina had won the day. At those altitudes, my competitiveness had been exposed as immaturity, and I paid the price. Lesson learned.

There was still plenty of scope for competitiveness elsewhere, though. I entered a few mountain-bike races. I was often the only girl, and I managed to beat the majority of the men. Then, for New Year we went to Pokhara, cycling the 200km from Kathmandu. With rucksacks on backs, we set off at 7 a.m. on the terrible roads, which were a lot of things but flat wasn't one of them. I just would not give in. One by one, everyone dropped out and finished the journey by bus, except for me and the Nepali mountain-bike champion. We arrived, showered and headed straight out for a night on the town.

And those morning rides with Sonam and his team were a daily opportunity to test myself against men at altitude. Kathmandu sits in a bowl, whose lowest point is 1,350m above sea level. When you cycle out of town, you are straight into the mountains surrounding the city.

I used to get up at the crack of dawn, which is actually an hour or two later than most Nepalese, who tend to rise at 4 a.m. just after the first cock crow has awakened the first dog, whose incessant barking wakes the next, and so on until they crescendo into a canine pre-dawn chorus: somewhat tedious.

With the sun rising over the foothills of the Himalaya, I would set out for the designated meeting spot with the team. The cows meandered drunkenly through the streets, the butchers slaughtered their goats, the Hindu bells rang and the poor children scavenged on piles of rubbish or sat slumped in doorways, breathing glue fumes from paper bags.

Each morning the riders met at a *chiyaa* stall. This milky, sweet Nepalese tea was drunk by the gallon out of vessels washed loosely with a swill of local parasites. I suffered from giardia and other intestinal issues almost constantly in Nepal. But after a couple of cups of *chiyaa* I was ready for anything, and off we would cycle into the foothills around town, where buffalo pulled their ploughs through the terraced paddy fields. We climbed through villages of ochre mud-houses and past elaborate temples. Scantily clad children would fly home-made kites from the rooftops, their freedom and weightless-ness a poignant image in a country crushed by civil war. In the distance rose the 8,000m peaks of the Himalaya.

Our morning bike rides usually took two hours, and I was back in time for work. (Well, I hardly ever was, but they didn't seem to mind my being a bit late. They liked the fact that I was getting out into the local villages.) At the weekend, the rides were longer. It was usually Cornelius, Billi, Tina and me, but others would often join us. We just rode and rode. We ate and drank whatever we could lay our hands on in the villages we passed – usually *chiyaa*, chick-pea curry, coconut biscuits (at four pence a packet) or deep-fried doughnuts. Wherever we ended up at dusk on the Saturday, we would seek shelter, sometimes in the house of a local, sometimes at a monastery. Dinner was always the same, as was lunch during the week. *Dhal bhat* – rice, lentil soup and curry. The Nepalese eat it twice a day. I loved it. Then, on the Sunday we wended our way back to Kathmandu by the most indirect route possible.

We would arrive back in town exhausted, sweaty and hungry, but with spirits soaring. We had no idea how far we had been, how many calories we'd burned, what heart rate we'd maxed out at. There was no data to download or logbook to tick. This was raw and elemental, the way sport and adventure has always been. I'm sure it was the making of me.

Then again, our sixteen-day bike ride from Lhasa, the capital of Tibet, back to Kathmandu via Everest Base Camp, might also have played a part. Billi, Tina and I pledged to make the trip while we were on our expedition in Langtang. At the end of April 2005, we flew to Lhasa and made our preparations for the 1,200km ride home. We called ourselves the Rangi-Changi team. *Rangi-changi* means 'multi-coloured' in Nepali. Our team consisted of Billi, a German; Tina, an Argentinian; Rupesh, a Nepali; Trond, a Norwegian; Chris and Kirsten, who were Danish; and me.

Tibet is very different from Nepal. Where Kathmandu sits in a bowl of lush vegetation, up over the other side of the Himalaya stretches the desert plateau of Tibet. Not much survives there, beyond clumps of course grass, chubby little desert rats and the yaks, which can cope with almost anything. As can the Tibetan nomads, who wander across the land setting up home for two months at a time, before moving on with their train of yaks, dogs and sheep. Tibetans are becoming a minority in their homeland as the encroaching tentacles of the Chinese take greater hold. What began as a violent annexation in the 1950s has become a subtler process of assimilation, as the Chinese move in on the roads and railways that increasingly penetrate the interior. I tried to talk to our guide about the situation, but he was reluctant to be drawn. He did reveal that he had spent three years in prison – for what, I don't know. On the morning of the day we set off, a few of us visited the Potala Palace, which was the residence of the Dalai Lama until he went into exile during the failed Tibetan uprising in 1959. It made a huge impression on me, standing tall on elevated ground over Lhasa, as if in defiance of the Chinese influence that closes in ever more tightly on the city below. Once it would have been a hive of activity; now, sadly, it is little more than a museum.

That afternoon, we began the long ride home. Arid it may have been, but the scale of the landscape was breathtaking. The plains stretched out with nothing but the odd dust tornado disturbing the peace. Beyond them, the land rose into barren mountains, and beyond those mountains lay the snowy Himalaya.

The going was tough from the start. We lost Trond and Rupesh to altitude sickness on the second day. They were taken by bus to Shigatse, to wait for us there. The rest of us soldiered on. This was Prem's second tour of duty in the Himalaya and he never let me down, even as we struggled against the stinging dust that was whipped up into our faces by the wind. At the end of the second day, I lay down in my tent with the horrible symptoms of altitude sickness overcoming me. We were at 4,800m and had much further to climb, but my body seemed to adapt overnight, even if my sleep never did. The higher we ascended, the lighter my sleep became and the more vivid my dreams.

We stayed an extra day to acclimatise at that altitude, which we spent with a family of nomads, whose temporary shelter of yak skin was just across the river. The ruddy-faced young son taught me how to use a home-made catapult, and inside the tent we were treated to the local Tibetan delicacy – yak butter tea. I'll try anything, but this blend of hot water, tea leaves, yak butter and salt tested that characteristic to the limit. It's vile, and it's ubiquitous in Tibet.

We struck camp on 1 May, but the maypoles of Merrie England

seemed a long way away. That particular day was a neat microcosm of the whole trip, taking in euphoria and despair, the heavenly and the hellish. By midday, we had made it to the top of a snowy pass at 5,400m. Tears were in my eyes at what we had achieved, and at the sheer beauty of the terrain we had cycled through, not to mention that which we could see in the distance. Having stopped for lunch at a small settlement of whitewashed houses on the plain the other side, we set off for the next pass that rose from the plateau to a mere 5,000m. This one, though, turned into an interminable slog. We regrouped at 5 p.m., and it was then that it started to snow. On we went, up through the hairpins as a full-on blizzard closed in. Conditions were even more horrific on the descent, as I lost touch with my extremities. The voices of Frank and Georgie rang in my ears: 'When things are tough, you are tougher.' Just as I thought my extremities could take no more, we came across a building, which turned out to be a workman's residence. Mercifully, we were able to bed down in the relative warmth of a spare room. We left our bikes outside, though, and in the morning the components were frozen solid. Solution? We peed on them. By 8 a.m. we were on the move again.

Most of the days contained highs and lows of epic proportions, geographically, meteorologically, physically and emotionally. But what a high, on all counts, we reached at Base Camp! I found it impossible to look at Everest without crying. When I rounded a corner in the National Park after yet another draining ascent, and the Himalaya hove into view for the first time, tears welled up in my eyes. I couldn't actually see Everest because it was shrouded in cloud, but just knowing it was there was enough. The next day, after a stay in a delightful little village, we set off for Base Camp. Everest rose majestically in the distance, but it seemed to take an age to reach the base. The rode was so bumpy it was like riding on rumble strips. The vibrations made our arms ache, but the pain paled into insignificance as the mountain drew closer.

We finally made it to Base Camp under an unrelenting sun that blistered my lips. More tears. Base Camp is incredibly civilised, with its rows of tents all colour-coded according to the different climbing parties. There are sleeping tents, mess tents, toilet tents, even internet tents. Billi introduced us to a group leader, and soon we were chatting away with the climbers preparing for the summit. I'm not sure I would ever be able to go up there. It's not the physical and mental demands, necessarily; it's more the sitting around, waiting for a window in the weather, waiting to acclimatise to each new level of altitude. That's what would break me.

We stayed the night at the monastery at Rombuk and spent a further day of rest at Base Camp, chatting to climbers about their motivations and the challenges they face. We visited the shrine, shrouded in prayer flags, commemorating those who have died on Everest. Still more tears. It was sobering to think that one or two of the climbers at Base Camp that day might have their lives taken by the mountain above us, which looked so innocent and charming in the warm sunshine.

The border with Nepal was only three days' ride away. The contrast in the landscape and conditions from one side of the Himalaya to the other is astounding. One day we were battling into a fierce, cold 60mph headwind, sandblasted for hours by the dust and gravel it blew into our faces, our heads wrapped in layer upon layer of fabric. The next we were cycling through verdant mountains of waterfalls, forests, birds and insects. After a torrential downpour at border control, we were back into our t-shirts floating through thirty-degree heat down the side of the mountains. Tibet and Nepal are stunningly beautiful in their own ways, but Nepal is so much more alive, and it was good to be back.

My time in Nepal wasn't all sanitation and flogging myself up and down mountains. I have always liked having a calming influence in my life. Tina played that role to a great extent. My relentless competitiveness meant I always had to be the first to the top of each mountain pass when we cycled across the Himalaya. I spent a lot of time waiting for the others. Tina, on the other hand, would never rush. She taught me so much about the 'smelling the roses' approach to life, the travelling over the arriving. So too did an older lady called Suzy. I met her through Tina, who was a work colleague. Like Tina, she had an aura of peace about her – an older version of Jude, my friend from South Africa. She wore her white hair in a bob and carried herself with a grace I found very settling.

We became very good friends, and used to meet for *chiyaa* at a café near where I worked. We talked about everything – men, Buddhism, development, films, books. Suzy loves to read (she is a qualified librarian) and recommended a lot of books to me. She also loves to write. Haiku are a particular favourite of hers – a Japanese convention of poetry that consists, in English, of three short lines. She did a lot of work in Nepal with a famous Nepalese poet, Janak Sapkota. They published a book of haiku together. We all attended the launch, where Suzy and Janak gave readings. I found it incredibly inspiring. I loved the simplicity of the haiku and its ability to capture a scene, a moment or a feeling. I started composing them myself, often when I was biking. Sometimes they just came to me; sometimes I had to play around with them a little. When I got home the first thing I did was to write them down. Looking back, they form a kind of diary of my life out there, snippets of feelings and images.

There's a place called Durbar Square in the centre of Kathmandu, where many of the Hindu temples can be found. I used to go there after work and sit on the temple steps, drinking *chiyaa*.

There was a woman who used to frequent the square. I couldn't say for sure how old she was – possibly early thirties. She had a daughter with her, who looked healthy, apart from her teeth, but bad teeth are very common in Nepal. And she carried what I had assumed was a baby. It turned out that this 'baby' was two years old.

The woman's name was Sita. She spoke no English, but my Nepali was just about good enough for us to communicate. I befriended her over a period of a few months. Her younger daughter, whose name was Parbati, could not walk and would feed only from Sita's bosom.

In Kathmandu, as in so many places, you see heartbreaking sights every day of families suffering the direst poverty and the most debilitating conditions. You have no choice but to pass them by, and so their plight never becomes personal to you. You feel powerless, because no matter how distressing their conditions, you can't possibly help them all. And the more you pass by, the more immune you become to the sight of the destitution.

If you can't possibly help them all, then how can you justify helping any? Well, when you find yourself getting to know a family on a personal level, as I did with Sita's, how can you not? It just happened that Sita and I became friends, over the months. I learned of Parbati's problems, and played with her elder sister. In time, I met Sita's husband, who earned a meagre wage as a porter. I visited their home, in a crumbling building, which was a tiny room with bare stone walls and a bed.

The further I entered into their world, the more I wanted to do something. Their cause became a mini-crusade of mine, particularly that of Parbati. I arranged for her to have some tests and, with a donation from my parents, paid for an MRI scan, which cost around £60. It turned out she had tuberculosis of the spine.

I raised a little bit more money, mostly from my own pocket, for an operation, which was successfully performed in a local hospital. Parbati's deformity was corrected, but she had to be fitted with a brace during recovery. I visited them in hospital every lunch hour.

Their plight also touched my mum, who, in addition to some money, sent over gifts for the girls from England.

This was now August 2005, and I realised I had done enough in terms of handouts. What we needed to do was to find a way of helping them earn a living. So I bought Sita a *chana* cart for about a hundred pounds. *Chana* means 'chickpea' in Nepalese, and these carts are portable snack stalls. There's a little stove on it, an awning and dishes from which you can sell chickpeas, popcorn, peanuts, and so on. Sita had really wanted one. It seemed a realistic way for her to earn some money without having to revert to begging. I also introduced Sita to my friend Nonna, who had founded a charity called Girls Education Nepal, and she agreed to accept Sita's elder girl on the programme.

Things seemed to be going well. I saw Sita at Durbar Square a few times after that, selling food from her cart. But I also saw her begging again, playing on Parbati's problems as a sympathy tool, which annoyed me after what she had been through to have the condition corrected.

Then, one day, I visited Sita's home and saw that the cart had gone. Sita confessed that she had sold it. I was so hurt and angry, but you don't express such feelings in Nepali culture, so I had to let it go.

From that day on, I would see Sita occasionally begging in the square. She wouldn't look at me, still less speak to me, so I think she knew I was upset. But the temptation to sell the cart was too great. Those in poverty are often forced to adopt a short-term perspective. It's hand-to-mouth. She would get more money from selling the cart than she would in a week of selling *chana*, so it was an inevitable decision, I suppose, even if her longer-term interests would have been better served by keeping it.

Unfortunately, a darker side to Sita was emerging. The first sign of it was when she asked me to buy her a watch, around the time Parbati was having her scans. This chilled me, not just because it was an aggressive line for her to take but also because of the possibility that she was adopting it because of the gifts I had provided up till then. Had it bred greed and dependency in her?

Soon she was flying in the face of Nepali culture. Certainly, her family was unusual in that she was the matriarch, where traditionally Hindu women are somewhat subservient. Things started to get out of hand, though, after she sold the cart. Her elder daughter was now going to a local school through the support of Girls Education Nepal. Sita strode into the headmaster's office to demand the money he had received from the charity to buy books; she did the same with the tailor who had been paid to make her daughter's school uniform.

Now, Sita and her family have lived through the kind of hardship that I, like most Westerners, could never begin to understand, so I will never judge her for her actions. But I became very disillusioned after that. It made me wonder what we Westerners can really do to help people in developing countries. I do still blame myself sometimes, worrying whether I went about things the right way. My approach was not dissimilar from the one the West adopts towards the developing world on a larger scale. We ride into town and hand things out, sometimes through guilt, but also through concern for our fellow human beings and a desire to make things better. But it doesn't work. The change has to come from within. My time in Nepal only reinforced my belief in Kamal Kar's community-led approach, which aims first and foremost to empower communities to help themselves. Only then can charity from the West have a chance of achieving the desired effect.

The trouble with Dr Kar's approach, though, is that it is time-intensive but not money-intensive, and most donors don't like cheap projects. They need to spend money, or they don't receive funding the following year. Donors like hardware, infrastructure and other tangibles. Short-term, quantifiable results are key. Dr Kar's approach, however, is subtle and qualitative and actively involves local communities. But this actually makes it unappealing to the large donor organisations. When NGOs switch to his Community-Led Total Sanitation programme, in place of programmes based on hardware and delivery, people benefit in a long-term, sustainable way, but directors are hauled up in front of their head offices to explain why they have spent less than a quarter of their budget. It is an insane and irresponsible attitude. It does nothing for the communities it is supposed to be helping, and it is economically and ecologically reckless.

As my first year in Nepal drew to a close, my mind turned towards the next move. My sabbatical from the civil service was due to end in September, but I managed to extend it for another six months. My friends Pete and Rachel were getting married in New Zealand that Christmas, so I decided to combine that with more travelling. It meant I left Nepal in December 2005.

I was ready to go. I had begun to see things in a different light. I had started detesting the pollution, loathing the barking dogs, despairing of the potholes and abhorring the caste system. I hated being sick the whole time. You couldn't drink the water; you had to soak your vegetables in iodine. None of this was new, but the beauty had always outshone any negatives. Now I was becoming short tempered at things that had once seemed mere frustrations or even quirks. I was incredibly sad to be leaving my job, though, particularly my work on the CWASH project. But the time had come.

I suppose it was like some relationships. You fall in love at first sight, then you get to know each other better, become familiar with the other's habits and mannerisms. Your love deepens, but so do your frustrations. Eventually, you have to decide whether there is a future in it. My fifteen months in Nepal were unlike any I had spent anywhere, and I came away from it so enriched.

I had also developed my aptitude for endurance biking, and that was to stand me in good stead. But my recently discovered enthusiasm for triathlon had remained unfulfilled. Sport is not so popular in Nepal. It is a different matter in New Zealand, though, which is where I headed next.

7

Prem and I

Another important thing I took away from my time in Nepal was Prem. What adventures the two of us had been on, and what adventures lay ahead! I packed up my worldly goods and flew with him to Auckland. We jumped on a bus down to Wellington, then took the boat across to the South Island. In Nelson, I stuffed those worldly goods into panniers, loaded up Prem and off we cycled to Marahua, the gateway to the Abel Tasman National Park.

Pete and Rachel were getting married on a beach in the park, so I left Prem in Marahua and joined the wedding party on a boat to Awaroa. The beach ceremony was idyllic, and afterwards we headed to a rustic resort just back from the water, surrounded by rainforest. It was here, swept along by wedding euphoria, that I reversed a policy I had been following for the previous five years.

We sat down for the meal, and, as a vegetarian, I dutifully contemplated the tomato-based dish in front of me. The guy to my right had a plate of lamb, to my left a plate of chicken. Maybe it was because Antipodean meat looks so good; maybe it was because I was so excited to be among friends in such a beautiful place; maybe it was because I was fed up with depriving myself. Whatever the reason, I took a deep breath, leaned over towards the chicken and whispered, 'Can I try some?'

My last plate of meat had been 3 July 2000. This was 22 December 2005. I took a bite and then leaned over towards the lamb and sampled that as well. Absolutely delicious; every bit as good as I'd remembered. The party moved on to the campsite on Totaranui Beach, where we spent Christmas. In between the beach games, the carol-singing and the fishing, there were barbecues – steak, sausages, fish. I ate some more.

Suddenly, I was a fully fledged meat-eater again. My willpower simply dissolved, I admit, but I also felt it was a return to the real me. I love food, and that includes meat. We have always eaten it in my family. Not that it is a guilt-free experience. I became vegetarian on my travels through Asia in 2000 mainly because of my disgust at the slaughter of animals, which in Asia is carried out in full view of anyone who cares to watch, rather than out of sight, out of mind, as it is in the West. The inhumane treatment of animals still troubles me even now, which is why I try to buy organic produce whenever possible.

But one of my resolutions going into 2000 was to be less hard on myself. Eating meat again was a step forward in that respect. Yes, there is an element of hypocrisy and therefore, to me, a loss of self-control, a weakness. But we all have weaknesses. Accepting that reality has been one of my greatest challenges, and still is.

Acknowledging those weaknesses is vital to our development. Some are real and can be overcome, but others are not so much weaknesses as imperfections – it is just our perception that makes them seem so. Willpower and discipline have always played a huge role in my life, and never more so than now, but if they are not applied selectively, they can wear you down as much as they spur you on. Pick your battles, and accept yourself for who you are. My love of meat has always been such that denying myself had been a lot of hard work. Better to accept that I just love meat, and to be happy.

With Prem left at the gates, I went on a few runs through Abel Tasman National Park. On one of them I fell in line with a man who introduced himself as Nathan. We got chatting, and he told me about a race called the Coast to Coast that was coming up in a few weeks. It involved running, biking and kayaking across the South Island from the west coast to the east. So a triathlon of sorts, even if I didn't know one end of a kayak from the other. (Actually I had done a bit of kayaking in Nepal. And Chertsey. But this was a very different type.) Then, just as suddenly as he'd entered it, this mysterious man ran out of my life.

I returned to the campsite and told Katherine about him.

'Nathan?' she said. 'Nathan Fa'avae?'

I shrugged and described him to her.

'That was Nathan Fa'avae,' she insisted. 'He's New Zealand's most famous adventure racer.'

Katherine, a friend of Pete's, was a Brit, who had lived in New Zealand for years. She knew all about the Coast to Coast, having completed it herself, and suggested I take part.

'But I can't kayak.'

'We'll teach you.'

'I haven't got a road bike.'

'We'll get you one.'

She insisted I stay with her in Wanaka, near Queenstown, and she and her boyfriend, Simon (who had already converted me once that trip, as the owner of the fateful plate of chicken), would help me learn to paddle.

I was convinced. After what was left of the wedding party had made it to Christchurch by New Year's Day, I bought a tent, loaded up Prem and set off on a six-day bike trip to Wanaka. Just me, Prem, my

CD player, a tent, the mountains, the sun and the stars – amazing.

I spent about five weeks staying with Katherine and Simon in Wanaka, and loved it. Sitting on a crystal lake with the Southern Alps rising beyond, it was the perfect place to live and train. It gave me my first taste of what life might be like as a professional athlete. I trained every day. I didn't swim much, but I ran and biked and earned my grade-two kayaking certificate, which was a requirement for the Coast to Coast. I also took part in an Olympic-distance triathlon in Gore, right down at the bottom of the South Island, near Invercargill, which I won quite decisively.

Then I spent a weekend with Katherine, Simon and a few others, practising on sections of the Coast to Coast course. It was the kayaking that concerned me. My confidence was low. The rest of the group were pretty advanced, so they went ahead, leaving Simon with me. The river winds through some gorges, where there are rapids to negotiate. The first few times I capsized I just emptied the boat and carried on, but then I capsized again, and I couldn't keep hold of my kayak. Off it shot down the river and smashed into some rocks. I had to be rescued by a boat. Not an auspicious start.

Out of the kayak and onto solid ground, I knew I had strong running legs. The main issue was that it was off-road; in fact, it was off-track. This was wilderness running. There were thirteen river crossings, some of them up to your waist. The terrain was rocky and unmarked. I wasn't used to this. While I may have been strong, I was not particularly goat-like. I liked having a surer footing.

The Coast to Coast can be tackled over one day or two, but in order to enter the one-day race, which the strongest do, you have to have taken part in the two-day race in a previous year. So I entered the two-day race. It started on Kumara Beach with a 3km run to our bikes, after which you cycle 55km, before a 33km run through the Southern Alps, up and over Goat's Pass. At the end of that first day, I was shocked to be leading the women. It was so exciting! There were camera crews on me, and helicopters swooping down. I'd never known anything like it. I might as well have been in a James Bond movie.

We camped in the mountains overnight and started the next day with a 15km cycle. Then it was time to face my fear. The 67km kayak down the Waimakariri River – five and a half hours of non-stop paddling. Just think of all the piss in the boat! It went well for me, though. I capsized just the once. But it was here that I lost time to the eventual winner, a girl called Sophie Hart, who was phenomenal on the water. The 243km course is rounded off with a 70km cycle to Christchurch, where the race ends on Summer Beach.

I came second in a time of 13hr 22min. They presented me with a new kayak. I left it with someone with instructions to sell. Not sure what ever happened to it. Still, I'd broken one kayak in New Zealand, and now I was leaving them with another, so this was a restoration of the karma.

Things were now becoming slightly surreal with regard to my sporting endeavours. I'd turned up to this event on a whim, learned how to kayak in a few weeks, borrowed equipment and very nearly won the biggest endurance race in New Zealand. Where had this aptitude for sport been all my life? Sure, I'd captained the swimming club at university and in a small market town in Norfolk, but it was nothing to set my county on fire, let alone the world.

Had this talent been lying dormant, or had it just developed as I'd grown older? I have asked myself this question repeatedly, and still do. I think it must have been dormant, lost amid my pursuit of other goals. I could easily have missed it, had I not been open to trying anything and everything.

Talent needs work, though, in order to flourish. In 2000 I ran the 14km City2Surf road race in Sydney, and I was overjoyed to finish in 1hr 14min. Of course, that was by no means fast (although I didn't think that at the time!), but it gave me a taste, and I worked and worked. Three years later I ran my first marathon in 3hr 08min. So I worked harder still, and then I tried cycling and worked at that. Another couple of years and I was cycling across the Himalaya. And now, less than a year after that, I was winning a kayak in New Zealand and attracting the attention of helicopters.

Hard work and an open mind – it's the only way to realise the potential that is inside every one of us.

I left New Zealand for Australia to go cycle-touring around Tasmania with Helen and Billi, who arrived with a broken hip – my muppet soulmate. It didn't stop her, though. She strapped her crutches to her panniers and gritted her teeth. Your body is capable of more than you could ever think possible.

Then I headed to Argentina to see Tina. I flew in to Santiago, from where I took the stunning bus ride over the Andes to Mendoza, Tina's hometown. There were ten days until Easter, which was when Tina and I had planned a cycle tour in the north of the country. Until then, Prem and I decided to head south into the beautiful lake-riddled landscapes of Patagonia. It was like being in New Zealand again. Our route took us through a small town called San Martín de los Andes, where we stopped for the night. This place satisfied my passion for breathtaking mountainous scenery, so the next day I decided to do some exploring. I relieved Prem of his panniers, and we headed out into the Lanín National Park, Lanín being the volcano that dominates the area.

I was cycling off-road when a jeep pulled up alongside. The passenger spoke to me in Spanish, and I told him I didn't understand a word.

'Are you training for the duathlon tomorrow?' he said in English.
'No.'
'Did you know there was one?'

'No.'

'Do you want to take part?'

'Why not?'

He told me to report to a hotel in the town, where all would be explained, which I did once I'd finished my 100km 'scenery' ride. The race turned out to be the Green Cup World Championships, the culmination of a series of Green Cup events held round the world. It was an off-road duathlon on foot and mountain bike, and I signed up. The organisers had flown in the winners of the qualification races. As I watched the professional athletes holding court at the press conference, I started to feel a little daunted. And then confused. There was a briefing, but it was all in Spanish. I managed to find someone to translate parts of it, but little details, such as the route and the rules, remained a mystery.

This one was definitely for Prem. Free of racks and panniers, I wanted to put him through his paces. The race was held in the National Park and comprised a 7.5km run, a 30km bike and another 7.5km run. Not very far, but it was technically quite tricky, off-road through mountain trails. On a lovely sunny day, I toed the line with a few hundred others. I took the lead from the outset. And I never lost it.

My Spanish may not have been up to much, but I could tell that the question on everyone's lips that morning in this small town at the foot of the Andes was: 'Who is this girl?' I'd beaten the professionals they had paid to take part. I'd beaten the girl who had won it the previous year. I was a cycle-tourist who had pitched up the day before. And I loved it. I also remember it just not being that hard.

I knew nobody in San Martín de los Andes, but all that changed at the after-race party. Everyone wanted their picture taken with me, and I was draped in the Argentinian flag. They presented me with a big cup (still got it) and a bouquet of flowers. There would have been prize money too, but because I wasn't a pro I wasn't eligible. I gave the flowers away, but I stuffed the cup into my panniers, loaded up Prem and headed off the next morning. I remember cycling on the road south to Bariloche and people leaning out of the window as they drove by: Beep! Beep! 'Hey, Chrissie!' I was quite the local celebrity.

By Easter I was back in Mendoza, just in time to go cycle-touring with Tina and another friend, Rata, around the desert landscapes of Salta and Tucumán in the north of Argentina. Then, in the second week of May 2006, after twenty months away, I flew back to the UK. I couldn't wait, but not because I wanted to resume my job, particularly (in fact, I knew now that a career in the civil service was not for me). I couldn't wait because I was desperate to throw myself into triathlon.

Within ten days of my arrival, I was lining up for a race – the National Sprint Championships in Redditch. It was a miserable, rainy day in the West Midlands, and as far as I was concerned, that was as good as it got.

As usual, I had borrowed equipment. First, there was the road bike. Paul Robertshaw, the very man who had introduced me to the idea of triathlon at the Birmingham Running and Triathlon Club two years earlier, lent one to me. It was a purple Klein, and this was the start of a special relationship. So: road bike, check. Now I needed to get hold of a wetsuit. Mark Hirsch, also of the BRAT club, had a spare. I tried it on the day before to see if it fitted, and it seemed all right.

It was definitely a day for wetsuits. I had recced the course with Rachel the day before. Her heavenly wedding on the beach in New Zealand five months earlier seemed a long way away. Let's face it, I'd been spoiled rotten with the life I had been leading and the places I had cycled in the previous couple of years, so I couldn't help thinking, as the rain teemed down in Redditch on the morning of the race: 'This is just not that exciting, is it?'

When I put the wetsuit on that morning, it suddenly seemed a lot larger than it had the day before. It was quite obviously too big. I don't know why I hadn't noticed. I climbed into the freezing water of the man-made lake in Arrow Valley Country Park, just before the gun went off. My wetsuit flooded on the spot. I couldn't swim, I couldn't breathe, I could barely lift my arm – and when I did it just let in more water. As the other girls disappeared into the distance, I realised I wasn't even going to be able to finish the swim. Maybe I should have soldiered on, but it would have taken me an age to swim the 750m, and at that time I wasn't altogether passionate about drowning in 14°C water in the pouring rain in a wetsuit that didn't fit. So a kayaker pulled me to the side. Race over.

Not that it put me off even slightly. Three weeks later, on 11 June 2006, I was lining up for the Shropshire Triathlon. This one had qualification for the Age Group World Championships riding on it. Ever since Ellie Rest, from the Serpentine Running Club, had qualified four years earlier, the idea of representing Great Britain had fermented in my mind. The more I had raced over the years that followed, the more serious I had become about the idea.

So serious, indeed, that in the build-up to Shropshire I bought Paul's Klein for £500 and called it Calvin. The night before the race, he taught me how to mount and dismount in my new clip-in shoes. I even borrowed a wetsuit that actually fitted. The sun was shining brightly for this one, and I felt in much better spirits. I took the lead on the bike and never let it go. And with that win I achieved my goal – a passport to the Age Group World Championships, which were being held that September in Lausanne. I won a mountain bike, which I gave to my mum, and I also won the right to buy lots of GB kit. I bought my race suit, and my proud parents bought me the full tracksuit as a present. My excitement and pride were uncontainable. I was going to the World Championships!

My joy was short lived, though. I was waiting at Snow Hill station in Birmingham for the train back to London that evening when I took a call from my mum. She had bad news. Nanna Chris, her mum, had died. I sat down on the bench, stunned, as the tears welled up. Suddenly, all excitement about the future evaporated, and memories of the past flooded back. How quickly emotions can turn. I thought back to our first Christmases at my grandparents' house in Halstead, Essex. My morning walks in the woods with my grandad Sid. The hours my brother and I spent playing in their big garden. When I was a girl, Nanna Chris used to call me Zola Budd, because I ran around so much and never wore any shoes.

That proved prophetic because, even if I was not exactly running barefoot, I had made it to the World Championships with a minimum of equipment or method. Paul knew I needed a coach, so he rang a friend of his called Tim Weeks. Tim was a very good Olympic-distance athlete, but his competitive aspirations ended prematurely when he was hit by a car while cycling. He was reluctant to take me on because of his workload, but Paul persuaded him, apparently, that I had a shot at winning in Lausanne. So Tim set me a ten-week programme, which was compromised by the fact that I could do barely any running. I had a pain in my sesamoid, which is a bone in the ball of your foot. It had started in Nepal and never gone away. It was thought to be a small stress fracture. Tim sent me for physio at Parkside Hospital in Wimbledon, which was where they first diagnosed a weakness in my core, my glutes and hamstrings, which I still have to work on today.

I had very little money, but Tim was kind enough to accept a nominal fee for his services. His programme had me training twenty-five to twenty-eight hours a week. I was back at Defra now, and every spare moment outside work was devoted to training or socialising. A typical day saw me bike to the pool first thing in the morning, swim 6km, bike to work for a 9.30 a.m. start, work a full day, bike home, exchange Prem for Calvin, bike to Richmond Park, cycle round it four times, then be home by 9.30 p.m. Repeat five times, then really up it on the weekend. One bank holiday I cycled with a friend to Brighton and back (a hilly 120 miles), then went to the pool and swam 5km. It was a lifestyle that demanded considerable reserves of energy, which, fortunately, I have always had, but the drive and determination that has shaped me from my earliest years was even more important, insisting that I complete my programme even when energy levels were waning.

At the end of July, without tapering my training schedule, I took part in the Salford Triathlon. I pitched up the day before on my bike with a rucksack, having slogged it up to Manchester by public transport. Tim told me I looked exhausted, and went off to get me a cup of tea. By the time he returned I'd fallen asleep on the sofa. He had organised for me to compete in the aquathlon that afternoon, and woke me up half an hour before the race. Despite my lack of run training, I came third, then went straight to bed. When I arrived for the triathlon itself the next morning, he told me I didn't look much better. I was determined, though, and I won by nine minutes. I stayed to watch the elite World Cup race that afternoon, and my time would have placed me among the top-twenty professionals. Tim was beginning to look excited. I set my sights on a top-ten finish in Lausanne, and maybe a podium place in my age group (25 to 29).

But it was the age group of my grandad Harry that was the cause of family celebrations before then. On 11 August he entered the 100-plus category. Grandad (he was my dad's father) was born and bred in north London and was a massive Spurs fan – which meant I was too. He had seen them win the FA Cup in 1921, before Wembley had even been built. In addition to his telegram from the Queen on his hundredth birthday, I managed to get Spurs to send him a carriage clock and a card signed by the players.

* * *

Three weeks later, I flew out to Switzerland for the Age Group World Championships. Easy had lent me his iPod and told me to listen to a song by Eminem. The flight out was very early in the morning. I remember taking a cab from Clapham to Gatwick in my GB tracksuit with the song playing in my ears: 'You only get one shot, do not miss your chance . . . this opportunity comes once in a lifetime. Yo.'

Never a truer word spoken.

But there was still an experimental feel to my preparations. The start time for the 25-to-29 age group was 12 noon, which is unusual. All my previous races had started at the crack of dawn. It meant I didn't know what to eat or when. And, of course, I had borrowed a wetsuit. This one fitted, although I tore it slightly in my rush to put it on. Muppet. There was a small hole in the arm the size of a penny piece. Enough to let water in and to throw me off mentally.

My swim wasn't great. After 1.5km of splashing in Lake Geneva, I was well behind the lead girls. But once aboard Calvin, I started passing a lot of people. You can't be sure who is in your age group, though, because of the different start times. Each athlete has their age group inked on their calf, so you have one eye on the road and one on the back of people's legs. I felt really strong, and I think I took the lead on the bike. My policy was simple: overtake everyone I possibly could. It's not a complicated battle plan, but it's one that has served me pretty well ever since. My run felt strong, too, even though I had done next to no running in training.

I crossed the finish line in a state of excitement. I felt I'd done well, but I still didn't know how well. Georgie and Tim had come to watch and were beaming from ear to ear.

'How did I do? How did I do?' I gabbled at Tim.

'You won!'

'What? My age group?'

'Yes. But you might win overall, as well!'

I fell to the ground and burst into tears. This was beyond my wildest dreams. I had hoped to sneak onto the podium for my age group, maybe, but to win my age group was another thing altogether. As for being the fastest woman in the entire field in a race that had the words 'World Championships' in its title – this was ridiculous! It hadn't even occurred to me. I felt as if there had been some sort of mistake, as if this were an accident. Surely someone would come along and say, 'Actually, you haven't really won. Sorry. As you were.'

But, no. Moments later, I was confirmed as the winner of the 25-to-29 category – by seven minutes. And when every last athlete had finished, it was confirmed that I was the fastest woman – by four minutes. In an Olympic-distance race, those are huge margins. I'd not just won, I'd smashed the field!

There was something very definitely unusual about all of this now, about my body, that hapless collection of skin and bones I'd spent so much of my life despairing of. It appears it had all the while been harbouring a world champion. Now, at the age of twenty-nine, that world champion had finally stepped out.

Almost immediately the thought occurred to me that I should consider turning pro. I still enjoyed my work at Defra – I was considered something of an authority on post-conflict reconstruction, and I helped shape Defra's policy priorities as part of the Comprehensive Spending Review. So I was still operating at quite a high level, but I wasn't altogether content. Most of all, the sabbatical had not quashed my doubts regarding rhetoric and action. If anything, it had deepened them. What I was doing was so far removed from my work on CWASH. I was becoming increasingly despondent at how little difference I was making on the ground. It was all talk.

So I was already craving a fresh direction in my professional life. And the feeling that it was the end of an era was heightened when Prem and I were forced to go our separate ways. The week before Christmas he disappeared from his usual spot outside the office.

Naturally, I took the matter to the highest level, and I watched, horrified, the CCTV footage of some bastard cutting the chain and making off with him. I was devastated to lose such a dear friend after all we'd been through.

All in all, I became very receptive to the idea of becoming a professional triathlete. Tim Weeks agreed that this was the way forward, but he was very busy and had a lot of things happening in his personal life. He confessed he had taken me as far as he could at that particular time. So he suggested I seek out a man by the name of Brett Sutton. He had coached Tim Don, who had won the elite World Championships in Lausanne the day after I'd won the age-group race, and, through Tim Don's manager, Tim Weeks put me in touch with him. I had never heard of Brett Sutton, but Tim explained to me who he was.

I was granted an audience – or a week's trial, to be precise. I had to make my way to Leysin, a mountain resort in Switzerland, not far from Lausanne. This was where Brett Sutton could be found. If I could convince him I had what it took, then the chances were I had what it took. It sounded like a rite of passage, a mission to test my worthiness. And that's exactly what it was.

8

The Wizard of Oz

In order to reach Leysin, you have to take the train from Geneva to Aigle. It's a grim, serious-looking chuffer, usually plastered with graffiti, but it is the views of the mountains and the lake that make it so special.

When I took the train that first time, though, the scenery was lost on me. Night had fallen, and I was completely oblivious to everything but my reflection in the train window. Fair enough. I knew this week was not about admiring the view. The focus was going to be on me, on my body, on my mind. Dispassionate self-analysis was the order of the week, so all that beauty in the darkness beyond the window could wait for another day.

At Aigle you change and take the chocolate-and-cream trolley train that hauls you up the 1,000-metre climb to Leysin. The carriage rattled as the ratchet pulled us higher, and I confronted my nervousness. At the end of the line I would finally meet Brett Sutton. I felt like Dorothy at the end of the Yellow Brick Road..

Meeting Brett Sutton was a big deal for a triathlete. It turns out he has trained some of the best in the world, and he is one of the most colourful characters in the sport. He revels in his reputation as the 'dinosaur' of triathlon, the Tyrannosaurus Rex. Tim Weeks had told me all about him. Eccentric, a certain way with words, very blunt. 'Don't be offended by him,' said Tim. 'Don't be offended by him.'

Why did he keep saying that? Either Tim must have thought me a sensitive flower, or this guy must be ferocious. If I wanted to turn pro, if I wanted to walk away from my job, my friends, my life as I knew it, this was the creature I had to convince, and soon I would be at his lair.

I had been ill the week before, and the week before that it had been Christmas and New Year. I wasn't in the best shape for this. Those mince pies and beverages weighed heavily on my mind and on my waistline. Would I be able to do myself justice?

And yet I had this chance to be accepted into Brett Sutton's team. Tim had filled me in on this as well. Team TBB was a new professional triathlon squad, founded by Singapore-based Dutch entrepreneur Alex Bok, who owns a chain of bike stores in Asia. Brett Sutton had been installed as its head coach, and with him came some of the best triathletes in the world.

When the train reached its destination I yanked open the door and tried as best I could to prance across the station platform like a thoroughbred. But lugging my 20kg bike across the snow was making it difficult. And anyway, when I looked around I couldn't see a T Rex anywhere.

There was an unremarkable-looking guy heading my way, though. If in my mind's eye I had carried an image of the archetypal sports coach, this man was the antithesis of it. He couldn't have been more than five-six – shorter than me, at any rate – and he wore a hideous pair of shapeless, blue tracksuit bottoms, held together at various points by elastic and tucked into a pair of Ugg boots. He had a paunch and thinning hair. He must have been getting on for fifty.

I was already taken aback by the sight of him, but I was really thrown when he offered me his hand and in a broad Australian accent confirmed that he was, indeed, Brett Sutton. Really thrown, but also strangely encouraged. I could handle this guy, surely. He was friendly, and one thing that struck me immediately upon meeting him were his large, soft blue eyes, which seemed to radiate kindness. I immediately forgot about trying to look the thoroughbred. 'Oh,' I kept thinking to myself. 'Oh. Right. So . . . this is Brett Sutton.' He seemed warm and welcoming. Maybe he was just misunderstood.

But there was another matter on my mind. Eight years earlier, back in Australia, he had pleaded guilty to charges of indecent relations in the late 1980s with one of the teenage swimmers he was coaching. This was a big concern for reasons of morality and safety. The crime had happened a long time ago, but I needed to give the issue serious thought. I would ask the advice of the other athletes; I would watch him carefully and challenge him on the subject, and I would make up my own mind.

It was a Saturday night, and my first glimpse of Brett's 'method' was when he dumped me outside the apartment of two of his athletes, Sam Renouf and Lizzy Hessing. There was no question of helping me to settle in or find any food. 'It's my day off tomorrow,' he said by way of farewell, 'so you won't see me. Sam's taking you to meet Andrew Johns and Stephen Bayliss at eight tomorrow morning. You're going for a run. I'll see you at the pool on Monday at seven.'

Sam and Lizzy, who were a couple, welcomed me every bit as warmly as their supposed monster of a coach. So far, so normal. The next morning AJ and Stephen were just as friendly, and we went for a jog with the snow falling round us. And it was very much a jog. I was itching to go faster. I could tell AJ and Stephen were paying me attention, and through them I started to feel Brett's eyes on me.

Back at the apartment, we were supposed to 'rest' for the best part of an entire day. This, it turned out, was going to be the aspect of the week I found the hardest – and it would be the part of being a pro I found hardest. I couldn't do it. It dawned on me that I never just sit down and do nothing. I'd never watched an episode of *24*, but Sam and Lizzy watched them one after the other. That was all they seemed to do – train and watch *24*. I sat down dutifully on the sofa with them, but I couldn't last much more than one episode. I did my Sudoku puzzles, I went wandering in the village. I did anything other than rest. I had a lot to learn.

The week began in earnest at seven the next morning. All of Brett's athletes were at the pool. I was struck by how regimented everything was – everyone was punctual throughout the week and there was precious little socialising. But I was also surprised that, rather than one big training session, Brett was overseeing many of them simultaneously. Each athlete had his or her own programme, specifically tailored. One of Brett's mantras is that no two athletes are the same.

The first observation he made about my swimming was that I was too weak in the upper body and over-reliant on my legs. How could I hold my own in the carnage that is the open-water swim of a triathlon when my upper body was doing little more than steer me in the right direction? I spent the rest of the session swimming with paddles and a pull-buoy. By the end, the accuracy of his initial assessment was all too plain. I'd just had my first brush with Brett being right about something.

It wouldn't be the last. He also told me, there and then, that he knew I had had an eating disorder. The man is bold and unrecon-structed, but, even if it took me a while to trust him unreservedly, he does know his stuff. And he knows he knows it. 'I'm so right it's scary,' is one of his favourite sayings. Even on those occasions when he's not right, it's still scary, and you learn to accept it. He may not be all that much to look at, but he has a will of iron, which he requires you to submit to if you want to be coached by him.

That makes it sound as if you have to be passive, or, better still, weak. No, you can't afford to be either of those. My first instincts as a fiercely independent woman were to rebel against him, which I would find myself doing a few times in the months ahead. Then the penny dropped that a triathlete has enough on his or her plate just enduring the physical and mental hardships of training and competing in their discipline. To be able to maximise their performance Brett believed it was essential for his athletes to cede to him all responsibility for strategic decision-making – in other words, to do exactly what he said without question. He often used an officer/ private analogy. He freely admitted that his aim was to brainwash his athletes, because we didn't know what was good for us and he did. All the same, if you're used to being your own boss, it takes a lot of strength to place your trust in someone so unreservedly. In many ways, that was the scariest part of what I was about to undertake.

It was on the Wednesday of that trial week in Switzerland that the idea of turning pro became a genuine prospect. Like the racehorse trainer he had once been, Brett had cast his eye over me in the pool, on the treadmill and on the bike. He tells me he had made his mind up about me that first morning at the pool, but it was after a bike session on that Wednesday that he sat me down to have a proper talk.

Brett had sent me and a couple of the other girls off on a set of hill repeats, cycling up and down an inclined road. Each repeat took about seven minutes, and we were told to do it for an hour. Brett doesn't always attend bike sessions, and you learn to dread the sight of his white Citroën Berlingo when it does pull up at the side of the road. In fact, it's not long before you jump out of your skin whenever you see any Berlingo. There are too many of them in Switzerland!

The sight of Brett that Wednesday, though, only encouraged me to go faster. I was the newcomer and I was so eager to impress. I didn't know about the etiquette of bike training. I didn't realise that you weren't supposed to go bombing off, and that cycling faster than the more experienced athletes in front of the coach just wasn't cricket. I didn't know, and, frankly, I didn't give a damn. Still don't, even now that I do know. So Brett turned up, and by the end of the hour I had lapped the girls on this training ride.

This sort of thing didn't endear me. None of the girls that week, other than Lizzy, was particularly welcoming, and, although it was too early for me to notice it, resentment was brewing.

But Brett loved all that. He summoned me to his flat that afternoon.

Lapping the girls on the bike that day was the first time I realised I could make a go of this, and Brett confirmed that this was how he was thinking. But he had some major reservations.

He lived in a flat with his Swiss wife, Fiona, and their two small children. The flat was on the fourth floor of an apartment block, and I climbed the stairs apprehensively. I was actually really scared of him at this point. I was learning more and more about his standing in the triathlon world, how many world champions he had coached. There was a kind of awe that all of his athletes exuded when they talked about him.

The flat was not big, but it was comfortable and open plan, and it overlooked the mountains at the back. There were kids' toys every-where, and he sat me down on their red sofa. So it was that the chat that would herald a new era in my life began.

I say chat. With Brett, it's more of a monologue, and you listen, although it's no less exhausting for the fact that you hardly have to say anything.

'Do you have a boyfriend?'

'No.'

'Are you a lesbian?'

That was one of our first exchanges, and it is the kind of blunt, confrontational method he delights in using. There was a purpose behind this superficially crass line of questioning. He needed to get to know me quickly if we were to work together, and there is no room for squeamishness in his world, or that of the success-ful triathlete.

'I think you have the physical attributes to make it as a pro,' he said, which was a revelation that had me buzzing with excitement. 'But I'm going to have to chop your head off.'

Oh.

My problem was that I couldn't relax. I went at everything like a bull in a china shop, he said.

On one level, this was great. He told me stories of some of his other athletes, and the importance of their aggression and bullishness. He told me about Loretta Harrop, one of his world champions, and how the guys never liked training with her because she would smash them and dent their egos. He told me about another, Emma Carney, and how she was at loggerheads with her sister in training. One day they were going different ways round the track, and neither of them would move, so they ended up crashing into each other. 'You've got to relish the fight,' he said. 'Sport is war.' And I just bristled inside. I wanted to be like Loretta. I wanted to be like Emma. He told me to read *The Art of War*, the ancient Chinese treatise on warfare, and I bought a copy as soon as I got home.

That aspect came naturally to me, but it was just as important to turn it off, which was my big problem. I had to be able to pour every ounce of my energy, both mentally and physically, into my training sessions and ultimately my races. At all other times I needed to be resting. And, most importantly of all as far as he was concerned, I must never let that gladiatorial instinct, accidentally or otherwise, turn itself on him. Pumped up to the eyeballs in competition I needed to be, but in my dealings with him I had to be as supine as a slave, never once questioning his orders. He wondered whether I'd ever be able to do this. This was where the removal of my head came into it. He also worried about my impatience. He had already picked up on my bull-in-a-china-shop tendencies, and I was impressed at how completely he seemed to have seen through me.

Just to reinforce that impression, it was Brett who brought up the other worry at the back of my mind – his past. In 1987, when he was twenty-seven, he had sexual relations with one of the teenage girls on the swimming team he was coaching. The girl was under age at the time. He was ashamed of what he had done; he had abused his position. Nothing more came of it until ten years later, when he was arrested in the build-up to the 2000 Olympic Games in Sydney, for which he was coaching the Australian team. The girl, now married, had decided to press charges. In 1999 he was charged with what the Aussies call 'indecent dealings' with a minor. The court found that it had been consensual and that it had been a one-off – he had never again abused his position in such a way.

Nothing with Brett is ever easy, and this already life-changing meeting with him that darkening afternoon took on an even more surreal tone as we delved into his past. But I was satisfied. Satisfied that it had been an aberration and that he regretted it more than he could say. Not once in the years since have I had any reason to think that similar 'dealings' have ever taken place with any of his athletes. Brett made a terrible mistake a long time ago, which continues to haunt him. It was weakness on his part, and we all know what it is to suffer from that. Case closed, as far as I was concerned.

I left that meeting exhausted. I had spent hours on that red sofa, surrounded by toys and bric-a-brac, listening to Brett talk about the qualities required for this new world of pain that I knew then I was about to enter. It would be financially hard, he said – it always is in the first year, even for the most successful athletes, and for most it remains that way. I would have to move to Thailand, where the team were to set up camp over spring. I would have to give up everything for a lonely, arduous pursuit, whose requirements would come as a shock to someone used to a varied life. I was far from convinced that I had what it took, mentally.

But I knew my course now. When Alex Bok invited me to join the team the next day, I said yes straight away. And when I took the train back from Aigle to Geneva for my flight to London, the sun was shining, the lake was icy blue and the mountains rose around me, thrilling and daunting at the same time.

First things first. Leave job.

I had taken a holiday for my week in Switzerland without telling anyone why, so now I spilled the beans and applied for yet another unpaid sabbatical. The request was referred to the powers that be, and it was granted after a suitable period of deliberation. This meant I didn't have to resign, which kept the door open for a return if things did not work out.

Then it was time to pack up my stuff and ship it all back to my parents'. Mum and Dad were incredibly supportive of my decision, although I think they were relieved that I was joining a team, not striking out on my own, and that I'd sought the opinion of an expert – I had done my due diligence.

The other matter that required my attention was the due celebration of my thirtieth birthday. I didn't know when I might next get the opportunity to push the boat out, so it was a good night. Naomi has a scar above her eyebrow to prove it. Thirty years old and only just about to embark on a career as a professional athlete – I knew it wasn't the conventional path, but that milestone was just another reason why I had to take the plunge. If I didn't do it now, I never would. And I would be left wondering 'What if . . .'

Mum and Dad took me to the airport, and on 20 February I flew out to join the team in Thailand. That makes it sound easier than it was. I flew to Singapore, then caught another flight to Phuket and managed to find my way to the place where the team were staying. The eighteen athletes were holed up in two Big Brother-style houses. I finally found the one I was meant to be living in at about 11 p.m.

It was dead to the outside world. I stood nervously at the door and knocked. Nothing happened. I hammered a bit louder. Eventually, one of the guys (I don't think I'd got him out of bed) answered the door. Everyone was asleep, he said. I could sleep on the sofa if I wanted. He had no idea I was coming. None of them did. It was another thing typical of Brett; a complete contempt for logistics. It wouldn't surprise me if he had deliberately not told anyone of my arrival that night, to see how I coped, but actually I think he just forgets. It's not important to him.

I settled down on the sofa for my first night as a pro athlete. I remember there were boxes of cornflakes everywhere. 'Is this all they eat?' I thought 'Bloody cornflakes?' This wasn't what I'd had in mind for my new life among the elite.

I hardly slept that night. The next morning the team met for our 7 a.m. swim session at the pool. Belinda Granger and Hillary Biscay were talking about the six-hour run Brett had made them go on the day before. *Six hours?* They'd run 60km. What's more, they actually seemed to have relished it. 'It was a smash-fest,' said Hillary. I wondered what I'd got myself into.

Stories I'd heard about Brett began to play through my mind again. Brett smashes his athletes, they said. They're like eggs to him. He throws them against the wall, and most of them can crack for all he cares because the ones that don't will become world champions. I'd heard he got the new girls to act as slaves for the older ones to toughen them up. He had weigh-ins. He got the guys to run in wetsuits with rocks on their backs.

We headed to the pool. I was apprehensive. Brett was waiting for us, and we all got into the water. Someone had brought their water bottle to the pool and left it on the deck. Brett went ballistic. He picked the bottle up and hurled it over a fence. 'You don't stop and drink during a triathlon swim, so you don't fucking do it here!' he yelled. 'The next time I see a bottle at the pool it'll be the owner who gets hurled over the fence!' This was more like T Rex.

And then I couldn't understand why my room-mate was being so hostile. I was let into my room for the first time later that morning.

She had told Brett that she didn't mind sharing with me, but that he had to tell her when I was arriving. Obviously, he hadn't, and they'd had a massive row at the pool. She was furious with him, and she was taking it out on me.

It was a pretty miserable start, and it set the tone for those early months. After two weeks in the Big Brother house, we all moved to new accommodation in apartments. Brett put me in with four of the boys – on purpose, he later told me. I remember when we moved – Brett drove a van while the rest of us got on our bikes to cycle the 100km in the heat of the day. Pretty soon the athletes split into two groups, and I went with the faster one. I tried valiantly to stay with them, but a lack of fitness got the better of me and I dropped off. I rode on my own for most of the way, not good enough to keep up with one lot but not wanting to drop back and join the other. God knows what either group thought of me.

It was symbolic. I'd never felt more alone than during that first spell in Thailand. I derived huge enjoyment from pushing my body as far as it would go in training sessions, that masochistic thrill of taking the pain just a little bit further each time. And doing it in the company of masters of their art, obsessive perfectionists all of them, was a great privilege.

But that was where the enjoyment ended. The typical day? Well, typical doesn't do it justice. Identical. They were all identical. And they went something like this: get up, eat, train, eat, train, rest, train, eat, sleep. Seven days a week.

Things weren't going well with my team-mates, either. They all knew each other, and most of them had been triathletes for years. I know they were just putting me through my paces, testing me like any new kid is tested anywhere, but there was a clique and I wasn't in it. Which is one thing when you're at the local school, but another when you're alone in a sweltering climate, thousands of miles from your friends and family, and all the while pushing your body to new limits. Snide comments came at me from all angles. The boys would goad me by flinging their filthy training kit around the kitchen, then watching as I picked it up, which they knew I would. They would steal my food. They – and I mean everyone – would go out for dinner and not invite me. I would be left alone with my laptop, trying to communicate with my friends scattered across the globe. I'd gone from being in the centre of a large, lively circle of friends to this.

I was desperately lonely, but I was angry too. I channelled the frustration, spurred on by emails from my friends urging me to stick to what I was out there for. But I was caught between the desire to smash everyone at training and the feeling that I ought to observe their petty conventions.

'Chrissie,' said one of the guys who we were on a ride with, 'do you know what half-wheeling is?'

'No.'

'You're doing it now.'

I was ever so slightly ahead of him as we cycled along, so that my wheel was half in front of his. This was how it was. You had to maintain perfect synchronisation with your training partner's bike wheels. You had to fall in line, literally. It made me realise how my lapping the two girls on our hill repeats in Leysin must have gone down. No wonder they all hated me.

I don't think they were too impressed with my bike, either. They all had top-of-the-range models and I had my beloved Calvin, who didn't cut much ice with anyone who knew anything about triathlon. Which was yet another problem. I knew nothing about my adopted sport, the history of it, or the personalities, even the rules. Yet triathlon seemed to be the only subject the others ever talked about. There was just no way I could have contributed to any of their conversations, even if they'd let me.

Meanwhile, Brett was in the background, stirring it up. I know he'd told them to make things hard for me. Every now and then one of the boys would break rank to apologise for the way I was being treated – one came in when I was crying in my room one evening; another sent me an email.

The irony was that Brett was the rock I clung to. While this sick trial of his devising was being played out, he seemed the closest thing I had to an ally. I could tell he was watching me; how I trained, how I coped, how I responded to the others. I knew he had a plan for me, although I didn't know what it was.

We had a common bond, as well, in our passion for international development and our desire to help other people. If I had grown disillusioned with the civil service over the impotence of our work and the hypocrisy of so much of what we had been doing, this self-indulgent, individualist pursuit I had now launched myself into was hardly an improvement.

I voiced my concerns to Brett a few times in the early months. I didn't know if I could carry on leading such a self-absorbed existence, I told him. I was missing a job whose purpose, in theory at least, was to try to improve the world and effect change.

He said to me once: 'Don't worry, Chrissie. You'll soon have a platform from which you can effect more change than you'd ever realised.'

He used to throw me mysterious one-liners like that every so often. I didn't know what he meant, but they helped to fuel my desire to succeed.

Brett was never more comfortable than when it came to tearing strips off you – and I was on the receiving end as much as anyone. One occasion sticks in my mind. It was in the pool in early May.

Swimming in this pool was disconcerting enough as it was. The local Thais can't have cared much about water quality. It was green and seemed to be radioactive. It made our teeth hurt, as if acid were munching away at the enamel. Like swimming in a puddle of Coke. We would come out buzzing.

This particular incident came at the height of my loneliness. At this stage I was still training to be an Olympic-distance triathlete, with the aim of making the Beijing Olympics in 2008. Brett had me doing a standard training set: two sets of a hundred metres at 1 min 35 sec each; then four at 1min 30sec, six at 1min 25sec and eight at 1min 20sec. Normally I would have to work hard to hit the 1min 20sec, but on this particular day I was so tired that I was struggling to make the 1min 25sec. The added issue was that Liz Blatchford was doing the same session with me. Liz trained on and off with Brett and was a high-class Olympic-distance triathlete, so she was one of my competitors. She is also a much better swimmer than I am. When we got to the 1min 20sec I was missing them all and falling well behind. Brett hauled me out of the pool and gave me both barrels in front of everyone. In his opinion, I had given up.

'You're fucking weak!' he yelled at me. 'Don't you realise you're giving something to Liz? You're giving something to one of your competitors! You never give a competitor anything! Never show them your weaknesses! Your heart's gone, Chrissie! You've gotta fight!'

There was no point arguing. I got back into the pool. My goggles filled with tears, but my heart was burning with anger, just as much as my teeth were burning with acid. 'You're wrong, Brett,' I thought. 'I haven't given up. I just cannot make those times today.'

I was exhausted. Brett always used to say that some sessions are stars and some sessions are stones, but in the end they are all rocks and we build upon them. That session was a stone, but it was one of the most important in my career. The fire that was ignited in my belly by that dressing-down I can still feel today.

I spent a lot of my time exhausted. I'm not sure I've ever quite mastered the art of switching off mentally, which Brett was so adamant I needed to do, but the art of switching off physically turned out to be pretty easy. You have no choice. When you're not training, you're not much good for anything other than lying around and resting. But even if I was exhausted so much of the time, I also felt stronger than I ever had. It was a strange sensation to feel my body changing shape and coursing with so much power, and yet to be so beset by fatigue.

By then I had already taken part in a couple of races, these gruelling events that nevertheless stood out in my mental landscape as the beacons to light the way. It was the races we were doing it all for, and you never stop loving them.

That said, another low in the early months was the moment I stood above the Chao Phraya River in Bangkok for the first time. This was the scene for the swim leg of the Bangkok Triathlon that Brett insisted a few of us took part in. The day before, I looked down into the water. The toxicity of it, the shit, the dead animals, a huge chemical factory on the other bank – these were the first things that struck me. Reinaldo Colucci, Benji Sanson, Harry Wiltshire, Lizzy and I were the ones Brett had entered in the race. We were taking part for promotional reasons, which I didn't like anyway – and Brett knew I wouldn't like it. This was a test to see if we would take orders.

Lizzy and I took photos instead and sent them to him. We're not swimming in that. Yes you are. Lizzy flat refused, which Brett seemed to accept, but he wouldn't let me back out. The race had been scheduled for April Fool's Day, and that was my only hope now. Maybe he would leap out just before the off to say it had all been a joke. But no, I stared down into the grey, sludgy water at the start, picking a path between the dead birds and industrial boats. There was to be no last-minute reprieve.

It was my first win as a professional. I collected £1,000 in cash, which brought its own kind of cleansing. Money at last. It was the first validation of what I was doing. I was particularly pleased with my bike split – 40km in an hour, and it wasn't just because I was trying to blow-dry the river slime from my body. Reinaldo won the men's race, followed by Harry and Benji. I was less than a minute behind Benji, in fourth place overall. I phoned Brett and he sounded pleased, although probably just as much with himself as with me. I hadn't died – I hadn't even caught anything – and I had my maiden win. He'd been right again.

The races broke the monotony. And, just as important for me in the early days, they took me away from camp. My first pro race was the week before Bangkok – the Mekong River Triathlon. I came second in that one, but it introduced me to the joys of the post-race party, none of which ever failed to disappoint. I remember dancing the funky chicken with the Filipino triathlon team and a group of Thai ladyboys at that one. My dancing must have impressed the Filipinos, because they invited me to compete in the Subic Bay Triathlon, which, like the Mekong River Triathlon, was an ITU (International Triathlon Union) points race. You raced in these to pick up points to qualify for the ITU World Cups and thence, if you were really lucky, the Olympics.

I leaped at the chance to visit the Philippines, and managed to persuade Brett that I should go out there for a week before the race. I stayed with my new friends, Analiza, Jefferson and August, three youngsters from poor backgrounds who had been discovered at local sporting events. I felt free of the politics and constant judgement of life in Team TBB. It was also a chance to travel again.

Come the race, I was recharged. It was the beginning of May, and the start time was 6.40 a.m., so that we avoided the midday heat. But by 8 a.m. the temperature had risen to around 35°C, so it was very much damage limitation. Nevertheless, I felt strong and won my first points race. Cue more dancing of the funky chicken!

It was a comedown to head back to camp in Thailand. I may have had a couple of wins behind me, but there was no thawing of relations with my team-mates, and my swim was going downhill. That was the week Brett hauled me out of the pool. I was constantly questioning whether the life of a professional triathlete was for me, and Brett was losing patience with my doubting. He was also concerned about my upper-body strength, so he had me doing fifty press-ups a day on my knuckles. I don't know if they did anything for my strength, but they certainly made my knuckles bleed.

At the end of May I left Thailand, and was grateful for a change of scene. I was heading back to the UK for the Blenheim Triathlon (another win and more money!), before we moved to Leysin for the team's summer camp. At last I was able to move into an apartment of my own. It was a stunning location. I had no TV, so I spent hours on my balcony overlooking the Alps. The cows ambled in the valley below, which echoed with the sound of the bells round their necks. I listened to the World Service on my pocket radio, I read books, I even dabbled with some writing of my own – more haiku, like Suzy had taught me to write in Nepal.

Not that I was in much of a transcendental state. I was suffering from stomach upsets and losing weight. We were based 1,000m up in the mountains, but the running track and flatter roads where we did much of our training were down in Aigle, at the bottom of the valley. Cycling back to Leysin was a feat of endurance in itself, an hour's slog up the side of the mountain after whatever hell we'd been put through in training. I loved that climb and was always chipping away at my personal best, but it took its toll. Brett thought I'd lost too much weight and turned up at my apartment one day with a block of Gruyère cheese and a slab of milk chocolate. 'I want this gone in three days,' he said.

Brett wasn't one for textbooks. Anything that came with the smack of 'expertise' he was immediately disdainful of. He believed he knew his athletes and he knew his sport, and anyone else's input was just going to corrupt his work. We were allowed massages, for example, but he didn't like any of us going to see physios because he didn't believe they understood the nature of triathlon. He hated science, he hated sponsors, he hated the various federations, he hated most of the other coaches and any mickey-mouse certificates they might have picked up. He was a law unto himself.

An insight into his mindset can be gleaned from the emails he wrote. Judging by those, he dislikes the norms of the written word as much as anything else. And yet there's a kind of poetry to them – difficult, unique and of searing insight.

A fortnight after the Blenheim Triathlon, I was back in the UK again. Brett had entered me for the UK Ironman 70.3. As a half-ironman, this was a sudden step up in length, nothing to do with qualifying for the Olympics, which had become the current focus of my obsessive nature. It was as if Brett's thinking was changing. Was he losing faith in my ability to make the Olympics? The thought made me panic. He even suggested at one point, apparently in all seriousness, that I change nationality to improve my chances. His suggestions were The Philippines, Nepal or Singapore. As much as I love those countries, it was not a ringing endorsement of my progress.

I struggled in the half-ironman, coming in fifth. A malfunction with Calvin's gears – the beginning of the end for the old boy – hadn't helped. Back in Leysin, the following week I had a terrible swim session (weight loss is not good for your swimming), and I sent an email to Tim Weeks despairing at my deterioration in the pool. I could see my goal of making the Olympics the following year slipping through my fingers with the water.

'I don't know what is happening,' I wrote. 'I feel like I have *no* power in the water. I am beginning to wonder whether to carry on with this. If I can't get my head and body around the swimming then it's a lost cause. I don't know what to do.'

Tim felt he could do nothing from the UK, so he forwarded my email to Brett. He responded in classic fashion with a long email to Tim, with me copied in, some highlights of which I reproduce here:

> i am not being rude, but chrissie is a doozy. fuck, what a handful. and she ain't even got good yet. she has the ability. i start thinking ironman, i start thinking podiums, i see hawaii. i am that impressed.
>
> but we have fucking hissy fits over nothing, and we both know that type of personality don't cut the mustard when the pain and blood are flowing. if i am wrong, let me know, but she smells tough to me under the cosh, but bloody pathetic, fragile, in normal, no-problem shit.
>
> i am at a loss for such rubbish. some people keep looking for the answers they want to hear, and some people confront themselves and dig in. such weakness displayed makes me question whether i am wasting my time.
>
> chrissie, i have this little saying that i think helps me be successful, more than anything else i do. and that is, i think, then i pick, and then i stick! and nothing shifts me from my view. no bad races, no bad sessions, no bad moods.
>
> tim, whatever decision she makes will be fine with me. but it's 100% my way or the highway. otherwise it's going to be a jibbering mess. the pressure will eat her inside out. so the best scenario is, either do her thing or learn to take orders like a good private. then she don't have to think of nothing, ensuring the over-enquiring and over-inquisitive mind don't destroy her physical attributes that are many.
>
> cheers, sutto

In the same email he questioned the wisdom of my pushing for the Olympics the following year. He wasn't sure I would qualify, and, even if I did, that would be two years gone from my career. The earliest I could hope to be competitive at Hawaii would then be 2010, by which time who knows what might have happened. If I were twenty-one, then maybe, but I was thirty, so we had to decide now where my talents lay. He was thinking my future lay in the half-ironman distance and beyond. 'Should we play the cards right,' he said to Tim, 'she's already going to the worlds now for 70.3 [half-ironman]. Then a crack at Hawaii in 2008.' At that stage, I had no more than the vaguest idea of what he meant by Hawaii.

What was abundantly clear was that I was pissing Brett off. I was fussing and flapping over the slightest imperfection in my training, let alone my race performance. Not for the first time I was put in my place. In my reply to the email, I thanked the two of them for 'the kick up the arse that I needed', and vowed to stop the soul-searching and 'hissy fits'.

I gave myself over to Brett at that point. Fighting it was just too much of a waste of energy, and I needed all my energy for what lay ahead. I still wasn't sure what that was exactly, but he seemed to have a clear plan. It was time to trust in his judgement and go wherever that trust took me.

9

Face to Face with the Ironman

My first experience of an ironman triathlon was spent safely behind the barriers, the very next weekend. It was in Zurich, late June 2007. The day before, I'd won the Zurich Triathlon, an Olympic-distance race. A group of friends had come over from the BRAT club to compete in the ironman taking place the following day, and their support spurred me on, as did the presence of Brett on the sidelines. I felt really strong – even the swim went well – and despite Calvin's refusal to shift into the low gears (again!) during the first climb up Heartbreak Hill, I managed to hit the front early on the bike. I held the lead to the end for my fourth pro win.

It was a great weekend. I was surrounded by friends from home, and able to be myself again – high spirited and all smiles. And I'd won! I could get used to this.

But there was no doubting that the main event of the weekend was Ironman Switzerland the next day. Up till then, that distance of triathlon was little more to me than something a few of my team-mates subjected themselves to. One of those was Rebecca Preston, and she went on to win the ironman that day. She ran the marathon in 3hr 18min, and I remember thinking: 'How on earth has she done that?' I was flabbergasted. It almost beggared belief that she could run that fast after nearly 115 miles in the water and on the bike.

But the atmosphere also thrilled me – the carnival of the occasion and the camaraderie, the pain, the joy of the athletes. I cheered from the sidelines like a deliriously excited child.

'Do you want to do this one day?' Brett asked me.

'Yes!' I shouted over the noise.

I wasn't put off by the distance. I just didn't know how competitive I would be at it. But the ironman had me in its grasp. I had been seduced.

What was becoming increasingly clear, though, was that Calvin's days were numbered. All of my recent races had featured some kind of malfunction, most often a refusal on his part to engage the small chainring. This meant I'd had to grind up hills in a big gear a few too many times. As much as it broke my heart, it was time to say farewell. He was too old, and bits were falling off that endearing frame of cheeky purple. I needed a younger model.

Which came along courtesy of the team's new sponsor, Cervélo, who kitted me out with a spanking new Soloist. My last race on Calvin had been the ITU Premium European Cup in Holten, Holland, where I came a disappointing fifth. My swim had been awful, and, loath though I am to point it out, Calvin's latest (and last) refusal to entertain the small chainring hadn't really helped. But a week later, I'd packed up the new bike in my life and taken it to France for the ITU Long Course World Championships at L'Orient. I came fifth again. The Cervélo and I hadn't quite gelled. I could hear Calvin saying, 'I told you so'.

It was at my next race that the bike and I bonded. And what a rite of passage it was for us both. Brett had entered me for the Alpe d'Huez Long Course Triathlon on the first day of August, and it was the most gruelling race I had yet taken on, another step towards an ironman.

Preparations hadn't been helped by an injury I'd picked up three days earlier. I suppose I had it coming – Calvin's retribution – but he had one last curveball to throw at me. I was trying to remove my bike computer, so that I could transfer it to the Cervélo, and in typical fashion I went at it with a knife and a lot of impatience. I slipped and sliced my hand open between the thumb and forefinger. The local doctor gave me four stitches in the webbing and an instruction not to get it wet.

Brett's response was typically unsympathetic and enlightening: 'Chrissie, you think these things just happen to you. They don't. It's because of the way you behave. You've got to learn to take control, to think before you act. Hurry slowly.'

At the time, I thought he might tell me not to race, but I know better now. 'You're racing,' was his curt assessment.

So the next day I was in the pool with a bright yellow rubber glove on. And the day after that I was in a hire car crossing the Alps with Brett's teenage daughter, Holly, who was the team masseuse, and Maxine Seear, an Australian Olympian who had joined the team soon after I had and quickly become a friend. I remember driving the road that climbs to Alpe d'Huez and thinking, Oh, Lord! Even the car was struggling. Twenty-one switchbacks on a climb of more than a thousand metres. We were going to have to bike this at the end of the 115km cycle leg. I bristled with excitement.

The three of us were sharing an apartment, and I didn't sleep well the night before the race – you never do. On the day, I removed the stitches from my hand with some nail clippers and cycled down to the start with the others.

The lake was freezing, and I didn't swim well. When I got on the bike, though, something clicked and I went into the lead and hammered it up the climbs. I felt so strong, and I loved it. It was like being back in Nepal. People started telling me my lead was growing. I remember seeing The White Berlingo on the sidelines at about 60km – and then Brett. 'Eat! Eat! Don't forget to eat!' he shouted.

Then disaster struck – well, the first of them. I picked up a flat tyre. I was about eleven minutes ahead at that point, they told me, and I dismounted and set about replacing the tube. By the time I was back on the bike, my lead was down to four minutes.

Cue Disaster Two. By then I was on the descent into the valley before the final climb to Alpe d'Huez began. Now, I'm a real numpty when it comes to descending. I'd sat on a road bike for the first time only three years earlier, so I was still a relative novice at cycling. The bike control and nerve required for a descent through hairpins at high speed was something I was still struggling with.

The situation wasn't helped when I came careering round one bend only to be confronted by some kind of jeep coming in the other direction. The roads at Alpe d'Huez are not closed for the race and I, in my numptiness, had taken this corner too wide, such that I was face to face with a vast, black four-by-four. There was no choice. Or, if there was, it was between death and heading straight for the barrier at the side of the road. And, who knows, death may yet have been waiting there as well.

I went for the barrier. There was a drop beyond it, but it wasn't sheer and it was forested, so I had a decent chance. I hit the barrier head on, and as I flew over the handlebars I pulled the bike over with me, and we both landed in a bush beyond. I was cut and bruised and had done something to my leg, but it wasn't terminal. My handlebars had been bent out of line, and so, swearing, I straightened them out, remounted and headed on down the hill again, before the serious climb.

That was when I started to overtake more of my team-mates – the males this time. I was in my element, and the kilometres were falling away. After 115 of them I arrived at the final transition, and so began the 22km run at 2,200m altitude. It was stunning. The mountains that surround you and the valley below take your breath away, which is not necessarily a good thing when you're trying to race at altitude, but it gives you a euphoric energy. The views help to make this one of my favourite races. My leg was hurting quite badly now, but I pushed on and won the race twenty-nine minutes ahead of the next woman and in ninth place overall. If I hadn't had a puncture or a crash . . .

That was a turning point. I knew I had something then, and I knew it was an aptitude for these longer races. This was still a way short of a full ironman, distance-wise, but because of the difficult terrain it was getting there time-wise. And I loved it. Long-distance racing was so much more enjoyable to me than the shorter events.

From that moment, I just couldn't wait to take on an ironman.

So when Brett asked me the following week if I wanted to do one, I knew the answer right away.

'Am I ready?' I asked.

'Yes,' he said.

'Then yes.'

And in three and a half weeks I was on the start line for Ironman Korea. It is staged, of all places, on Jeju, that tiny island off the south coast of South Korea where I'd had my epiphany about the civil service, under the erupting volcano. This is a seriously difficult race, mainly because of the heat and humidity. So Brett sent those of us who were racing out to our base in Thailand for some acclimatisation training. The trouble was, it was monsoon season. Water was cascading everywhere, including down the steps to the pool. Naturally, I slipped at the top of them and went bumpety-bump all the way down on my bony backside. I was in agony. I felt as if I'd shattered my coccyx.

X-rays showed I hadn't, but that knowledge did nothing for the pain. I sat for hours in the local Thai hospital, waiting for a diagnosis, surrounded by men and women with all kinds of horrific ailments. Not an experience I'd want to repeat. With a week to go I could barely walk, and I couldn't run at all. I spent two days sitting on a hot-water bottle in my bedroom. After that I was able to swim and bike again, but I couldn't see how I was going to complete a marathon. Just sitting down on the flight to Korea was agony.

Brett was thousands of miles away in Leysin. I voiced my concerns to him in an email. The response was typical.

> it means we fix the back and tell no one. your mind has got to be focused on recovering and being ready for korea. plenty of big dollars await you there. not as many as were there before you went over the barrier, and now a little less after you fell down the stairs, where you have seen others go head over apex – and even coach showed you twice about how dangerous it was. oh, and that is not counting the self knife attack.
>
> i hope you are receiving the point i am making here. it's time you forgot about, 'woe is me, all these coincidences,' and got some self-discipline in your head. the training you got a handle on, the walking around in nerd land you have not. you get over that the same way as improving an athletic weakness. BY KNOWING AND BY TRAINING IT OUT.
>
> life is nothing but a habit. get to work.
>
> cheers, sutto

Of course, there was never any mention of my not taking part in the race. I would be on the start line whether I could run or not. I obeyed.

But even without the injury, it was a big gamble to throw me into an ironman only six months after I'd turned pro. Everything I'd done so far had been geared towards Olympic-distance triathlon. Ironman athletes usually followed a different training programme altogether. I had no conventional grounding in the discipline. Most rival coaches would have called Brtett mad if they'd known. But I was a nobody, and so none of them did.

Maybe, in a strange way, the injury alleviated the pressure. I wasn't nervous at all beforehand. And from the moment I got in the water, I never felt the coccyx again, even after the race. The body does weird and wonderful things.

Unfortunately, the same can't always be said of the bike. I'd had a really good swim and I left the water as the first-placed woman, which was unusual. It was in the ocean, which I love, but I'm not supposed to be leading come the end of any swim. I couldn't believe how well things were going.

But then I got to my bike. The front tyre was as flat as a pancake. Aarrrgghh. Stay calm, Brett would say, stay calm. I've been here before.

Seven minutes later we were back in the game but in sixth place. Vij the Velo (as I had named my steed) and I were motoring through the ranks. We'd moved into second place within twenty miles, and after sixty-five we hit the front, going past Rebecca. It was tough – the course was far hillier than I'd expected, the temperature was 37°C, humidity 95 per cent – it was a veritable sauna. After nearly an hour in the water and 5hr 17min on the bike, I peeled myself off the saddle. Only a marathon still to go.

Forget the sauna: the run was conducted in what felt like an oven. The starting gun had fired at 7 a.m, but it was now early afternoon. The run was three laps up and down a newly laid highway. It undulated all the way, and the heat radiated off the asphalt as it would off a frying pan. There was no shade anywhere. No trees, no nothing. It was hellish, a war of attrition. People were dropping like flies, staggering around like drunkards, trying so desperately to finish a race that had miles still to run.

And yet I felt all right. I faded a little around the seventeen-mile mark, but by mile twenty-two I had my second wind. (Or was it my fourth or fifth?) Cruel though it may be to say it, there was also something strangely encouraging about the sight of athletes, some of them pros, falling by the wayside. They were really struggling. And I wasn't. Sure, it hurt. My feet were like a war zone when I finished, and you don't want to know about the chafing. But I never doubted that I would finish, and finish strongly.

I crossed the line in a time of 9hr 54min, and I'd won. I couldn't believe it. Well, I would never have believed it if you'd told me beforehand, but, in truth, nothing happens suddenly in an ironman, and I'd known for a good while before the finish that, as long as I didn't break down, I was going to win. The girl in second place came in more than fifty minutes behind me. I was seventh overall, including the men.

The prize was a cool $20,000 and a place, if I wanted it, at the World Ironman Championships in Kona, Hawaii, the daddy of all ironman races. It was seven weeks away, in October. I phoned Brett on the finish line and told him I'd won.

'Good job, kid.'

'They've offered me a place at Kona. Should I take it?'

'Why not? At least we'll have it if we want it.'

'It costs $500.'

'Take it.'

The next day the customary post-race party took place in the Lotte Hotel on Jeju – yes, Hotel Erupting Volcano. It was kind of cathartic to be back, this time not wearing a suit and carrying UK Government policy documents, but competing in an ironman and sleeping on the floor of a cheap-as-chips apartment with two other team-mates. I was happier with things this way.

I was happier, full stop. I had shared the apartment in Jeju with Luke Dragstra and Vinnie Santana. Luke, in particular, was a hardened pro, and I think he expected me to be worried and nervous before my first ironman, asking endless questions and generally being a royal pain in the arse. But I wasn't any of those. He and I started to get on a lot better on that trip. I later heard from Brett that I had surprised Luke with how calm, confident and well prepared I'd been. That made me happy. It was a breakthrough in my relations with the team. And that weekend, among the ironman brethren, I felt as if I belonged at last.

Brett was happy too. He sent me an email the following week. Here it is:

> i am so proud of you, and a little for me this time. because you know the pressure i feel when i make these sutto-type decisions. all the people are happy to tell me i am nuts and hurting your career, but they never ring back and say, 'well, you old bastard, you were right again. How do you know they can stay all day?' no! they just lay in the darkness waiting for something to go wrong and then have a smart-arse crack at me.
>
> you shut them up good and proper.

It suddenly dawned on me how much pressure he'd been under, sending me to Korea. It could have gone horribly wrong. He was taking a punt, almost as much as I was. No ironman training, I didn't even have the basic equipment – I was racing on a road bike with drop handlebars and training wheels. I'd borrowed kit off my team-mates and worn an old black vest – not great in the heat – onto which I'd ironed the team logo. And then there was the coccyx injury he'd told me to ignore. He was going on little more than a hunch that I could 'stay all day'. It was all wild, anti-textbook stuff.

As was his next trick – to insist that I went the very next weekend to Singapore to compete in a half-ironman. This was ripping up the textbook and pissing on it. No other coach would have endorsed the programme I was on. I'd done two long-course triathlons, Alpe d'Huez, an ironman and now a half-ironman in the space of a few weeks – and six weeks later I was meant to be doing Hawaii. In anyone else's book, that's over-racing; it's too much travel and not enough rest.

In the case of Singapore, they might have been right. There was pressure to race, because this was a big promotion for the team in one of the world's largest financial centres. During that race I came the closest I ever have to bonking, as we say, which others might describe as hitting the wall. I ran like a tin woman – it was really painful. Belinda Granger, another team-mate, won that day, and I came third.

But it was out of the way, and I returned to camp in Thailand with six weeks to prepare for the biggest race of my life.

They rewarded me with a proper time-trial bike after Singapore, complete with race wheels! Brett had taught me not to care about having the latest equipment. He felt that far too many people spent too much time worrying about expensive, aerodynamic gear and not enough about the engine that drives it. All the same, now that I was going to Hawaii he agreed that a time-trial bike was a prerequisite. I spent much of the following six weeks learning to ride it. A time-trial bike requires a totally new cycling position.

As the big day approached, the other team members who had qualified in Hawaii left for Kona. But Brett told me to stay behind in Thailand for a few more days. He didn't want me to get caught up in the hype out there – Hawaii-itis, he called it. I had no idea what he was talking about, but I was quite happy to stay behind. Although relations were thawing between me and the boys on the team, I still felt very much like a high-school geek shunned by the prom queens when it came to some of the girls. Now that I had a few races under my belt, I'd thought I might become more accepted, but jealousy seemed to be the latest issue for us to get past. I just couldn't win – or, rather, I could, but it wasn't helping matters.

Before they'd left, Brett had made the others do a mini-race simulation, and two days before I was due to fly out it was my turn. The session was a 3km swim, a two-hour bike ride and twelve 800m on the track. It was pissing down, monsoon-style. I remember running round the track with the rain coming down, splashing through the puddles, with only Brett and a couple of rabid dogs looking on at me. I nailed that session. Brett didn't say anything, other than his customary, 'Good job, kid', before he walked off. But I knew how the others had done in their test sets, and I know that the times I did in that session got back to the girls in Hawaii.

When Brett saw me off in early October, nine days before the race, he gave me a scrap of paper torn from his notebook (still got it) on which he had written, almost illegibly, his final words of wisdom. He told me to keep my head down and stay well away from the hype. This was just another event. And, most importantly, he told me not to defer to anyone.

It was only when I arrived at the airport in Hawaii that I began to get an inkling of what he meant by the hype. It was a complete circus. There are not too many places to train, so you end up going up and down the same roads. Everywhere you turn there are people training. Everybody's looking at everybody else – it's like a catwalk show.

The media are out in force, conducting interviews with all the well-known pros. People descend on the huge sponsor expo, buying their last-minute pieces of equipment, or lining up under the midday sun to get an autograph from ironman champions. And those that want to relax go to the nearby coffee shops watching others go past and gossiping about who has raced where, who is fast, slow, injured or on form and predicting the top ten finishers. I know I wouldn't have featured in any of their conversations.

It was a relief to be able to slip under the radar. Nobody knew who I was. I'd struggled even to find some accommodation. By the time we knew I was going to race, everywhere was booked. I managed to find a room – actually, it was a bed within a room – in a little apartment that I shared with two guys I'd never met before, Scott Neyedli, a British pro, and Eneko Elosegui, a Spanish age-grouper. It turned out the apartment was five miles out of Kona, halfway up the mountain, reached via an incline with a 20 per cent gradient. That meant a torturous bike ride just to get home after each session. I remember lugging my shopping up the hill on my bike, wondering if this was how everyone else was preparing.

Then there was the apartment itself. It had two bedrooms. Scott took the main one, since he'd rented the house, and Eneko and I shared the other. It had a desk, a fan and two single beds, each of which sagged in the middle like a trampoline. The kitchen was outside, under an awning. Next door there lived a couple with a barking dog, a screaming baby and a propensity to scream at each other just as much. It was all decidedly suboptimal.

As were my levels of organisation. I had no kit, other than the second-hand shorts Rebecca had lent me for Korea (still got them). So I bought a race suit and shoes that week. How did I make my choice? Simple. Whatever was cheapest. I couldn't believe some of the prices for a top. I ironed on the team logos. If only I'd had any sponsors of my own to advertise. Then one of my pedals broke. I was so tight, I fixed them with industrial glue.

On the Monday before the big day, Eneko and I were out on our bikes and we bumped into Belinda, Hillary and Rebecca. Team-mates we may have been, but we'd had no contact that week. I was sure they didn't want to spend time with me, and anyway, I had been told to stay away from everything and everyone and to concentrate on the race. Eneko and I were on a four-hour bike ride, and it was at the turnaround, after two hours, that we met them. You could practically hear the claws being sharpened – Eneko didn't know where to look.

We started cycling back together, but almost immediately Belinda shot off ahead. That gentleman's agreement about staying in line with your training partners had gone out of the window. There was no malice in it, though. I understood it was her way of putting down a marker before the big race, and it's the sort of psychological ploy I've probably used myself since. It had the desired effect, too, because I remember thinking then that she was so much stronger than me on the bike.

Come the day itself, I do believe I had a major advantage in my anonymity and ignorance. So many people know everything there is to know about the race, the terrain, the conditions and the competitors, but I knew nothing and no one knew me. I didn't think. I just raced.

And there were definite benefits to staying in our ramshackle apartment, which looked down on Kona, well away from the circus. Not that the night before helped at all. Next door were in good voice, even by their standards, and when the police turned up at one in the morning with the sirens wailing and the baby screaming and the dog barking I lay on my saggy bed in the single room that I shared with a man I barely knew and thought: 'I've got the biggest race of my life tomorrow, and I haven't had any sleep.'

I eventually dozed off at about 2.30 a.m., which meant I had two hours' sleep before I had to get up. At 4.30 a.m., the alarm went off, and the three of us went about our preparations, bleary eyed. Three English muffins, honey, a banana and a cup of tea was my race breakfast of choice. Kipling's poem 'If' is my pre-race reading material, without fail.

Scott's mum and dad picked us up and drove us down to the start at 5.30 a.m. We performed last-minute checks on our bikes, and I headed down to the swim start to prepare. World Championships or not, I just didn't feel nervous. I hadn't the same respect – or fear – for the race as everyone else. I was simply very excited. There are so many people there, around 1,600 competitors, and thousands of spectators lining the shoreline and streets.

I entered the water at around 6.30 a.m., warmed up and then muscled my way into a good position on the start line where we skull on our front until the cannon fires into the morning air. It is one of the most awe-inspiring sights. The sun has risen over the volcano; the ocean is calm and crystal-clear. I watched the fish in the water below, and beyond them were the scuba divers with their cameras trained on us as we hovered, waiting for the start.

The 150 pros head off at 6.45 a.m., a quarter of an hour before everyone else. My target was a top-ten finish. During my two-hour sleep I'd dreamed that I'd come fourth, and I'd been overjoyed with that.

The cannon fired, and we were off. I didn't have a great swim. It was like a washing machine, a complete free-for-all. But there's energy to be taken from the fish and the coral beneath us – more so, at any rate, than is to be had from the endless straight black lines in the training pool. Belinda and I swam side by side. She breathes to the left, and I breathe to the right, so we kept looking at each other throughout that swim, and we exited the water together. It was a strange way for our relationship to start improving.

As we entered transition one, I was about six minutes off the leaders, which is quite a lot at that stage. For the first twenty-five miles of the bike leg, I felt really lethargic. The frustration built as it looked as if I wasn't going to be able to do myself justice. But I plugged away, overtook a few people and started to feel a lot better. I overtook Hillary and felt better still, and then came the climb to Hawi, a small town on a headland on the northernmost point of the island and the turnaround point on the bike. It is a steady climb into a headwind, which means I was in my element – I'm at my best on the climbs, and a headwind only magnifies that. I overtook a lot of people on that twenty-mile stretch. As I approached Hawi, I passed a group of women coming down the other way with motorbikes and cameras trailing them. I knew then that I was gaining on the lead group, although I didn't know at that point that there were actually two more women ahead of them. They would have passed by a little earlier, but it's not always easy to tell the sex of the athletes coming the other way when you're cycling at 25 miles an hour.

I realised then that if I just kept going at my current pace I would probably catch them. On the way back from Hawi, there's a small town called Kawaihae just before you return to the Queen Kaahumanu Highway. A few minutes on, the road bends to the left, and there were the girls a little further ahead. I had a decision to make. Either I had to sit at the back of the group, or I had to overtake the whole lot of them, because they were too close together for me to slot in somewhere in between.

So I overtook them. I acknowledged Belinda as I went past, and I now know that another athlete, Sam McGlone, asked her who I was. Belinda replied: 'That's the winner of the race.'

There's a motorbike that carries a board with the split times on it, and I could see my race number was in ninth, although you don't know how up to date it is and I didn't know who the other numbers represented. It turned out I was actually in third, with two more girls ahead of me, Dede Griesbauer and Leanda Cave. With about fifteen miles of the bike to go I'd overtaken them both, each on an incline. And I still felt strong. I was having a whale of a time.

All of a sudden, the cameras started to appear. I wonder if any of my friends are watching at home, I thought to myself. You can get coverage of the race live on the internet. Look at those helicopters overhead. Listen to the cheers. Wow, there are a lot of people lining the streets. Isn't this surreal?

Surreal is the word. During a race I feel as if I'm in a kind of bubble – it's as if I'm swimming underwater. I can see and hear all this pandemonium – helicopters, cameras, media and spectators jumping up and down – but it also feels as if it is happening just slightly somewhere else and to someone else.

Transition two went smoothly enough, and soon I was out pounding the streets of Kona, out and back along Ali'i Drive and then onto the Queen K. You never know whether your run legs are going to be waiting for you in your transition bag, but they'd been there all right, and now they were whisking me away.

Not that people were taking me too seriously at this stage. I think there was still very much a feeling that I was some silly rookie who had gone off too fast and would fade on the run. On the commentary there seemed to be more interest in the fact that I wasn't wearing a hat or visor. This was Hawaii – everyone wore a hat in Hawaii. But I'd never liked headgear – it makes me feel as if my head is in a vice. All I had were the $20 sunglasses that I'd bought in a gas station in New Zealand two years earlier.

The commentators were desperately trying to think of things to say about me. My friends watching online were screaming at their computers as the poor experts floundered in the dark.

Roughly five miles in, Belinda and I crossed paths. I was now a couple of miles ahead of her and she screamed at me: 'Chrissie, it's yours! Just remember to eat! Don't forget to eat! Focus!'

From that point on, our friendship blossomed.

In my excitement, I suddenly remembered that England had played against France in the Rugby World Cup. I asked a guy who was waving a St George's flag if he knew the result, and he told me that England had won. They were in the World Cup final, against all the odds.

There must have been something in the stars for the English that weekend (we won the football, too). I was even more of an underdog than the rugby boys, and yet I was still winning. From the moment I'd taken the lead, about five and a half hours and a hundred miles into the race, I'd just assumed it would be temporary. They'll catch me, they'll catch me, I thought as I got off the bike. They'll catch me, as I headed out on Ali'i Drive. They'll catch me, as I hit the Queen K.

Where are they? The gap just grew and grew. With five miles or so till the end, it dawned on me that this was mine to lose. Brett had always said that the race doesn't start until this point. You can be feeling great and suddenly it hits you, the proverbial wall. His words rang in my head. I didn't think my body was going to break down, but I couldn't let myself believe I was going to win, either. If I let my concentration drop, my body might be next.

I remember seeing my old friend from Birmingham University, the nutrition expert Asker Jeukendrup. He was halfway through the run as I was coming towards the end. We high-fived each other.

I ran down the hill into town, and I could almost see the finish line. I was half laughing, half crying, totally bewildered. I saw my friend's boyfriend on the side of the road, grabbed the Union Jack off him and belted for the finish, waving, weeping and grinning.

Then, much to my surprise, the lead motorbike turned left at the bottom of the hill. 'Oh, no,' I thought. Muppet strikes again. I hadn't looked at the map properly, and it turned out we had to do a loop through town before we finished. There was another mile to go, another mile carrying this huge flag and continuing what I'd started on the waving, weeping and grinning front.

As I finally reached the last couple of hundred yards, I heard this low-frequency humming sound and I suddenly thought: 'They're booing me!' No one knew who I was, this irritating flag-waving Brit, and my win was clearly not welcome. It took the wind out of my sails for a moment or two. Until I noticed two large islanders blowing into their conch shells to welcome the world champion across the line – another Kona tradition I'd been ignorant of.

At five months old with my mother, Lin.

At home in Feltwell, Norfolk, where my parents still live. The perfect platform for any wannabe Wonder Woman.

At the Thetford Dolphins Swimming Club, with my nemesis in the water, Julie Williams, holding the trophy.

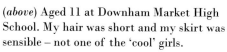

(*above*) Aged 11 at Downham Market High
School. My hair was short and my skirt was
sensible – not one of the 'cool' girls.

(*right*) With Gabriel at Beaver Country Day
School, Boston in 1996. We had so much in
common, not least an obsession with body
image.

(*below*) And with Jude in 1998, the person
who changed everything.

After the 2002 London Marathon, with Dad, Matty and Mum. I was stunned by my time of 3hr 08min.

(*left*) In sight of Everest, with Tina, whose example of calmness keeps me grounded even now.

(*right*) I'm no mountain goat, but I entered the famous Coast to Coast race in New Zealand, a bike-run-kayak triathlon, in 2006 and managed to come second.
(© *Paul's Camera Shop*)

(*above*) On the occasion of my grandfather Harry's 100th birthday, with my mum and dad, brother, cousins, Rob (centre) and Tim, my aunt and uncle, Jen and Tom, and, seated, Grandad and Nanna Romey.

(*left*) The Boss. Life was never boring with Brett Sutton around – the man who turned this nobody into a world champion.

You cannot be serious. Winning my first world title. No one can believe it, least of all me.
(© Rich Cruse)

One of the inspirational
messages on the
roadside at Ironman
Australia. Also my
screensaver.

In 2008, after my second
world title, I pushed bikes
where no bikes had been
pushed before on a cycle
tour through the Andean
mountains in Argentina. Here
I am, taking my turn at one
of the many river crossings.

Settling down for a night in the Andes: from left, my soul-mate Billi, Helen, me, Tina's husband, Seba, his friend Ricardo (or 'Rata') and Tina.

In the hills outside Boulder.

Make sure you remember where your bike is. It's one among thousands.
(© Jesse Hammond/Active.com)

The all-out brawl that is the start of an ironman. *(© Rich Cruse)*

Out on the Queen K Highway during the 2009 World Championships, knifing through the unforgiving lava fields. (© *Rich Cruse*)

Winning my third consecutive world title in 2009, breaking the seventeen-year-old course record, and enjoying the moment with Mum and Dad. (© *Rich Cruse*)

On the turbo three days after breaking my arm in January, 2010.

With my manager, Ben Mansford, Tom and Cat Morrison.

The Wellington support crew at Roth, 2010.

(*left*) With Tom at the Ironman Arizona finish line in 2010. Breaking the official Ironman world record was the best way to bounce back from the illness that had ruled me out of Kona that year. Sharing it with Tom, who broke the British ironman record in his first attempt at the distance, made it even more special. (© *Rich Cruse*)

(*below*) At the wedding in 2011 of my brother, Matty, and his bride, Kelly.

In thought before Roth 2011. The words of 'If' are written on my water bottle. (© *Kristen WinterKamp*)

The legendary climb of Solarerberg. The atmosphere at Challenge Roth is unlike any other. (© *Challenge Roth*)

A new world record and my third consecutive victory at Roth (© Rebecca Marshall)

My traditional 'Blazeman' roll, a few seconds later, ended in tears of joy.
(© Rebecca Marshall)

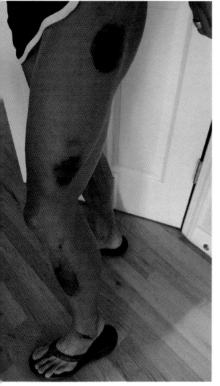

(left) Displaying my 'road rash' shortly after the crash I suffered two weeks before Kona 2011.

(right) Leanda Cave gives me a pat of encouragement as I pass her during the marathon at Kona 2011. There is such a wonderful camaraderie among the ironman athletes.
(© Larry Maurer)

The win to end all wins. My fourth world title and my thirteenth ironman win out of thirteen, during which I was forced to dig deeper than I ever have before.
(© Larry Maurer)

And there it was in front of me – the finishing tape, and the first inkling that things were going to be very different from now on. I had won – Chrissie Wellington, World Champion. I took a bow in front of the crowd, who were definitely cheering now, and at around 3.53 p.m., 9hr 8min 45sec after I'd started, I reached out for the tape, seized it with both hands, brought it down to my knees and hoisted it high over my head.

Everything fell out of me at that point – tears, laughter and any remnants of British reserve. Important-looking people shook my hand, a lei was placed around my neck and a garland on my head. An excited guy in a white baseball cap, whom I now know to be Mike Reilly, the Voice of Ironman, grabbed me and thrust a microphone in my face.

By now everything was blurred. Someone else grabbed me for an interview, and I followed his lead blindly. My eyes were full of tears, and the fixed smile was making my mouth hurt almost as much as did my feet and legs.

People have often asked how it felt. It's the hardest question to answer, and I still can't do it properly. Surreal is the adjective that I use most often, but there are lots of other words that hint towards how I was feeling, without ever truly getting there. Words like elated, confused, satisfied, delirious and proud. The coming together of all that you've trained for at the moment you secure your sport's biggest prize is a rush of euphoria much discussed by other champions, but it doesn't make it any less powerful when it happens to you. And no less difficult to capture in words. I do remember feeling sadness, too, that my parents weren't there (they had long before booked a holiday in Sicily, never knowing I was going to be in this race, let alone win it) and that Brett wasn't (he doesn't go to Kona, partly because of his controversial past, partly because he feels his job is done by then).

I was whisked away for a drugs test and then to a nearby restaurant for the most amazing buffet, where I ate my body weight in food.

Then it was back up the side of the volcano to salvage my things from the apartment. I now had a hotel to stay in, and it struck me that moving out of our hovel into it could prove symbolic. I was no longer Ms Anonymous. I knew barely anyone in that town down below, seething with thousands of racegoers, but suddenly they all knew me. I would be shaking a lot of hands for the next few days; I would have a big target on my back at all future races; and my funky chicken would be scrutinised like never before. Oh, Lord, I thought, my life is never going to be the same again.

That fact was brought home to me powerfully in the hours that followed. I was grilled at the hour-long press conference by a range of journalists who had never heard of me, before returning to the finish line, where I stayed till midnight when the race comes to an end and all competitors still out on the course are gently told that they will have to stop. I shook hands, signed autographs, threw things into the crowd, cheered on the other athletes as they finished, danced . . .

But I was also overwhelmed. I had no mechanism in place to deal with all the attention I was receiving, all the offers. Asker was really the only person there I knew and trusted, so he acted as a kind of manager. I just handed him all the business cards as they were thrust at me. Bike manufacturers, shoe companies, management companies, we can do this for you, we can do that. I tried to smile through it all, but inside I was in turmoil.

I managed to get through to my overjoyed parents to tell them that their little girl had just done something that she feared was going to have major repercussions – and for once, it wasn't because of some accident I'd been in. Which was just as well, because my mum revealed that she'd been in hospital for three days, having tripped on a kerb in Sicily, landed on her arm and damaged her gall bladder and one of her kidneys. You see where I get it from.

And I got through to Brett.

'Good job, kid,' he said, simply, just as he always did. Those three words meant everything to me.

The next day I sat down to write my victory speech for the awards party that night. I didn't have a dress either, so I had to borrow one. Standing up on the stage with the other girls in the top ten, who included Belinda and Rebecca, was intimidating not just because of all the people in the audience but also because of the calibre of athletes lined up alongside me. It was a long speech, I'm afraid – they always end up longer than you think they'll be – but it was straight from the heart.

And I used it to foist upon everyone my passion for international development. 'I worked as a swimming teacher at a day school in Boston,' I said, 'and I saw at first hand what a difference sport can make to children's lives. And again in Nepal, where sport was one thing that could bring conflict-affected communities together. Sport has a tremendous power, and can be a force for considerable change.'

It was a crazy night, a crazy weekend. I finished it the only way I knew how – low-key and with friends. I might have met Scott and Eneko for the first time only a few days earlier, but we had bonded, and after we'd danced into the small hours at the after party at Lou Lou's, the three of us headed out to Denny's fast-food joint for the most disgusting, polluting, delicious meal of chicken wings, chips, mozzarella sticks and every other deep-fried delicacy you could dream of. The boys gave me a silver necklace with three turtles, one for each of us, and I still wear it.

It took a while for me to get to grips with where I was, all of a sudden, after Kona. All year, I'd simply completed the next task that was put in front of me, and I'd never considered my progress to be much more than doing just that. I'd certainly never expected to become a world champion. Now that I could stop for a moment and look back, it was plain that, yes, it had been an extraordinary few months. I'd turned pro in mid-February as a wannabe Olympic triathlete. And here I was, in mid-October, the champion of the world in ironman. I had a cheque for $110,000 in my back pocket, I'd just registered the eighth-fastest time ever recorded on the course by a woman, and my marathon split of 2hr 59min 58sec was the second-fastest ever. I had people clamouring outside my door and was being showered with praise, the like of which I'd never known before.

It was the sort of thing that could go to a girl's head. I knew my challenge now was to make sure it didn't.

10

A Triathlete's Life

Of all the body parts we train for this unforgiving pursuit of ours, none is more important than the head. There is a culture in triathlon for logbooks and data, obsessing about how far and how fast we have gone in our latest session. People think that if their logbook is in order, then so must their preparation be. Then they hit kilometre thirty in the marathon, their bodies racked with pain and fatigue, and they despair that there are another twelve to go. That's when they are in danger of breaking down, and certainly of slowing down. That's when they most need a mind that is as honed and as powerful as their butt cheeks.

The best coaches will tell you this. It is more or less the first thing Brett said to me when I turned up to be assessed by him, even if his observation that he would need to cut my head off was a somewhat unconventional way of letting me know I had work to do. I was fretful and obsessive when I first turned pro, running at everything like a bull in a china shop.

'The training you got a handle on,' as Brett had told me in one of those emails. 'The walking around in nerd land you have not. You get over that the same way as you improve an athletic weakness – by knowing and training it out. Life is nothing but a habit. Get to work.'

At the start it seemed daunting. 'But I can't relax,' I wanted to say. 'I can't slow down. I can't not be a muppet. It's the way I am.' These protestations, though, were no different from saying: 'But I can't lift that weight, I can't run that fast, I can't complete an ironman.' You may not be able to right now, but, with a positive frame of mind and a willingness to work, anything is possible.

Remaining positive really is one of the most precious faculties for any athlete. That, and an ability to stay focused and disciplined. Develop a mind bank of positive images and thoughts – family, friends, previous successes, favourite places, a big plate of chips. You need to build it up as you would any collection, but soon you will have a range of thoughts to flick through when next your body and soul are screaming out for relief.

There is a lot of repetitive activity in an athlete's life, particularly in ironman, and you need to learn to handle it. The best way of improving your capacity to endure boredom is to endure boredom. Spend time training on your own and challenge your mind to stay focused. We had a room in Leysin that we called the dungeon, where the treadmill was. It was airless with no windows, and if you stretched your arms out you could touch either wall. It smelled of the sweat and tears of previous workouts. The radio was broken. Brett used to send athletes down there for sessions. He made some, such as Hillary Biscay and Bella Comerford, run entire marathons down there. Hillary once forgot to charge her iPod and had to do the whole thing with no stimulation at all. Now, I'm not necessarily recommending you try that at home, folks. Brett knew what he was doing when he picked and chose certain sessions for certain athletes. But it gives you an insight into the sort of techniques with which you can train your mind as well as your body.

You should maintain the same level of concentration in training as you would when racing. It's no use imagining you will miraculously develop that focus on race day. It won't happen, and you will have

140

neglected a fundamental part of your programme. You wouldn't go into a race without any physical training, so why would you go in without any mental?

The mind constantly wanders when you are engaged in repetitive activity for a prolonged period. Many's the time I have been thinking of other things, only to snap out of it and say, 'Wake up! You're in a race here!' This is natural, but you have to be aware of it and to learn to stay in the moment. If your mind wanders, so does your body. You should constantly be asking yourself questions. Are my arms relaxed? Is my face? Am I working as hard as I can? Am I breathing into my belly, or am I stopping in my throat? On the swim, it should be: is my hand entering correctly, am I finishing the stroke properly, am I on feet? There should be a regular check/feedback mechanism, whether you're in training or in a race. If you lose that continual self-assessment, before you know it your face and shoulders have tensed up, you're clenching your fists and you're holding your breath or gasping when you don't need to. It all adds up to a waste of valuable energy and loss of form.

But it's not just out on the road, in the water or in the dungeon that you can train your mind. I find I do some of my most valuable work on the sofa. Visualisation is a hugely important tool, one that requires little more than some peace and quiet. Close your eyes, relax, then go through each stage of the race in your mind. Picture yourself performing at your peak. Then imagine all the things that could go wrong, and picture yourself dealing with them. What will I do if my goggles are knocked off? What will I do if I suffer a puncture, or cramps? Visualise each situation and rehearse your response, so that, if problems do arise, you are able to react decisively and calmly, despite the chaos and adrenaline of race day.

Things will go wrong – of that you can be assured. Not only will it help to have visualised your reaction, but in the heat of battle it is also essential to carry your own mantras and motivational material.

Soon after I joined his camp in Thailand, Brett introduced me to one of my most valuable sources of inspiration. 'There is a poem I want you to read,' he said one day. 'You might not like it because of its patriarchal wording, but it captures the qualities you need to be a successful athlete and a good person.'

The poem was 'If' by Rudyard Kipling. Brett gave me a photocopy of it, and I remember the shiver of excitement I felt as I read the opening words: 'If you can keep your head when all about you/Are losing theirs and blaming it on you.'

That photocopy is now dog eared and torn, but I carry it with me everywhere. 'If' has become my favourite poem. I write its words on all of my water bottles. I have drawn reassurance from the poem's teaching of fortitude and level-headedness, and tried to apply it to all areas of my life. In addition, I write my own mantra on my race wristband: 'Never ever give up – and smile'.

It might not be the same for everyone, but smiling, for me, is crucial. First of all, it relaxes my face and gives me a lift. Second, it shows how much I love the sport and the occasion. We need to take triathlon seriously, but ultimately it is something to be enjoyed. Through my smile I like to convey that joy and passion for what I am doing. And, third, I hope it affects the mindset of my competitors. If they see me smiling, they might think I'm finding it easy. Sometimes a smile is useful to mask the pain.

In an endurance athlete's life, pain is never far away. As pain is little more than a conversation between your body and your brain, this is another reason why a fit mind is so important. The brain is the master computer of the body. Even when we are working on the efficiency of the peripheral components – the legs, the arms, the butt cheeks – we can recruit the seat of all power to enhance the effectiveness of our work. It's a question of testing limits.

For a start, there's the importance of keeping an open mind. The brain is programmed to protect us, and that can mean imposing limits on what it thinks we can or should do. Constantly push at those limits, because the brain can be way too cautious. Not so long ago I would have laughed at you if you had suggested I do an ironman. Imagine if I had allowed that attitude to persist. It is up to each and every one of us to change 'I can't' into 'I can'.

I am motivated above all by that little voice inside that urges me on to fulfil my potential. Everyone has that same voice in them somewhere, but many are too scared to listen to it, too scared to try, too scared of failure. That fear is immobilising, but it is also our own personal construct and therefore doesn't exist in reality. Never imagine anything is impossible, and never stop trying out new things. My life has taken me to so many wonderful places and has truly enriched me. None of it would have been possible if I'd let timidity overcome the impulse to explore.

If we think about our training for sport, the same principles apply. The brain is constantly trying to impose limits on what it thinks we can achieve. We should constantly question it, fight it. That means enduring pain. Successful ironman athletes relish their relationship with pain. Not the mechanical kind, necessarily, which warns us that something has broken down – although even there I have found time and time again that it is possible to overcome certain 'injuries' by making myself train and/or race through them. What the good triathlete should relish is the pain that is our brain's way of telling us that it doesn't like how hard we are working. I have completed training sessions I would never have thought possible, usually on the orders of a coach who would not be disobeyed but also through my own thirst for pushing back the limits. The key is not to be afraid of failing.

This is not gratuitous masochism. There is a very real process of refinement going on. You are not just working your muscles and lungs, you are working your brain to learn to accept each new level of exertion as something that can be endured safely. The brain – at least, the safety-first part of the brain – will try to dig its heels in.

Eventually it will prevail, because, of course, there *are* limits. We can't launch into an ironman as if it were a sprint, so a sense of what really is too much is always crucial. The key is to push that point back as far as possible. The interface between the conservative and ambitious impulses in the brain should be a front of continual struggle. And remembering the pain of previous sessions or races we have successfully endured gives us the confidence to go through it again, and the evidence to present to the brain that we are capable of handling it. That way, the next time we hit kilometre thirty of the marathon and want to stop, we know that a) we have been here before, and b) our discomfort can be overcome.

I would stress to any athlete the importance of this intuitive approach, based more on perception than on data. There is a temptation for many athletes to surround themselves with all the latest gadgets, and to base their routines on what their heart monitor or their stopwatch is telling them. The danger then is that you start to judge your limits by these devices rather than by the one that matters – the one inside you.

There would be little point here in trying to lay out a comprehensive guide to triathlon training. Every athlete is different, and besides, experienced coaches with a long track record in triathlon – in other words, people far more qualified than I am – have written entire books on the subject. I am just an athlete, albeit a successful one. This doesn't mean I understand why coaches set the sessions they do, nor does it put me in a position to prescribe programmes.

If I had to stress one thing, though, it would be to keep it simple. It's not rocket science. I think a lot of athletes make things more complicated than they need to. My training is pretty much the same from week to week, in terms of the disciplines I tackle on a given day. We do need to be flexible and to adapt, tweaking here and there, but consistency is key.

In keeping with the simple approach is this emphasis on feel over gadgetry. I do use quantifiable indicators in my training, such as speed on a treadmill or time on a track, but not as much as you might think, and certainly not as much as many others. Tangible results in training are important, especially if you are being coached by someone from a distance, but they are not as valuable an indicator as perceived effort. You might end up training within yourself one day for fear of exceeding a predetermined level on your heart-rate monitor; on another you might train too hard when you're not feeling 100 per cent in order to reach that predetermined level. In both cases, you would be better served listening to yourself.

The other problem with obsessing over numbers, I think, is that it takes some of the enjoyment out of what we do. We should never lose the ability to read our bodies, but we should never, ever lose the joy of the wind in our hair, the joy of sport for sport's sake.

Although my programme is specific to me and has changed very little over the years, any athlete's programme should consist of four basic types of session. Steady-state sessions, which are aerobic and do not raise the heart rate too high; strength sessions, which involve drills such as hill repeats on the bike or run, or swimming with paddles in the water; race-pace sessions, where you are training as fast as you would race, using drills such as time trials; and faster-than-race-pace sessions, incorporating interval work, short, sharp bursts where you go beyond your limits, sessions that really hurt and are supposed to.

If an age-group athlete could find time for one of each of those session types for each discipline across a week, or even two weeks, then they would have the basis of a sound programme. I would particularly urge them to make time for the faster sessions, especially as the season develops. Long, slow and steady plays a crucial part in our training, but if that is all you do then you will race long, slow and

145

steady. As the season gets into swing, it is important to incorporate those harder, faster intervals.

Another key component to my training these days is strength and conditioning. For many triathletes, lifting weights is synonymous with body-building and, as such, is avoided. Brett is in this camp, although he did set me that programme of knuckle press-ups to strengthen my upper body. He feels that the majority of strength and conditioning comes from the swim, bike and run sessions and that additional gym work, as well as being unnecessary, could cause injury. Later, when I started to train under Dave Scott, I was introduced to a new philosophy. Dave is a huge proponent of a targeted and structured strength-and-conditioning programme. Such training is about much more than lifting weights and Mr Universe competitions. If applied carefully and specifically to you and your strengths and weaknesses, it promotes physical development and resistance to fatigue and injury. I wouldn't be without it.

If I was to give you an idea of my typical week's training, insofar as there is such a thing, it would look something like this:

MON	Swim: aerobic (total 5km)	Bike: 3hours with 5x3min intervals and a 50min TT with mixed gearing		
TUE	Run: 75mins with 30–40min of intervals at faster-than-race-pace	Swim: 4.5km, with at least 2.5km at race pace, or above	Run: 45min steady jog	S&C work
WED	Swim: 4.5 with sprints, followed by paddle work	Bike/Run brick: 3hour ride, with hill repeats and 60min of TT intervals followed by a run of 12–17km which includes faster-than-race-pace intervals		

THUR	Cycle: 2hours, with hill repeats (2x15 and 4x5min)	Swim: 4.5km	Cycle: 2hours with 60–70min IM pace TT	
FRI	Run: Mixed hill repeats with intervals on the flats	Swim: 4–5km steady	S&C	
SAT	Swim: 5km with 3km at race pace and above	Cycle: 4.5–5hrs with 3hours of IM and Half IM pace		
SUN	Run: 22–32km depending on phase of training, with at least 10km of varied pace, including faster-than-race-pace efforts	S&C		Massage

Before you start any training, though, it is essential to plan and set goals, both long term and intermediate. Patience is key. We should never be in such a rush to achieve our goals that we are not willing to take the small steps needed to reach them. Trying to make giant leaps can result in injury and overload. The long-term goals for a triathlete will usually be their A (main) races. The intermediate goals will be little milestones along the way – either in training or B races – to be celebrated whenever they are reached. The journey between these must be planned in advance. Begin by establishing where it is you want to get to by the season's end, then establish where you are now, and then set about drawing up the journey in between, working backwards from the end. It is no use knowing where you are now and assuming you will get to your goal somehow, nor will it help knowing where your goal is and ignoring your current state. Start the season with a time trial in each of the three disciplines, so you have a benchmark, say, for a 1,500m swim, a 20km bike and a 5km run.

As you embark on your plan, measure your progress against your times. An important technique is to write everything down – your goals, your plan, your progress.

It may not surprise you to hear that I am a great believer in quality over quantity. I would urge all athletes at least to bear this policy in mind, but, as discussed, it might not suit everyone. Brett knew this as well as anyone, so in Team TBB we all had different programmes. I was more racehorse, he kept telling me, fast, yet liable to break under high-volume training, while other girls, like Belinda, Bella and Hillary, were more shire horse, strong with big engines. That's why he sent them off on those marathon (literally) sessions in the dungeon, or on crazy 60km runs.

There was a competitiveness between us all. You know what girls are like! Sometimes Brett would actually split us up. I was often told to train with the boys. It played on my mind that the other girls were so often given longer sessions than I was. Early on, in Thailand, Brett set me a two-hour run for my long run session of the week. I knew the others were doing three hours, and I wanted to show him I could do three hours just as well. So I did. He came down on me like a ton of bricks. Same with the cycling – at the end of each day's training in Switzerland, we had the 16km climb up from Aigle to Leysin to negotiate. He would tell me to take it slowly; I would disobey, constantly trying to chip away at my personal best. But Brett was often watching from his white Berlingo without our knowledge. One day he sat me down to tell me that I was undermining everything else by pushing up that hill when I should be taking it easy.

Then again, sometimes he allowed that kind of thing. The following year, while training in the Philippines, I was suffering, as usual, from diarrhoea one day. Three of us had been set a session on the track – ten one miles on six minutes with a 200m jog for recovery after each. I had to rush off to the bushes after each mile and then catch up with the others. I was so frustrated at having to stop the whole time that I stayed on to do another set of ten 800m, even though Brett hadn't told me to. He stood there watching with a smile on his face. For some reason he let me smash myself that time.

We always had a long ride on Saturdays. Some were truly epic. Once the whole team cycled the 200km around Lake Geneva – followed by the climb to Leysin, obviously. Another time, the girls went on a five-hour bike ride in the pouring rain. It was freezing, but we forced our way through it. Donna Phelan fell on the tramlines. We didn't know it, but she had actually broken her elbow. She finished the ride without so much as a complaint. There was something about Brett's training – there was something about Brett – that made you suck up pain. In so doing, it raised your threshold for it. He loathed the idea of any of us going soft, physically or emotionally. A pity party, he called it, when people sat around and felt sorry for themselves. Needless to say, we weren't allowed any.

Brett used to organise birthday sets, whereby everyone followed the routine he had devised for the birthday girl or boy on their special day. Which meant we were all in trouble on Hillary's birthday. Hillary is a masochist at the best of times, but for her birthday in Leysin in 2008 she asked for agony – and we all got it. The day started with 100 reps of 100m in the pool, all on 1min 30sec – that's a 10km swim. Erica Csomor had made us muffins, which she placed by the poolside as a treat for when we'd finished. Then, at lunchtime we had a two-hour ride with an hour of hill repeats, followed in the afternoon by a two-and-a-quarter-hour ride with a 20km time trial. We finished off, of course, with that 16km climb up the mountain to Leysin. I had horse steak for dinner that night.

After that kind of session – after *any* kind of session – it is vital that you recuperate. I would go so far as to describe recovery as the fourth discipline of a triathlete. This is a very hard thing for me to say, and it was even harder for me to put into practice. The idea of rest flies in the face of every value I have lived my life by. I should be the last person to preach downtime, having indulged in so little of it during my life before triathlon, but I am fully converted now. I realise it is not the actual sessions of swim, bike and run that make you fitter, it is the periods you spend recovering in between, during which your body adapts and regenerates. That's why I say that I train 24/7 – recovery is training. It's the most important part of it, in fact.

Again, it might take another book to explore properly the different techniques and disciplines of recovery. Each athlete will have a personal take on what works best, each equally valid. What follows are the brushstrokes.

Around 10 per cent of your physical training should involve 'cooling off' (or warming down), by which is meant gentle (really gentle, almost unnaturally so) swim/bike/running at the end of each session. This can also include targeted light stretching.

I rest two days a month, which might not sound like much, but then I'm a pro, so I have the luxury of hours of downtime during my normal week, which the majority of amateurs are not afforded. There is no rule here, but I would suggest incorporating a rest day every seven to ten days in a typical training regime. Whatever feels right – again, listen to your body, irrespective of pre-planned training schedules. And spending the day shopping or gardening doesn't count as rest. It has to involve sitting down, preferably on a sofa. This is not wasted time. Banish that guilt and rest assured that your sofa is making you faster, stronger and more resilient.

Wearing skin-tight compression garments is a must, albeit it in a tasteful manner. These increase blood flow to the muscles, enhance the removal of waste products and support the muscles. Massage, too, is an important means of recovery, if time and finances allow.

And, of course, there's nutrition and hydration. Again, as detailed elsewhere, there have been periods in my life when I have been in no position to hold forth on this subject. But I have, despite myself at times, always loved food, and finding out that healthy practice does not rule out a diet of almost anything – as long as it is in moderation – has been one of the joys of recent years. Sports nutrition is another subject that could stretch to a book in its own right. Asker, my friend from Birmingham University, has written two of the best, and has played a key role in shaping my diet into what it is today. I have also read extensively on the subject, and would encourage anyone else to do the same. I am amazed at how many neglect this part of their training and fail to fuel their bodies with what they need in order to function effectively. The basic principles are these: keep it simple, eat natural foods as much as possible, balance intake with output and have everything in moderation. If you follow those principles, nothing is 'naughty', unless it's eaten (or drunk) to excess. That's when the balance is corrupted.

So what does my daily diet look like? It is healthy and balanced, with fresh fruits and vegetables, whole grains and good fats (with some saturated ones thrown in too).

I have two breakfasts. One when I wake up, before my first session. This is a couple of rice cakes or a frozen banana, with sunflower butter and honey on top, washed down with an oversized cup of Joe. Decaf is not in my vocabulary. After my first session I have my second breakfast: either hot oatmeal with some nut butter mixed in and covered with honey, or a huge bowl of raw oats, nuts, seeds, dried fruit, coconut and yogurt mixed together. For lunch I have either a baked potato, some wholegrain bread or brown rice salad with a combination of either tinned tuna, sliced meats, pulses or eggs, as well as a bigger-than-average bowl of cereal and some nuts or fruit as a snack.

I eat meat most evenings, either fish or white meat – with red meat once a week to keep my iron levels up. I also love liver and kidneys. On the side I have salad or veggies and a big pile of 'complex' carbs or potatoes. Dessert is always a bowl of cereal and frozen berries with Muscle Milk. I have olive oil on everything. Even porridge.

I don't deprive myself of any foods. A few pieces of dark chocolate a day definitely don't do me any harm, and as for pizza – well, I can always squeeze one of those in. The key is to find out what fuels work best for you, and to see nutrition and hydration as part of training your body to be the best it can be.

Lastly, I would stress the need for an off-season. As with a day off, this can seem like the most heinous crime of decadence to any self-respecting sport obsessive. Well, feel guilty if you have to, but make yourself do it anyway. Six weeks is my chosen length of holiday, which begins after my last race of the season. For the first two weeks, I do nothing but enjoy myself with friends and family, reliving the life I once had – theatre, concerts, eating out. I do no exercise whatsoever. Then I embark on a two-week period of sporting activity that doesn't involve swimming, biking or running; just enough to fire up the aerobic system once again. The third stage of my off-season is when I venture out again to the pool or on the road, but the exercise will be much less intense than normal. I can still lie in each morning, and there will be no sign of a logbook anywhere about the house. Only then, after six weeks, will I start to build up for the new season with something that might be recognisable as focused training, albeit still with an emphasis on aerobic fitness. That off-season will have given you a break from your routine and rejuvenated your body and mind. You will feel refreshed and ready to pursue new goals.

But it is at the races that we enjoy the fruits of our labour. It's every bit as important to develop a routine for these, as it is for your weekly training.

I arrive a week before an ironman (ten days for Kona), or three days before a half-ironman, having gathered beforehand as much information on the race as I can. In the days before, I run part of the course with an iPod in my ear. That way, when I am out there during the race, I can hear those well-chosen motivational songs at certain landmarks. I have a gentle massage two days before to relax the mind and muscles (not the day before, as that can leave you feeling sluggish). By then I will have cut down on fibre and the more complex carbohydrates, sticking to plain foods such as white rice, bread and pasta. Together with the reduction in training, it ensures my glycogen levels are full but not overflowing. The day before, having racked my bike, I walk through the transition areas, checking where I'll come in and leave, and picturing myself doing so. Then I will go home, close my eyes and visualise the race in my head, reinforcing my plans for dealing with the inevitable ups and downs. My pre-race meal is tuna pasta, before some time in front of the television.

It's early to bed (around 8 p.m.). I will have set two alarms to wake me two hours and forty-five minutes before the start, which usually means around 4 a.m. Very often I don't need waking. Everyone gets nervous before a race – it's human. I would be worried about any athlete that didn't. It's a sign of how much we care. The key is to trust in your preparation. You have done all you can, so focus on that fact. You will remain the same person before, during and after the race, so the result, however important, will not define you. The journey is what matters.

After rising, I will shower, breathe deeply, massage my muscles, think positive thoughts and study 'If'. Breakfast is taken two hours and fifteen minutes before the start. This has changed for me in the course of my career, but the key recipe is 500 calories (for an ironman) of low-fibre, simple carbs and a small amount of fat and protein. These days I have hot rice cereal made with water, with nut butter and honey stirred in. I sip water and drink a cup of coffee. I dress warmly for the start and leave myself plenty of time to take into account the traffic and avoid a last-minute rush.

Your bike will be one of a few thousand in the transition area. Coming into T1 to be confronted with so many bikes always reminds me of the story my dad used to tell me of Mr Mole, who couldn't find his home one day because of all the other molehills that had sprung up while he'd been out. So make sure you have identified a landmark to help you locate your bike when you return after the swim. Leave it and your biking gear exactly as you would hope to find them, so that you are in and out of there in as little time as possible. Once you are happy, smother yourself with lubricant – the ironman's best friend – in all of the areas prone to chafing. Just make sure you apply it with rubber gloves on, or a plastic bag – oily hands can affect the 'catch' in the swim.

Fifteen minutes before the race I start to warm up in the water. The swim is when you are at your freshest but also at your coldest. For this reason, and in order to get among a pack with the fastest swimmers, the first 200 to 400 metres are an all-out sprint. When the gun goes off, I get my head down and plough my way through the flailing hands and feet, then settle into my race pace. Once settled, I breathe once every two strokes.

As I come into T1, I kick my legs harder to prepare them for the next stage of the race. I rehearse the transition in my mind. Remove goggles and swim cap first, and strip wetsuit down to the waist while heading for the bike. Then remove wetsuit completely, remaining calm if it doesn't come off easily. Sunglasses on first, then helmet, then race belt with number on back. Wheel bike to mount line and start pedalling.

Hopefully, it all goes as smoothly as that.

It is not until I have settled into a rhythm that I first start to take on nutrition. In an ironman I take on one gram of carbs per kilo of body weight per hour. On my bike there are two bottles of energy drink (430 calories each), two gels and a chocolate bar. My first bottle is slightly less concentrated than my second to make it more palatable early in the race. The aid stations are crucial as a means of breaking up the race, and you can use the bottled water to cool your body on a hot day. Other vital techniques involve adjusting your position in the saddle and getting out of the saddle altogether in order to recruit different muscles and prevent fatigue. On the bike you will start to suffer, of that there is no doubt. That's when the mental strategies discussed earlier will come into their own.

In the last 500m I increase my cadence, and about 100m from T2 I loosen the strap on my bike shoes and slip my feet out. I dismount barefoot, run into transition while unclipping my helmet. I put on my pre-talcum-powdered socks and my shoes and grab my gels for the run. The race belt must be rotated so the number faces forwards. I take a few breaths. Now for the marathon.

The first thing to do is to ignore the legs. After the bike, they feel heavy and wobbly, but within a kilometre I have settled into my rhythm. I try to maintain a shorter stride length, keep my shoulders and elbows down, lift my hips and look forwards. Following the nutritional formula above, I take one gel every twenty-five minutes, washed down with water. I think of the marathon as four sets of 10km with a little bit more at the end. It's a way of tricking the mind into thinking the run more manageable than it might seem as an unbroken 42km haul. Landmarks can also be ticked off as I pass them as a measure of progress. I find male athletes similarly useful.

The energy from the spectators is vital, too. My wonderful family and friends can be relied upon to appear at strategic points round the course with their Chrissie banners and t-shirts, and to indulge in the kind of antics that would have them arrested under normal circumstances. The boost this gives me is incalculable, as are the cheers of the many complete strangers. I smile and smile as much as I can. And as the pain really kicks in, I dedicate each of the final few kilometres to people or causes I care about.

Every moment in that finish chute, whether as a professional or an age-grouper, is one to savour and remember. Look up and smile, and let the race photographer give you a tangible record of the moment you crossed the line.

Then, one of the best parts of the day: put flip-flops on. Ahh, the relief!

After the cocktail of emotions has abated slightly, it's time to listen to the body and do whatever it commands. Mine usually says, 'Pizza!' 'Burger!' 'Kebab!' and 'Chips!' Whatever the command, it is your duty to obey. Two half-pound burgers, two plates of chips, one plate of onion rings and fifteen doughnuts is my ironman record. It's one I'm as proud of as any. Moderation is swept aside. You've just finished an ironman. You deserve it.

11

Wearing the Crown

It should have been the best time of my life. Instead, it was one of the hardest.

I had just become a world champion. The truth is, though, that the period following a triumph like that is often difficult. There's always a different reason for any downturn, but a downturn there so often seems to be. It's probably not a coincidence.

Brett was at the centre of the first one. He suffers as much as anyone in these periods. He has always borne a feeling of doom when his athletes become successful. He'll tell you that money is the problem, something he has never been motivated by. As far as he is concerned, success is not only the motivation when it comes to coaching; it is also the great enemy. His methods demand that he has total control over his charges, but when success comes along, he knows that its trappings will provide a new threat to that control. Suddenly, he is not the only voice in their heads. He becomes fatalistic about his ability to remain the prime influence. The moment I crossed the finish line in Kona, he probably thought it was the end of our relationship. He certainly thought it well before the idea ever occurred to me.

Nothing was occurring to me back then. Everything was a

bombardment and a blur. I was even weepy at times, as I took refuge under Asker's wing. His was one of only a few familiar faces out there. Thousands of miles away in Asia, Brett and our team manager, Alex Bok, were aware of this, too. I could tell Alex was seriously regretting his decision not to accompany the team to the biggest race in the triathlon calendar. Now I was out there on my own, naive, vulnerable and, in Brett's view, at the mercy of the sharks who swim around at these events.

Amid the chaos I received an email from my old coach, Tim Weeks. He knew someone who worked as a sports manager for the Wasserman Media Group, and thought I should speak with him. As it was Tim, I agreed to speak to this contact, Ben Mansford, on the phone on the Monday. I was exhausted and hoarse, but we spoke for about 45 minutes. I immediately liked him. He suggested I come back to the UK to meet up. Alex and Brett wanted me to go to Singapore. I was caught in a horrible tug of war.

In the end, I went to Singapore. I owed Brett that, at least, and I trusted him and his judgement. I owed Alex, as well. We met at the chaotic Team TBB offices, above Alex's bike shop, down a back alley. Nothing up to that point had ever been signed between us – it had all been gentlemen's handshakes and back-of-the-envelope stuff. But this time there was very definitely something to sign, and it was pretty much thrust in my face upon arrival. Brett was there, as was a girl called Steph Cox, whom Alex had recently met in Thailand. Alex introduced her as my PR manager. Although she didn't stay in the role for very long, that did turn out to be a happy relationship. Steph remains a good friend to this day.

I felt under huge pressure. There was a voice in my head saying, 'Whoah! Take your time. Something's not right here!' But overriding all that was the desire to stay with Brett. It felt as if I had no option if that was what I wanted, so I signed. Alex would be my manager, Brett my coach and Steph would do the PR.

Immediately I knew it was something I hadn't wanted to do. I wasn't given enough time to discuss things with people, or to straighten myself out. Why couldn't I just go home to Norfolk for a while? There were definitely no sharks there.

The next thing I knew, Alex was whisking me off to the airport again. He and I flew to the UK, where we were going to meet with sponsors and journalists.

My parents greeted us at the airport with a Union Jack. This was the kind of homecoming I'd had in mind. I went straight to Norfolk – home at last. After just a few hours, a peace descended, and I regained the clarity I had lost since the race. From there, I rang Alex to voice my concerns. I didn't feel he had the time, as manager of the team, to focus on me as much as someone else might. Now was the moment to make hay. Professional sport is a precarious business, and if you have a chance to secure your future, you must take it. I wanted a manager of my own to help me with that.

We disagree over what was said next. I maintain that he said I could speak to other potential managers. He would tell you otherwise. Nevertheless, he was there at the meeting I organised, through Asker, with Ben Mansford at Birmingham University. It was awkward. I sat quietly and let Asker do most of the talking. Alex tried to be his usual charming self, but he was clearly not happy with the way things were going. Ben held court for much of it. I immediately warmed to him, although I was aware of the fact that he was an agent. They don't have the most wholesome of reputations, do they? I was struck by how young he was – about twenty-eight. And I enjoyed putting a face, a cheeky round face, to the dulcet Humberside tones I'd first heard on the phone in Hawaii a week earlier. He looked like a car salesman, and he made me laugh. He also seemed to know his stuff. We struck up a strong rapport from the start.

By the end of the meeting I had decided I wanted him to be my manager, which I think Alex realised. We had another meeting in

London a couple of days later, where the deal was confirmed and its details thrashed out. I would continue to be a part of the team, wearing their logo and, of course, most importantly of all, being coached by Brett. I would also be free, with only a few restrictions, to have Ben negotiate sponsorship deals for me, independent of those negotiated for the team. I don't deny it was the best of both worlds. I was happy, for the time being at least.

My next assignment was to fly out to the team camp in Thailand to prepare for the Laguna Phuket Triathlon.

I knew Brett was extremely upset with me. He seemed to feel I had defied instructions in speaking to Ben, which was absolutely not the case. The atmosphere had changed. I was heavy-hearted about that, because Brett was the one – more than anyone – I wanted to celebrate my win with, and I felt I couldn't. Sure enough, when I arrived in Thailand, he was distant and just went about his business. No congratulations, no nothing.

He did make one devastating gesture, however, which knocked me for six. He had a stash of cigars, which he had always said he would smoke when he had coached an ironman world champion. Now that he had, I'd given him a few more when we'd met in Singapore after Kona. Almost as soon as I arrived in Thailand, he wordlessly handed them back to me. To have made so angry the man I had always been so eager to please hit me very hard.

But I know now that Brett struggles in the aftermath of a win like the one in Kona. He gets very depressed. I understand, because I feel it too, to a degree. You go through this euphoria, then all of a sudden you feel quite empty when it subsides and the long road ahead is revealed again. I can empathise with that, but I found this breakdown in our relationship incredibly difficult. I craved Brett's approval. I had just won the biggest race in the world, and was so sincerely grateful to him for getting me there, yet I was unable to share it with him. He didn't want to acknowledge any of it.

Another part of my pain was that I could see where he was coming from. All he had ever wanted to do through the team was to find athletes, make them successful, manage them and with their help, bring on more. I was undermining that, he felt, or at least, the last part of it. He'd made me a star very quickly, and now, in his view, I was chasing the money.

This notion touched a nerve, which I'm sure Brett realised. He knows how important the question of development is to me. Helping those less fortunate had been my career before I became a triathlete; it had been my reason for going to Nepal. It has been my life. I spent hours every week helping mentor the other athletes in the team, particularly the Filipinos who had come to train with us. In the season to come I spent many more hours working with Alex and Brett to formulate a coherent development strategy. I hated the idea of my commitment to those projects being questioned. But I also had my own security to think about. I didn't see why the two had to be incompatible.

I hated, too, this icy relationship with Brett. I appreciated everything he had done for me. I wanted so much to continue to work together. I needed him. I didn't feel I was capable of succeeding without him.

Things got worse before they got better. I raced averagely at Phuket, which was a unique race, length-wise – basically, Olympic distance but with a longer bike – and came fourth. From there, it was back home for Christmas.

Trouble was brewing, though, on a number of fronts. First, the team had yet to decide on the bike sponsor for next season, who were also the main sponsor. One of the conditions of my staying on the team was that I had to take the same bike sponsor. Cervélo were up for renewing, but now, not only did we have Alex negotiating with them on the team's behalf, we had Ben negotiating on mine. Second,

I still had to be paid my prize money for Hawaii, which meant I still had to pay Brett his win bonus. Third, while we were in Thailand, Brett had been electrocuted in the shower. He was thrown across the bathroom, and now he was suffering short-term memory loss and occasional seizures. Fiona, his wife, was 'scared shitless', as he put it. I'm not sure he's fully recovered even now.

It made for an explosive cocktail. Brett was already bothered by all the advice I was suddenly getting from people on 'Team Chrissie', another of his phrases. This was not how he worked. He liked me to take orders from him and him alone, but now I had other people offering me their tuppence-worth on all kinds of matters, from sponsorship to training to physio. Brett was getting riled. He was also worried about the bike deal going through. He wanted it finalised as soon as possible, so that the team's future might be secured for the year ahead. We agreed a package in the end, but there was a delay with the contracts. This meant a delay in the deal being signed. Brett, naturally, blamed this on Ben and me.

He was also getting jumpy about the fact that I hadn't paid him that commission on Hawaii. There was an agreement Brett had with all of his athletes, whereby they would pay him 20 per cent of their winnings from their top three races. This meant I owed him more than $20,000 from Kona. I couldn't pay him until the World Triathlon Corporation (WTC) had paid me, and that still hadn't happened. He was worried, though, in view of the money monster he so obviously thought I had become, that I was not going to pay him at all.

Early in the new year, we exchanged a few emails. He seemed calm and philosophical, but there was the undercurrent of an uneasiness building in his words, and strong hints of melancholy. He was in Switzerland with his family, still recovering from his electrocution; I was in Norfolk with mine.

'I am the lone ranger, kid,' he wrote in one email. 'That's why I have grave doubts it will work. Now I am thinking I can no longer make you the best you can be. However, you are already world champion, so not a big problem.'

He said that all these advisors would be coming at me, armed with qualifications and letters after their name, and that their advice would always conflict with what Brett the maverick had to say. He said the academic in me would instinctively lean towards them, or at least make me nervous about following the advice of the boy who left school at fourteen, or at the very least make me angry if I took his advice and then something went wrong. He remembered how I'd told him I would be the one to break the pattern of his successful athletes leaving him. He also said that we humans can live with absolute misery, but it's hope that destroys us. He was clearly dejected.

About a week further on, though, and still with no money from my win in Hawaii, he was getting angry:

> you want to be alternative, but you also crave the normality. it sounds great to you to have all these advisors, as it is to go train in places where you got people you like, and the atmosphere is lovey-dovey and relaxed. but you are a product of the atmosphere you're in. you, girl, work best athletically when you're a demon, a fucking omen, and you might not like it, but we both know you have it. i just exploited it, while using a whip and a chair to keep it under control.
>
> now, you want normal. sorry, you're not, and your old boss is not. we rail against the system. the difference is, you also crave to be accepted by societies.
>
> i don't.

To my surprise, it was only when I had been paid the prize money for Kona and had the $20,000 ready to transfer into his bank account that things started to improve between us. I say surprise, because it suggested he really had thought that I was not going to pay him. Surely he knew me better than that, even if he felt I had been corrupted by financial considerations.

He offered me an olive branch – just after he'd sent me his bank details. He outlined his vision for how we could move on:

> you pay the money. you tell me team chrissie is:
> coach, b sutton
> strength and conditioning, b sutton
> sports scientist, b sutton
> exercise physiologist, b sutton
> shrink, b sutton
> the reason: i went thru it very carefully, and they are the best
> in their field in each speciality in triathlon. if these appoint-
> ments are acceptable then i will see my way clear to deal
> honestly with ben, as long as he sticks to his job.

With Alex mediating, we settled our differences by email and on the phone. I was staying on the team.

It had been a horrible, horrible stand-off, one that had rattled me to the core. To my mind, I still needed Brett, so to feel that he was turning me away was to feel completely exposed. But I knew, as well, that he was not in the best of states, emotionally or physically. He'd gone back for downtime in Switzerland, suffering from the repercussions of his electrocution. For him then to turn over and over in his head the impression that I was about to do what he claims so many of his other successful athletes had done – leave him after he had coached them to success – would have done nothing for his mood. I understood all that, so it wasn't long before I was able to view his barbs in context. I was glad to be staying with him.

And I wanted to stay on the team. I had paid my dues and since Kona I had felt much more accepted. Maybe Brett was right about my need to belong, or my desire to, anyway. I've always had friends in my life. It had taken me a while to crack my triathlon team-mates, but now that I had, I wanted to enjoy their friendship for a bit longer.

So it was with relief that I was able to join up with them all at our new training base in Subic Bay, an old US naval base in the Philippines. Relief, mixed with sadness, because my dear old grandad, Harry, passed away peacefully in his sleep just before I left, aged 101. One of the first things I did when I was interviewed after my win in Kona was to pay tribute to him, an inspiration whose long life put into perspective any feats of endurance I might have been attempting. Now he was gone. It felt like a new season, all right. Kona already seemed a long time ago.

Things were fine between Brett and me once we got to Subic Bay. It wasn't as if nothing had happened, but we were both keen to make it work. Alex may not have been my manager any more, but Brett was my coach, and I had no problems falling in with the usual routines – in other words, surrendering any notion of free will. I followed his every order, as I always had done, and that helped our relationship enormously, as it always had done. I think he respected me for it. He knew then that Hawaii hadn't gone to my head.

It was a head that now wore the crown, as he kept telling me. He lectured me a lot on the wearing of that crown, and in doing so he was back to his best; the usual, strident Brett.

'Train right, and let the cards fall where they may,' he said to me. 'I've seen too many world champions not adjust for the pressure. They fret about their performances. They train and they race with the crown on their head. It's too fucking heavy. Take my tip. Take it off, put it in a box and place it in the cupboard. It'll be there when you're finished. Don't let it kill you or stop you from putting a few more in there to go with it. Don't debate this. I'm so right, it's not funny.'

There was little prospect of any crown-wearing out in the Philippines. I love the country, and I love flogging myself under Brett's tutelage, but there were no airs and graces out there. The former naval base is about 40km long by about 10km wide. It is now what's known as a free port, a kind of economic haven with tax and customs breaks, all contained within the fence that used to surround the base. We rarely ventured beyond it. We were ironman triathletes, so that meant a lot of bike work up and down what were essentially the two main roads in the complex. I have an unusually high capacity for enduring boredom, which was just as well, because we soon knew every inch of those roads.

The accommodation left a bit to be desired. I was sharing a house with two others, and in the first week it was broken into. So Brett moved us into a hotel. Which was also a brothel. There were girls screaming throughout the night and doors were banging. I couldn't imagine professional athletes in many other sports having to deal with this. But we knew better than to complain.

All of which was in stark contrast to what greeted me at my first ironman of the season – Ironman Australia in Port Macquarie at the start of April. All of a sudden, everything was laid on. I was flown over for the race; Ben had negotiated an appearance fee; they put me up in a stunning apartment overlooking the ocean. I don't deny that it was great – certainly, it made the job of preparing for a race a lot easier. I didn't miss the poverty of my race accommodation the year before. Besides, I had had plenty of that back at the brothel.

But if life was cushier, it came with the added pressure of being the champion. Everyone knew who I was. I sat in front of press conferences. I posed for photographs. I have never felt entirely comfortable in front of the camera, but winning in Hawaii seemed to have given me confidence. And, when I saw people wanting to be photographed with me, and how my story seemed to energise them, the pleasure of inspiring such enthusiasm swept all self-consciousness away. I loved being world champion. To me it meant pleasure, not pressure. It gave me a platform. I like to be able to speak to people about issues I'm passionate about, to convey messages and to inspire, and it's so much easier to do that when you have a voice.

The race went well. It was pouring with rain, and I was overtaken quite early on the bike by Kate Major, but I'd regained the lead 30km before transition and then finished with a three-hour run. I won in a course record of just over nine hours.

That was the first time I performed a 'Blazeman roll' over the finish line. After my win in Kona, I had met Bob and Mary Ann Blais, parents of Jon, the ironman athlete who had died of ALS, a form of motor-neurone disease, only six months earlier. I never met him, but his story, discussed later in this book, cannot but touch your heart. Bob and Mary Ann have become close friends, and I am a patron of the charity in his name, the Blazeman Foundation. At the end of every race since I met them, I have performed a Blazeman roll across the finish line in honour of Jon.

To have been doing it in first place was a huge relief. However well Hawaii had gone, there's always the nagging fear that it might have been because the others had had a bad day, or that it had simply been a fluke. To back it up with another win, my third out of three at ironman distance, was very important. You start to feel that it might not be a fluke after all.

Which was all well and good, but Brett would never let me rest on my laurels. He still thought I should keep my hand in at Olympic-distance racing. There was almost no chance of me making the Beijing Olympics later that year, but all the same he had convinced me to enter the ITU World Cup race in Tongyeong, South Korea, three weeks later. There were problems, though. The first was that Olympic-distance races require a road bike, not a time-trial bike, and I didn't have a road bike. The second problem was that, well, it was three weeks after an ironman, and on a different continent. Such details tend not to concern Brett. So it was up to me to find some road bars for my time-trial bike, which turned out to be a headache. And nobody could do anything about the issues relating to time and space.

Racing Tongyeong wasn't a wise decision. I came twenty-second. By that point, I didn't think I was ever going to make Beijing anyway, but I definitely wasn't going to after that. It drew a line under any aspirations I might have had in that direction, but it also made me realise how much I preferred ironman. I would have liked to have arrived at that realisation on my own terms, rather than to have had it thrust upon me by an impossible schedule, but it probably didn't make any difference. I don't believe you can juggle ironman with Olympic-distance racing, so we were always going to have to make the choice, and it was pretty obvious by now that ironman was the distance for me. My spam box keeps telling me that size matters, and in this respect I agree. There's something about the sheer length of the ironman that inspires awe among all triathletes, and I was happy to devote myself to it, even if it meant no Olympics. Kona would be my Olympics, and I got to do it every year.

So with that matter cleared up, it was back to Leysin in May for the summer training camp. I felt focused and at ease – a happy place to be. I love Leysin. What more could you want than to be 'at work' in the Alps? It's beautiful, it's remote and it's peaceful. And the training is great. Life is very easy there. What's more, I now had a far nicer apartment closer to the centre of town. I had friendships with my team-mates that were really blossoming, particularly with Belinda Granger, Donna Phelan and Hillary Biscay. You know you've bonded with girlfriends when you go with them to see *Sex and the City*. Belinda, Donna and I watched it in the room with a big screen that passes as Leysin's cinema. We went for dinner beforehand. It was such a treat, as we generally led such monkish lives. And, just as importantly, I had organised it. In my previous life I had always been proactive in organising friends and functions, so this small development made me feel a bit more normal again. To have gone from that previous life to feeling ostracised and alone had been so hard, but now I felt as if I had found my place again among friends, not enemies. The on-going intensity of the training meant that I was physically in the best shape of my life, but this new happiness was doing great things for me mentally, and that kind of contentment is so important when you are an athlete.

The relationship that dominated, as always, was the one I had with Brett. By the time we got to Leysin it was better than ever. Mainly because I was no longer quite so scared of him, and yet I was still desperate to please and impress him, to win that rubber stamp of approval. We used to do hill repeats, up and down the hill outside Brett's apartment, and he would be standing there in his misshapen, baggy blue tracksuit bottoms, tucked into his equally misshapen beige Ugg boots, with some kind of shirt – he had a lilac one, a blue one – buttoned up all wrong. But I would always sneak in a glance to check he was looking at me. Then he would pull me aside afterwards and simply say, 'Good job'. That was enough.

We talked about things at length that year – not just training, but politics and international development, even my relationship status. Or he would talk at me, anyway. I remember one 'chat' at the poolside on a beautiful day, overlooking the mountains, which lasted for about an hour and a half. He told me that I'd achieved so much, yet a huge part of my life was missing because I didn't have a partner. Brett was convinced that I needed someone to share things with and that I was lonely. He wondered why I didn't have a boyfriend and hadn't had one for a long time. Again, he asked if I was a lesbian. A love interest, he said, was the piece of the jigsaw that was not in place. I wouldn't be complete until I had a boyfriend. This was what he wanted for me now. He didn't give a damn about results. It was about making me into a well-rounded person.

He seemed deadly serious. He didn't want me to become so single minded in my pursuit of physical excellence that I shut out everything else. That really surprised me, to think that Brett put so much emphasis on my having a boyfriend. A lot of people might think that he would hate anything distracting me from the training, but the opposite was the case. Besides, he thought it would improve my performance. That was part of it. But part of it was a heartfelt desire to see me truly happy. Everyone sees him as an authoritarian, performance-driven ogre, but he actually cares for his athletes. Of course, he wanted me to reach the top of the sport, but more important to him was that I be, in his eyes, a good person and be happy. And that's the other side of Brett, which people don't see.

The only bust-up I remember having with him was over my race schedule. In a reversal of our usual roles, which so often saw him reining me in, I was shocked at the amount of racing and travelling he was demanding of me in July and August. The schedule for April had been bad enough, with Ironman Australia, followed three weeks later by the Olympic-distance race in South Korea. But that was just a gentle warm-up. My schedule for the summer started off with a full ironman in Frankfurt on 6 July, followed by the Alpe d'Huez Long Course Triathlon with its mountains and switchbacks on 30 July, followed by a quick nip across the Atlantic to race in Timberman 70.3, a half-ironman in New Hampshire, on 17 August, before returning to Europe for the ITU Long Distance World Championship in Almere, Holland on 31 August. Four races; seven and a half miles in the water, 315 miles on the bike and 72 miles on foot. In eight weeks. And I don't know how many thousands of miles of travelling. It was too much, I told him, but Brett was deaf to my concerns.

In the end, I got sick of fighting with him and just did it. I won them all. Obviously, he felt it was a vindication. Yes, but only if I'm in a fit state to win in Kona, was my retort.

Truth be told, I felt in good shape. It had been an exhilarating eight weeks. I set a course record at Ironman Germany, where I went under nine hours for the first time. It turned out afterwards I'd missed the world record by thirty seconds. Unfortunately, I hadn't known what it was, and spent a bit too long high-fiving and celebrating with the crowd on my way to the finish line. Since half a million spectators turn out for this event, that can take a while. The world record, which had stood for fourteen years, was smashed a week later anyway by Yvonne van Vlerken at Challenge Roth. But Frankfurt is a remarkable race. With all those people, it is more of a spectacle even than Kona. And on a personal note, this was a special event, because it was the first time my parents had been able to make it to a big race of mine.

Then came a return to one of my favourites, the Alpe d'Huez Long Course Triathlon. That one was special, too, because I nearly won it outright, finishing second overall, just over a minute behind Marcus Ornellas. It remains a goal of mine, but to have come so close to beating all the men was significant for women in triathlon. I was, though, the fastest of either sex over the infamous twenty-one-hairpin climb on the bike.

But then came sad news. The day after Alpe d'Huez, my dear Nanna Romey, the last of my grandparents, passed away in her sleep, less than six months after her husband, Harry. She had been suffering the ravages of cancer, so her passing was, in many ways, a relief, but she was one of the most enthusiastic, energetic, selfless and courageous people I know, and her death hit me hard. I travelled back to the UK ten days later with a heavy heart for her funeral, which was as much a celebration of her life as a mourning of her death.

From London I hopped across the Atlantic for Timberman 70.3, breaking the course record and, of course, dedicating my win to a woman I so dearly loved. Then it was back to Europe for the ITU Long Distance World Championship in Almere. Brett had been particularly keen for me to race in this one, so that I could go up against Yvonne van Vlerken. He saw her as one of my main challengers at Kona, and he thought it was important for me to put down a marker against her in her native land, which I did. She finished third, nineteen minutes behind me. All in all, Brett was pleased with his decision-making.

But it was a decision he had made many years earlier that, even now, kept coming back to haunt him. Some people feel that Brett should never have been allowed to coach again after he had had sexual relations with a teenager in 1987. As a result, a lot of people question the morals of those who choose him for a coach. The issue had flared up briefly after my win in Kona the year before, when an article in the *Sunday Herald* had character-assassinated him. We were quite philosophical about that, but in the build-up to Kona this year the issue suddenly burst onto the forums, and fingers started pointing at me.

Brett is big enough and ugly enough to take the flak, but he hates it when his athletes are made to suffer, or to have their achievements overshadowed, because of his indiscretions. We were alerted to the threads, and together we agreed we should both post a response. Brett did not try to defend the indefensible, other than to say that it had all been dealt with in the courts and that the testimony of many of his athletes from the time and since had lent context to the charges brought against him. But he appealed to his critics not to bring his athletes into it.

'Make me the pariah and go your hardest,' he wrote. 'You can't go down to the level I feel about myself. But do a rethink on these champions. Their character is not, and should not, be placed in question, because of their ability to forgive.'

Brett seemed to spiral into depression. Those of us racing at Kona that year were now preparing in Jeju, South Korea. He went from being very engaged in our training to becoming more distant. First, he wouldn't get out of the car at the track, then he wouldn't come out of his room. We grew increasingly worried about him.

He emailed us our training schedules and told us to get on with it. I developed a niggle in my ankle and shin and wanted to speak to him face to face. He wouldn't answer his door. Even though I was in the adjacent apartment, I emailed him, asking if I could pop round. He said no, he would rather talk about it online. So I took a photo of the leg, drew an arrow pointing to the problem area and emailed it to him through the wall. This was ludicrous, I thought. I've got a coach and he won't even come out of his room to talk to me.

He stayed in there for a day and a half. That was the worst I'd seen him.

But then, almost as quickly as he'd spiralled, he snapped out of it again. And the week before I left for Kona he made me do a session that I would never have thought possible. Three hours on the bike, one hour at ironman pace, one at half-ironman, one at Olympic pace, followed by fifteen reps of 800m on the track, each one coming in at 2min 50sec, with 200m recovery jogs in between. As I worked through the reps, something went wrong with the sprinklers and they all came on, so that it felt as if it were pouring with rain under a burning hot sun. I powered my way through, kicking up puddles as I went. Brett was watching high in the stands, and he knew I was hitting the times. He didn't say anything afterwards, but I thanked him for realising I could do it, because I might not have believed myself. My confidence was soaring, and I knew I was ready for Kona, even if I was still troubled by my sore ankle and shin.

Brett didn't shield me so carefully from Hawaii-itis this time, and I went out a bit earlier than I had the year before. I was overjoyed to be back. I love Hawaii – the smell of the place, the open-air airport, the weather, the flowers. I was met by John and Linda Oery, friends I had made the year before. They are Kona locals, and had organised an apartment for me in the complex where they live. My mum and dad came out, as did other friends and family. Ben was there, Asker, even Alex this time. It meant I felt as if I had a support network. If I needed something, someone was always on hand to help. I had a lot of media commitments, but I was able to keep myself to myself and concentrate.

The Sunday before the race, though, after my long run, the pain in my shin intensified, and I became deeply concerned. It was so sore I couldn't hop on it. How could I possibly run a marathon? I did no running at all during race week. I told no one, other than my physio and close friends, and when I strapped it up I hid it under compression socks. Never give your opponents anything. I took confidence from my experience at Ironman Korea, when my coccyx agony miraculously vanished on the day. So I approached the race in good spirits. I was more nervous than the year before, but not debilitatingly so.

That said, I shat myself at the start. Literally. Diarrhoea struck as I was in the water waiting for the off. I had suffered from gastro-intestinal issues in every ironman I had raced, but never this early. This is going to be a long day, I thought to myself. The race hasn't even started, and I'm shitting myself already. That kind of thing sets the thoughts racing through your mind. First of all, there's the dehydration aspect. Then there are other practical issues. It's all very well crapping into your swimskin when you're in the water (not so great for your fellow competitors, admittedly), but doing it on a bike is horrible. And trying to run a marathon with poo dribbling down your leg is not much more fun. The key is not to let those problems affect your performance. It is what it is, and you've just got to get on with it.

The swim went well, and I came out of the water in eleventh place after fifty-six minutes, an improvement of about a minute and a half on the year before. On the bike, I felt strong from the word go, much better than at that stage the year before. I took the lead at around the 30km point and felt great, despite the rumbling in my bowels. By 80km I'd opened up five minutes on the other girls and was working my way through the men.

It was around then, halfway up the incline between Kawaihae and the turnaround at Hawi, that things went wrong. Any cyclist knows well that horrible feeling when each bump on the road suddenly shudders right through you. I looked down and, yes, the rim of my wheel had hit the tarmac – the rear tyre was flat.

I dismounted. First of all, before I'd even looked at the tyre I knew I couldn't waste this opportunity to relieve myself. There were cameras trained on me, so NBC viewers were treated to the sight of a girl from Norfolk crouching in a bush by the road giving the inside of her shorts a break.

Back to the bike. I took the wheel off and removed the inner tube. I checked the rim for any debris that may have caused the puncture, but couldn't find anything, which is always concerning. But I replaced the tube and then the tyre without any trouble. I was pretty impressed with myself at that point. I was handling this mechanical glitch with some efficiency, by my standards.

I should have known better. It didn't last. Despite Brett's disapproval of anything vaguely flash (in this case, anything other than an old-fashioned pump), I was carrying two gas canisters. I released the first canister's gas before I had attached it properly to the tyre, so it spewed its CO_2 uselessly into the Pacific air. Cursing, I turned to the second one. It was faulty and didn't work at all. I was in real trouble now. How I wished I'd just taken a pump, as you-know-who had insisted.

I was stranded, waiting for technical support to arrive, which could be any time. But I remember feeling quite calm. I wasn't exactly relaxed, but I wasn't flapping. I kept thinking of what Brett would say. Don't panic. Stay calm. What will be, will be. A mechanic will arrive eventually. And when I'm back on the road I'll fight and fight. The thought never crossed my mind that my race was over.

But if I could get a canister from somewhere else . . . I knew I couldn't receive help from anyone outside the race, other than the technical support team, but I wasn't sure if I could get it from fellow competitors. With the clock ticking, I took a chance and called out to the increasing number of athletes overtaking me.

'Has anyone got any gas?'

But the bikes were flashing past too quickly for my cries to register. After a few minutes, the message that I had a flat had made it down the road. Athletes started to shout encouragement to me and apologies for not being able to help.

Then, after ten minutes on the roadside, my saviour rode into view. Rebekah Keat had a spare canister on her bike, which she gave to me as she went past.

'You owe me one!'

'Thanks, babe,' I said, setting to work immediately.

'No worries, mate,' she cried. 'Keep going, keep going!'

It summed up everything that is great about ironman. For Bek to give up something like that to a rival takes huge heart. Let's not forget how hard we all train to achieve the best for ourselves in this individual sport. To lend someone else a hand in the heat of competition is a sign of something special. It's a gesture I will never forget.

This time things went without a hitch, and I was soon back in the race. I'd lost eleven minutes, and I think five or six girls had overtaken me. I was more than five minutes behind Belinda Granger, who was now the lead woman. There was no water left in the bottle on the front of my bike, because it had all leaked out when I'd turned the bike upside down to get the tyre back on. And I had diarrhoea.

But I do remember this strange feeling flooding through me that the pressure was off. No one will expect me to win now. Except me.

About twenty minutes later I was turning round at Hawi, and I'd made up two minutes or so on Belinda, Dede Griesbauer and Leanda Cave, the three leaders. My friends and family were all there, decked out in their blue Chrissie t-shirts, all screaming their encouragement, jumping up and down.

I shook my head at them. 'I've had a bloody puncture.'

'Go get 'em! Go get 'em!'

Seeing them gave me a huge boost. I launched myself into the downhill. Normally I descend like a grandma, but this time I rode as if I had a firework up my backside, which in a way I did. I was conscious of the danger of overworking myself in this game of catch-up, but I was on a mission. I didn't care about the howling wind, or the rising heat. These were the hardest conditions they'd seen at the World Championships for a few years, apparently.

I made up a lot of time on that downhill. By the 130km mark, I'd overtaken everyone apart from Belinda. Another 10km after the Kawaihae intersection, on the Queen K. Highway, I suddenly happened upon her. I hadn't expected to see her so soon, as the splits I was getting had her further ahead, but by the time they get to you they are about ten minutes out of date. I remember these purple bougainvilleas on the roadside, so vibrant and beautiful, and as I passed Belinda she seemed to do a double-take.

'Stick with me!' I said to her.

'Go on, chick!' she said. 'You can win it!'

I felt strong now, despite the hellish headwind that buffeted us on that long stretch back into town. I started to pick off some of the guys. My stomach had eased off a bit. Things were looking good again. As with the year before, the memory endures of the helicopter hovering as I approached the end of the bike. It makes you feel so special.

I knew I had put a bit of distance between me and Belinda by the time I set out on the run. It turned out I had a lead of seven minutes. Yvonne van Vlerken, the new world-record holder, meanwhile, was closing in on Belinda. She is a very strong runner, too, so I knew I had to be on my mettle. At least it was just me and the road now. Any further malfunctions could happen only in my body. I pushed all thoughts of the shin injury to the back of my mind.

It took me some time to find my rhythm. The heat seemed so much more intense than the year before, partly because, well, it was, and partly because of the dehydration from my diarrhoea and the emptying of my water bottle.

You go into a kind of tunnel where everything outside your head, including the rest of your body, becomes peripheral. Never once did I feel the pain in my shin.

Then, with five miles to go, I knew I was going to make it. My hamstrings were tightening and my form was starting to fall apart, but I felt I could relax and enjoy the final stretch. I told the camera crew that this one was for my grandparents.

The crowd support was phenomenal as I ran that last mile through the town high-fiving and waving like a madwoman. People knew who I was this time.

I was crying as I trotted to the tape, crying and gasping at the intensity of it all. I raised my hands above my head, trailing the Union Jack from them, and, standing for a second to savour the moment, I seized the tape and hoisted it high in the air. You never get tired of that moment. Then I took a step back, lay down on the ground and rolled over the line in honour of Jon Blais.

I'd won. My time was 9hr 6min 23sec, an improvement of just over two minutes on last year and fifteen minutes ahead of Yvonne, who came in second. And I'd broken the Kona marathon record in a time of 2hr 57min 44sec, with two diarrhoea stops. If it hadn't been for the flat tyre, I might have threatened Paula Newby-Fraser's sixteen-year-old course record.

But just the fact that I knew now who Paula Newby-Fraser was, and all the other legends of the sport, moved this win onto a new level as an experience. The year before it had all been a bit of a blur. I had had no idea what to expect, or who anyone was. Now I did. I appreciated everything so much more. I felt so privileged. And I was so happy with the way I had performed. I'd overcome the flat tyre and I'd dealt with the pressure of being the champion.

And, most of all, my mum and dad were at the finish line with my cousin, Tim, who was in tears. To share the moment with them meant so much to me.

I was whisked away for drug testing, and then for the press conference. The rest of the night was spent down at the finish, greeting the hundreds of other athletes as they ran, walked and crawled across that hallowed line. We pros devote our lives to preparing for this race, but seeing what the finish line means to people who prepare for it in their spare time, and seeing their courage, never fails to move me. As we joined hands for the traditional Hawaiian song after the midnight bell had tolled, my winner's lei on my head and my family by my side, tears flowed down my cheeks.

The celebrations continued the next day. A storm blew over, which disrupted the awards ceremony. I had just started my victory speech when it had to be abandoned because the sound system broke and, anyway, people were taking shelter under tables. More a reflection, I hope, of the torrential rain than what I had to say. But it frustrated me, because I believe one of the most important parts of winning a race is to be able to convey a passionate, inspiring message in your speech.

Otherwise, the night went with a bang. I couldn't tell you how I got home. But I can tell you that I woke up the next morning to an email from Brett. It was long and it was to everyone in Team TBB. Once I'd deciphered it and worked through the implications, the message came through loud and clear.

I was off the team.

12

My Own Two Feet

I guess we'd all known it was going to be our last year together. Brett knew it as well, which might also have been affecting his mood. He had tried various things to keep us together, including an attempt to convince Ben to manage the whole team. He seemed to be warming to Ben, which was positive, but one of the things that frustrates me about Brett is that his sense of reality is so often far removed from anyone else's. Ben was employed by WMG and had a range of athletes under his management. We did discuss the idea, because I still wanted to stay with Brett, but Ben couldn't see a way of reconciling it with his current commitments. He, effectively, would have had to resign from his day job in order to make Brett's plan work. To Brett, this was totally reasonable. Needless to say, it didn't happen.

Which left us with a problem. From the following season, any athlete with individual sponsors that did not align with the team's would be asked to leave, as would any with a manager who wasn't Alex. This had often been talked about, but now it was becoming policy. Brett laid down the law in that long email he sent to all of us the Monday after Kona.

The end was nigh. The new policy was going to hit me hard. I now had relationships (and long-term deals) with a range of sponsors, all of whom I liked. I couldn't have walked away from those, even if I'd wanted to. But, if I had, I would have been settling for my share of a team pie split with twenty other athletes. Brett would often talk about this. Would I rather be a mediocre athlete with my own deals, or part of his team and a champion? In other words, who was more important, Brett or my sponsors? His answer to me or anyone else with similar issues was simple. Without him, there would be no prize money, and there would be no sponsors clamouring at the door. We would actually make less money. I was far from convinced, even then, that I could succeed without him, but ultimately I wasn't prepared to get rid of my manager (and Ben had become so much more to me than just a manager) or my sponsors. We used to appeal to Brett that the priority of professional athletes was to maximise their earnings while they could. And triathletes are a very long way from being the highest earners in the sporting world.

To have stayed on the team under this new arrangement would have been a logistical nightmare. I wouldn't have been able to accept any sponsor without that sponsor agreeing to take on the team as well. Brett and Alex did try to persuade my two main sponsors to extend their patronage to the whole team, but they were not keen. It just wasn't realistic. And, after I'd gone, it frustrated me to see that the policy of one team, one set of sponsors was relaxed, and that some team members were allowed to stay on with their own separate deals and their own managers.

It was clear that I would be leaving, along with the majority of my team-mates who had similar dilemmas. I didn't like the idea any more than I had done when these issues had first arisen a year earlier. The prospect of parting with Brett scared me, and he didn't hesitate to play on those fears, constantly sowing seeds of doubt in my mind about whether I could succeed without him. But I was braced for it now, and, who knows, maybe I could achieve things without him.

* * *

Belinda, Hillary and I decided quickly that we still wanted to train together. But who was going to coach us? We started batting around some names and emailing a few coaches. One was Cliff English, who was based in Tucson, where Hillary lives, and was engaged to Sam McGlone, who'd come second at Kona in 2007.

Hillary and I flew to Tucson to meet him. We got on very well. He was a young guy, about our age, and very friendly, with the pedigree of having coached the US and Canadian triathlon teams. Hillary, Belinda and I decided there and then to work with him.

And yet I felt as if I were suffering from déjà vu. I couldn't help thinking back to the same time the year before when I had been rushed into signing with Alex. Having left the team now, we were all anxious to choose a coach and move on, and I put myself under pressure to make it happen.

Then, as per the year before, I went home to Norfolk, and the doubts started to close in. The post-Kona euphoria was wearing off fast, and I had plenty of time to reflect on the decision to go with Cliff. Was this arrangement the best for me? Or was it best for Hillary and Belinda?

While in Norfolk, I got another long email from Brett, signed 'ex-boss' this time. He thought I was insane. He told me I could not possibly have picked a worse option. Hillary lived in Tucson, so she was happy. Cliff was the fiancé of one of my biggest rivals – how was that dynamic going to pan out? I would be revealing myself to him, my playbook and my strengths and weaknesses, and thus I would be revealing them to Sam. Never imagine I was so good that I could afford to give the opposition anything.

I was in a tailspin again. I might have left the team, but Brett would never let a little detail like that stop him from giving me advice. I appreciated that he still felt passionately about my choices, even after we had parted, although I also realised he might be feeling uneasy about another coach picking up tips from him via his former athletes.

I was also the opposition now. He was no doubt playing his mind games. Not that it helped to be aware of that. I have always been torn between taking on board what Brett says and ignoring it as his way of getting to you. I've never been able to separate the strands. I listen to him, and he gets to me. It's the Brett package. Either way, he was inside my head again. I had already been harbouring doubts, but now Brett had crystallised them in that way only he can.

To complicate matters further, I attended the British Triathlon Awards Dinner, where I met Simon Lessing, a legend in triathlon. He was starting up a coaching business in Boulder, Colorado and was curious to know why I had chosen Cliff. He laid out his own training ideas, which involved high intensity and low volume. It was a philosophy that chimed with mine. And so another ingredient was thrown into the mix.

I knew almost immediately that I wanted him to be my new coach. I also wanted a coach who was right for me, rather than right for me, Hillary and Belinda. The trouble was, of course, that I had agreed a course of action with them, and I couldn't see a way out of it that wouldn't damage our friendship.

The upshot was that I agreed to go with Simon – and then I told Hillary and Belinda. It was the wrong way round, I know. It doesn't sound very world champion, but the truth is, I was worried that if I told Hillary and Belinda first, as I should have done, they would have tried to change my mind. I didn't want things to get even more complicated than they already were. I had arrived at a decision at last, in the quiet little corner of the world that I call home, and I just didn't want any more input.

Belinda took it really well. We talked it through on the phone, and she totally understood. She ended up being coached by her husband, Justin.

Hillary didn't take it so well. She felt I had let her down. My pulling out had led to the collapse of the plan. Belinda did her own thing, Cliff was having second thoughts anyway, and Hillary's dream of having the three of us training together in her hometown was ruined. She stopped speaking to me for months after that. Once again, what should have been the happiest time of my year had turned into the worst.

Nothing for it, then, but to head to Argentina for a dear friend's wedding, followed by the torturous bike trek through the Andes that doubled as her honeymoon. Yes, honeymoon.

Tina from Nepal and her beau, Seba, had decided that they could think of nothing more romantic than to push bikes where no bikes had been pushed before, through the mountains of northern Patagonia, with four of their equally deranged mates. This would not be many people's idea of an idyllic honeymoon. Even I was impressed!

The wedding itself was fresh and informal, which was just as well, because we arrived in Lycra. It was a Nepal reunion. Suzy took the elegant route, but Billi, Helen and I cycled the 80km from Mendoza to Tina's *finca*, only to discover that our wedding clothes had been delayed. I don't suppose Tina, looking radiant on her big day, even noticed. She certainly didn't care. The day went with a swing and lots of sunshine, slabs of Argentinian meat and vats of Argentinian wine.

A day or two later, we headed south with the bride and groom to Malargüe, from where we struck out on our trail. It was one traditionally tackled by adventurers on horseback, but mountain bikes were to be our steeds of choice, each one laden with 35kg of equipment – sleeping bags, clothes, tents, ropes, stoves, food, and so on. We had no idea what we were letting ourselves in for. Our route was about 300km. No one had ever biked it. There turned out to be a very good reason for that.

Our group consisted of me, Billi, Helen, Tina and Seba, and their friend Rata. We set off in high spirits along wide, very passable fire trails, surrounded by the stunning scenery of the Andean mountains. This was all right, we thought.

Soon, though, our passage deteriorated into narrow, sandy tracks heading upwards, and then no tracks at all. This was no longer all right; this was mercilessly hard work. It gave new meaning to the term pushbikes. And these were mighty cumbersome bikes to push. On one day we averaged 2km an hour.

We encountered rushing rivers along the way. At the first, Billi, who is a high-altitude climber and for her next trick climbed Everest, looked at me. We just thought, well, this is the last straw, we can't go on. But Tina was having none of it. She is one of the most incredibly positive people I know. In our group we had a double ironman world champion and a climber who had conquered several peaks higher than 6,000m – and they were probably the most negative people there!

'We can do this!' Tina chirped, over the noise of the roaring river that barred our way. 'We have ropes, we have harnesses, we have spirit! *Vamos!*'

The boys managed to make it across the river (I still don't know how), so that we could rig up an improvised rope-and-pulley contraption across the torrents. One by one we winched our panniers, bikes and selves across to the other side, each teetering precariously above the swirling waters. We did that three times in one day. And then there was the glacier we had to climb up and over – again, pushbikes are not much use on one of those. A yak would have been preferable.

The trip was one of the hardest things I have ever done – harder than any race, certainly. There were times I didn't think we would make it, times when we turned another corner only to see the path snaking up the side of yet another mountain, biceps screaming as we hauled our tractor-bikes over rocks the size of houses, the wind blowing sand into every orifice.

But what a backdrop! All around us, against clear blue skies, soared the Andean peaks. Among the rocks were vivid fossils and wild flowers, and overhead circled vast condors.

We ran out of food on our last night, having spent a day cycling downhill, albeit on sand with a headwind whipping it up into our faces. A local weather-beaten farmer and his wife took pity on us and welcomed us into their humble, stone home. They slaughtered one of their goats, there and then, and served it up spread-eagled on a plate. Billi and Helen are vegetarians, but even they had some of this fresh, delicious meat. The next day, full to the brim with goat, we made it back to Malargüe, battered, bruised, blistered and bitten.

It was the best honeymoon I'd ever been on! I felt so grounded with my old friends, who'd all known me pre-triathlon. I was just Chrissie again, and it felt good. As it did on the bus I then took from Mendoza across the amazing mountain pass into Chile to catch my flight from Santiago. There was a traffic jam at border control, which is in the heart of the mountains. They check every single vehicle and all the people in them. The estimate for the wait was five hours. I would have missed my flight, but I managed, with my pidgin Spanish, to get myself through. I made it to the airport just in time, having hitched a ride on a ramshackle local minibus, with gubbins piled high around me. It was an appropriate way to finish a trip that had so revived the spirit of my time in Nepal. Dear friends, beautiful mountains, some never-say-die spirit and a goat. I left invigorated.

There were times on the trek when I thought of Brett, and the situation awaiting me on my return to reality – a new season, a new coach. There were times when I wondered what a triathlon coach would think of what I was doing in those mountains. Brett, I feel sure, would have approved. He knows I need to switch off, and he was always encouraging me to do that. He told me never to read the internet forums, never to become obsessed with the sport. He wanted me to take another degree, or to learn a language. Trekking through the Andes, however incompatible it may have been with a conventional training programme, represented just such a refreshing change from the norm.

The trip did me the world of good. I did think of ironman, but it seemed a long way away. I was able to find myself again, to feel independent.

From Santiago I flew to Boulder, where I spent three days with Simon, his wife, Lisa and their two girls. Simon was certainly confident that I could succeed without Brett. The self-assured part of me agreed, but still the nagging doubts plagued me. I had been Brett's puppet for two years. Could I still dance without him above me to pull the strings? I was determined to try.

It meant that I went home for Christmas ready for life without him. That feeling was further sharpened when I was greeted upon my return by more posturing from Brett over the payment of his bonus. The dynamic was exactly the same as the year before – he wanted me to pay him his 20 per cent cut of my Kona prize money now; I couldn't pay him until they paid me, which was going to be in January. There was never any question of my not paying him, just as there hadn't been the year before. He got his money when I'd been paid mine, and he spent it on a new bathroom. The Chrissie shitter, he calls it. He sends me emails intermittently, saying, 'I sit there thinking of you.'

But as one man left my life (or took a back seat, at least), another walked in.

It was January, and, while I was waiting for my US visa to come through, I headed to Club La Santa in Lanzarote for some warm-weather training. It wasn't very warm, though, so on this particular day I was wearing a puffer jacket, £9 from a discount store. They were holding a duathlon, and I was the starter. Brandishing my gun, I noticed this tall, good-looking guy hanging round the finish line. He was wearing a puffer jacket just like mine (only somewhat more expensive), he had streaky hair and I vaguely recognised him.

I thought no more of it, but the next day I received a message through Facebook from a guy by the name of Tom Lowe. I get a lot of messages through Facebook, but he made reference to the puffer and looked mighty fine in his photo, so I replied. It turns out he was there to train with the winner of the duathlon that day, Joerie Vansteelant. And we had met once before, at the British Triathlon Awards in 2007. We flirted by email and then arranged to meet at the TCR (Triathlon, Cycling and Running) Show the next weekend.

This is an annual expo for all things triathlon, held at Sandown Park in Esher, on the fringes of south-west London. I was doing a signing when we met again. It was difficult for us to talk, because I was being pulled this way and that by sponsors and fans. He seemed relaxed and undemanding of my time, which I liked.

After the awards dinner, though, we got to talk properly. I was immediately attracted to him. He was so engaging, funny and seriously good looking. I remember thinking that this was someone very special.

Me being me, at midnight I ran for my pumpkin. I was with Steph Cox and a friend called Caroline. I said goodbye to Tom, but at the moment of reckoning we didn't kiss.

I walked downstairs with the girls to get my coat. 'Nothing happened! Nothing happened!' I practically wailed at them. 'In a few days I go to Boulder, and that will be it!'

Steph said, quite decisively: 'Wait here, I've left my scarf behind!' Off she bolted.

Moments later, I heard her calling out behind me: 'Chrissie! I brought him back!'

I turned round, and there he was, smiling awkwardly.

This is sounding like one of those situations at a disco when you're about twelve – and it was exactly like that. Steph and Caroline went out to hail a cab, leaving the two of us face to face under the glaring lights. We said goodbye again, and this time he gave me a hug, and I went in for the kiss. Being world champion really had given me confidence! He didn't resist, and in the taxi home we girls were wild with excitement, all the more so when I got my first text from him before we'd even left the venue. We went back to the room I rented in Putney and gossiped the night away over a whole tub of chocolate Carnation milk and a huge bag of crisps.

Tom and I spoke on the phone a lot over the next week. My birthday was coming up, and I had organised a party at a bar near Waterloo for around forty to fifty friends. I suggested he come along. Without a thought he said yes, which just showed what a warm and open person he is, up for anything. This is a big deal for me. I had always said that the most important attribute in a prospective boyfriend would be an ability to fend for himself in a large group of my friends. He passed the test with flying colours. I more or less dumped him among them, coming back every now and then for a kiss and a chat. Everything felt so natural. I was on a cloud.

He came back with me to Putney and stayed the night, which was very unusual for me, to have that level of intimacy so quickly. The next day, as luck would have it, was Valentine's Day. We had both bought each other a card, and he had gone so far as to buy me a rose. More brownie points – he could stay again.

So he did. We went for a pub dinner at the Telegraph on Putney Heath. The next day I was going for lunch with my parents and brother, to say farewell before I left for Boulder. After Tom had stayed again, I took a deep breath and told him I was meeting my family that day, feel totally free to say no, I mean, this is all a bit soon, isn't it, but I'm going to America tomorrow, you probably won't want to, but do you think, um, would it be a not totally stupid idea if you, er . . . Do you want to come?

He smiled and said, yes, of course he did.

Oh, wow, this was getting serious, I thought. I'd known this guy for barely a fortnight, and he was about to meet my family! But I knew it was the right thing to do. I was off the next day, so there had been no choice but to force the pace in our relationship, and he handled it effortlessly. We went to my brother's flat in Streatham and then for a pub lunch. He got on so well with them. My brother, in particular, really liked him, which was very important to me.

Even if I was off to another continent, I was determined now to make this work. I hadn't had a boyfriend for the best part of a decade, but for the first time I had found a man who made me want to change that. Tom is easygoing, yet authoritative. He is accommodating, but not the sort to be walked over. He didn't seem to be at all bothered about the fact that I was world champion. Indeed, he made it clear from an early stage that he intended to beat me at ironman.

He had been in the army for twelve years, working on tele-communications. They had given him time off to train and race competitively at middle-distance running and duathlon, in which he had represented Great Britain. He was fighting a three-year battle with a knee injury, but he was about to leave the army to train full time. In other words, he knew what kind of life I was leading. He had the same aspirations, too – the pursuit of sporting excellence, a desire to travel and an open mind. He was perfect.

The next day, he drove me to Heathrow, and I flew off to Boulder to start training properly with Simon. Everything went smoothly from the moment I got there. Simon went to great lengths to settle me, showing me round and introducing me to people. I took a room in the house of a friend of his, Mark Gavach, just round the corner from where Simon lived.

Boulder is a great place, liberal, relaxed and vibrant. The University of Colorado dominates the city, which is politically left of centre, until you venture out into the rolling farmland beyond, where it swings the other way. The bumper stickers at any point will tell you all you need to know.

In the centre of town there is a pedestrianised precinct, lined with independent shops, buskers and street artists. You never have to go far to find a vibrant bar and music scene and alternative therapies, including legalised marijuna, are popular. But there is another side to the place, which attracts athletes by the bucketload – its sporty, health-conscious spirit. Triathletes of every level flock there. Dave Scott and Mark Allen came and made it their home; hordes of others have followed.

In terms of training for a triathlon, it has everything. Boulder lies on a plateau around 1,600m above sea level. From out of that plateau rise the foothills of the Rocky Mountains. The city is overlooked by a famous rocky structure known as the Flatirons, five smooth flat faces each rising to a peak, which have the look of five irons resting on the ironing board of the Great Plains. Beyond them, the hills swell into the Rockies.

It is perfect for cycling and running. There is rolling farmland, there are the climbs through the hills into the mountains. For runners there are some wonderful trails, and then there is the Res, as it is known – a large reservoir where all manner of water sports are accommodated.

Flatiron Athletic Club is where most athletes train, elite athletes right the way down to Dave Scott's father, Vern, who is still cranking out 4km swims, aged eighty-seven. This was not Leysin, where we were tucked away in a mountain retreat. Here you were thrown in with hundreds of other athletes, only a few of whom were pros. I found it hard initially. I felt as if I were being watched, as if I had to put on a performance the whole time. As someone who loathes showing any weakness, I hated it if I had a bad day in front of everybody. But it also helped me to let go. I began to realise, as I do now, that people weren't judging me as much as I presumed they were. If I had a bad swim session, for example, no one thought any less of me for it.

But the goldfish-bowl phenomenon formed the background in those early days to what quickly became an unhappy relationship with Simon. It was always going to be difficult, I guess, for whoever coached me after Brett. I probably did Cliff a big favour by not going with him, and I probably did Simon none by choosing him instead. But Simon didn't do himself many favours, either.

He has mellowed a lot since then and now has a deservedly successful coaching practice, but at this stage he was only recently retired from his glittering career as an athlete. It seemed to me as if he couldn't let go of it. These weren't training sessions he was organising, they were competitions. We would go on a three-hour ride, and he would shoot off into the distance. Then he'd come back and say, 'Chrissie, you're pushing too big a gear,' and I would think, 'How do you know? You're ten miles up the road!' They felt like Simon's training sessions, not mine. It was also demoralising to spend your time chasing, literally, the man you were paying to be your coach. I think he still felt he had a lot to offer as an athlete, which – believe me, as someone who has spent so much time trying to keep up with him – he did. It was as if he was constantly trying to prove himself to us, physically. But I didn't want someone who could prove himself physically, and being a competitive sort myself I really didn't enjoy the way he kept proving how much faster he was than me. I wanted someone who could watch me as I trained and make sound judgements on what was happening, rather than on what he thought was happening from several miles down the road.

And, OK, I admit it – I couldn't shake off the shadow of Brett either. I was constantly comparing Simon's programmes with his. I was constantly asking myself what Brett would say about this and that.

In most cases, the answer was unprintable. I would challenge Simon with this, but he stood his ground. Who would want to have their methods constantly compared to those of someone else? Simon felt he was always playing second fiddle to this ghost, but he had consummate faith in his programme and remained inflexible. A coach does need to have faith in his methods – Simon was no different from Brett in that regard – but, if you can't convince your athlete, the relationship is doomed.

Very quickly, I started adding and removing things from my programme. I started forging relationships with other people. The British Olympian Julie Dibens was one pro I bonded with especially quickly. She coached herself, and that sowed some seeds in my mind. I started going to places and people other than the ones Simon told me to go to – new bike fitters, Dave Scott's swim sessions.

The upshot of it all was that I drifted apart from Simon. By the end of March, barely a month after I had moved out there, our relationship was strained and uneasy. When I flew to Sydney for the defence of my Ironman Australia title, it was with relief to be getting away.

I love flying into Sydney. The Opera House, the Harbour Bridge – it's a beautiful, beautiful city, and it reminds me of so many happy times. It was not at its best then, though. It was pouring with rain. Pouring when I got there, pouring when I got to Port Macquarie, pouring all week. There was doubt over whether the race could go ahead at all, but there was a real possibility of its becoming a duathlon, with the swim dropped. The water at an ironman has to satisfy certain standards of quality, and the swim for Ironman Australia takes place in an estuary. All kinds of things had been washed down from the farmlands and hills into the water. Not knowing about the swim made the week's preparation hard to handle, mentally.

They had put me up in the same place as the year before, The Observatory, a beautiful apartment block, even when the rain is lashing non-stop against the french windows onto your balcony over the ocean. Also staying there were Nicole and Tim DeBoom. Tim has won at Kona twice. I had never met them, but they are fantastic people. I shared with them my fears about whether I could live up to expectations at the race. My confidence was not overflowing, just because I knew Brett didn't have my back. I was in the enemy camp now, and, what's more, the girl to beat was Bek Keat, whose generosity with the gas canister had saved my bacon in Kona. She had just changed coaches, too. You guessed it: she was with Brett now. I knew he would have revised a plan for her. It was unnerving.

We ended up racing the full triathlon, which I am particularly glad about, because it was the strength of my swim that set me up for what followed. The water might have passed the tests, but it was brown, warm and full of debris – weeds, logs and if rumours are to be believed there might have been a cow in there somewhere. I didn't feel I was going particularly fast (who would, wading through all of that?), but I came out of the water first, neck and neck with Bek.

On the bike I started to pull away. The rain was torrential at times, and I developed a niggle in my leg, which started to concern me. Would I be able to run? All you can do is block it out and believe that it will go away.

The roads were lined with umbrellas and waterproofs – not that the Aussie spirit was ever dampened. At no other ironman do the spectators offer you beer at regular intervals. At no other ironman have I been offered seven proposals of marriage, as I was on that race, two of them from women! And I think the flasher in the raincoat who appeared out of a bush towards the end of the bike leg was offering me something as well.

It all served to keep the adrenaline pumping, and by the time I was out on the run I was feeling comfortable. The niggle, whatever it was, had gone, and the miles fell away to the sound of crashing waves, cheers and the offers of alcohol. I finished in under nine hours, for only the second time, and I had my sixth ironman win out of six, twenty-four minutes ahead of Bek in second.

I have read Brett say somewhere that it was my complete race. It was certainly an important one. Brett was gone, and to win my first race without him as comfortably as I did was a huge boost to my confidence. For him to acknowledge that I was racing better than ever felt strangely as if I had his blessing.

It did a lot for my confidence, which meant it didn't do much to help my relationship with Simon. When I returned to Boulder, I pretty much developed my own programme. Mentally, I had all but left him, even if our professional relationship would run for another few months yet.

My next ironman was to be Challenge Roth in July. Before then, I had a short-course race in Columbia, Maryland. This ended up being a defining race for me. I had entered it almost as a training exercise, to break me out of my long-course comfort zone and to work on my speed. It was also important to me as a means of supporting the Blazeman Foundation, the nominated charity. But I didn't respect the race, I didn't prepare properly and I simply didn't perform. I came sixth. It felt as if my world had caved in.

It was not the first time I hadn't won a race, and certainly not the first time I hadn't won a short-course race. But this was my biggest flop relative to expectations. I had come twenty-second in Tongyeong the season before as a world champion, but that had been only three weeks after Ironman Australia and against a top-class field of Olympic-distance athletes. In this race, however, I really should have made it onto the podium, at least.

I could bore you with all the reasons why I didn't, but there are no excuses. The controllables were not controlled. Something, I am ashamed to say, approaching arrogance was the root problem. I did not shut myself away in the build-up, as I would have done for an ironman. My days were spent meeting people and eating out irresponsibly – heavy meals I would never have dreamed of eating before an ironman. There were other things I couldn't have controlled, such as the fire alarm that went off at my hotel the night before and wouldn't stop, and, possibly related, the wild party in the room next door. I kept telling them to turn it down, but of course that only made it worse. They were very definitely not controllable.

When I woke up in no state to race I had only myself to blame. I just couldn't get my body to cooperate. This can happen. It happens in training, it happens in the ebb and flow of even an ironman, when the body is screaming at the mind; but it usually passes. Here, it stayed throughout the race. And when it does happen there's a good reason for it, and it's usually to be found in some inadequacy in your preparation. As a control freak, failing to control the controllables is something I cannot accept, because it means I have left myself open to failure through malpractice. I was incredibly hard on myself after Columbia. For a week I was in turmoil, utterly despondent. Simon got it in the neck. He, perfectly sensibly, told me to bank it and move on. I found myself pinning yet more blame on him, which in this case was totally unfair as I had stopped following his programme. I was in tears on the phone to Tom.

It made me draw lessons, certainly. Most of them about the importance of preparation.

But it also made me question the concept of winning and losing. I hadn't won; therefore I had lost. But what did losing mean to me? Surely, I had visited a part of the world I had wanted to come to. Maryland is beautiful, very like home, with rolling farmland and deciduous forest. I had supported the Blazeman Foundation. I had met some amazing people, including the race organiser, Robert Vigorito, who remains a friend to this day. I'd stayed at the finish line and hung medals round the necks of all the other age-groupers. In so many ways, even if less tangible, the trip had been a success and so worthwhile. It forced me to learn to accept so-called defeat. There's still a lot for me to learn on that front, but the importance, which Brett was so keen to impress upon me, of being able to separate out what happens in the race from those other things that might enrich me is brought home when I reflect on Columbia.

Things went better in June, when I won a half-ironman in Lawrence, Kansas. I hadn't been able to resist the chance to race in the state of *The Wizard of Oz.* As a child, my Scarecrow had taken the Feltwell Fête by storm, so this was a special pilgrimage for me. I stayed with the race organiser, Ryan Robinson, in his beautiful house. He and his wife, Jenni, and their boys, Hunter, Hayden and Hudson, looked after me royally. Hudson, who was three, was in fancy dress at the finish line, alongside Dorothy, Scarecrow (a rival version), Tin Man and the (not so) Cowardly Lion. Hand in hand, he and I ran down the Yellow Brick Road to the finish line. What a thing, to marry victory with such iconography from a girl's childhood!

As usual, we partied at the finish till the last competitor had made it home. It was a wonderful weekend, but one of the highlights would have to be my chance to meet an institution of Lawrence, the legendary Red Dog. He is a guy in his seventies, who reminded me of Frank Horwill. Since 1984 he has led community workouts, called Dog Days. The set-up is basically Red Dog (or Don Gardner, as he was more boringly named), a megaphone and a field of as many as a thousand locals. He and his wife Beverley run three of these gatherings, every day in the summer, at six in the morning, midday and six in the evening, and twice weekly in the winter. They use the city's sports stadium, entry is free, and the assembled masses include people of all ages and all standards. Red Dog belts out the instructions for his off-the-cuff routines, and hundreds of people of all shapes and sizes follow his lead.

I was truly inspired. Every community around the world would benefit from this sort of activity. It reaffirmed for me the power of one individual to effect change, and the power of sport to unite people. There were two-year-old children taking part, eighty-year-old grannies and everything in between. In these fragmented times, when people go to the gym, stick an iPod in their ear and work out alone, this simple model represented a heroic counter-revolution. It left me buzzing with excitement.

Back at Boulder, I was now, by early July, to all intents and purposes my own boss. I was doing bike sessions with a few pros, including Julie. I attended the swim sessions at Flatirons run by Dave Scott and others. I drew heavily on Brett's programme, with a few ideas from Simon thrown in. The goldfish-bowl aspect of living in Boulder was getting easier to handle, and I found it actually had much to commend it – a world away from the isolated, claustrophobic bubble of life on Team TBB.

The next event on my schedule now was Challenge Roth. This is one of the oldest and most famous races on the circuit. It used to host Ironman Europe, but it is no longer part of the WTC series of official 'Ironman' races. It is run by a family company headed by the passionate Felix Walchshofer, who inherited the organisation from his late father, Herbert. The politics that led to their split with the WTC in 2001 are complicated, but they have grown their race in Roth, a town in Bavaria, into a series of races around the world, called the Challenge series. It is a rival to the Ironman series, which means that the latter do not recognise the records of the former. This is a shame, because Roth is and always has been a fast course, and the fastest times over ironman distance have been recorded there. The men's world record of 7hr 50min 27sec had been set there in 1997 by Luc van Lierde, which was OK because that was pre-split. The women's world record, however, was not officially recognised by the

WTC, because that had been set at Roth only the year before by Yvonne van Klerken, in other words post-split.

It's all a bit of a shame. Nevertheless, there was a lot of speculation before the race over whether I would break the women's world record, unofficial or otherwise. I couldn't wait to try. Roth was one of the first ironman races I had known about. When I turned pro, I remember Belinda raving about it. She had raced it five times and regularly used to wax lyrical about the atmosphere, the organisation and the race itself. The year before, I had found Ironman Germany in Frankfurt incredibly special. I could only guess at what an event this must be. And, yes, maybe I could become the fastest female ironman (note the lower case!) athlete of all time. At least this time I knew what the record was.

I felt in great shape, but about ten days before the race I was overtaken by a strange condition. I was in Boulder when I developed an odd sensation in my right upper arm. It was somewhere between an itch and somebody stabbing me. I thought I'd just been bitten by something.

It didn't go away; in fact, it started to get worse and was keeping me awake at night. I did a Google, and all the symptoms indicated it was shingles. Ice was the only thing that alleviated the pain. A week before the race I was running round getting blood tests, seeing neurologists and my sports doctor. Nothing came up in the blood tests, but they put me on anti-viral tablets anyway. On the plane over to Germany I was beside myself with discomfort. Not for the first time, I was wondering how I was going to race. I didn't feel ill or particularly run down, but I wasn't getting any sleep, and I was just so tired.

Kathrin Walchshofer, Felix's sister, met me at the airport and was my first introduction to the unparalleled care and support that Challenge provide for their athletes. She dropped me at my apartment, and as it was Sunday and all the shops were shut she brought me a basket of goodies to tide me over. I confided in her about my condition, imploring her not to tell anyone, not even her brother. To my knowledge she kept her word, and she did everything she could to help me seek treatment.

We went down the natural-remedy route. It turns out that for shingles, which all of the medics were assuming it was, there are three. I spent the week munching chillies, drinking vinegar and crushing leeks with a pestle and mortar, then rubbing them into my upper arm. I stank. I told Tom and Ben about it and spoke to my mum, who had suffered from shingles. Oddly, I wasn't getting the rash that commonly goes with it; just this awful stabbing sensation in my arm.

But let's leave me there, stinking from a cocktail of vinegar, chilli and leek, my mouth burning, my skin seething; let's focus on Roth. It is a picturesque town in typical Bavarian style, about 25km south of Nuremberg, surrounded by equally picturesque Bavarian villages, through which the race wends its way. Around 4,500 competitors take part, cheered on by around 120,000 spectators. The Germans are incredibly passionate about the sport. In places, the support is like that at the Tour de France. The Solarer Berg climb is unlike anything else on the ironman circuit. Crowds five deep on either side roar you on up the incline. In places they close up to leave a passage only a few feet across, and a motorbike has to carve a way through them. Spectators play chicken with the riders as they lean forward to cheer them on, then pull away as they pass, precipitating a kind of Mexican wave as each rider runs the gauntlet. The noise of their rattles, whistles and cheers is non-stop. Then there is the Beer Mile at Eckersmuhlen, where tables and benches line the route, at which spectators sit down to watch and drink beer from seven in the morning. And, yes, the temptation just to stop and join them is almost unbearable.

The course is closed to traffic, and the signs directing you on the route are permanent, making the whole event feel like a part of the local landscape. It does inspire you, constantly. It's no surprise to me that the fastest times in ironman history have been recorded there.

On the day itself, the conditions were perfect, and the journalists were wetting themselves with excitement. I hadn't been confident at all because of my arm, but if there is one talent I do have it is an ability to put such doubts aside on the big occasion. I don't know how it happens. For no obvious reason, I performed as if I didn't have a care in the world. Not once throughout the race was my arm a problem. Then, at the press conference afterwards, it came back and continued to plague me in the days that followed.

Mine's not to reason why. The important thing was that I raced as I'd never raced before. The swim was good, although there was room for improvement. It reinforced the need to concentrate at the start and get in among the flying body parts and on the feet of the fastest swimmers. Leanda Cave held a clear lead, but I came out of the water only slightly behind Bek Keat, who once again was shaping up to be my main rival. Brett had been working his magic on her, and she was responding.

The bike ride was the best I had ever ridden. And, it turned out, the best any other woman had ever ridden. The road surface at Roth is immaculate. There are climbs on the course, but there are also some nice, gentle descents. It took around 40km before I could put any distance between me and Bek, which I needed to, because she can run like the wind. As can Catriona Morrison, the Scottish athlete (and another good friend) who was racing in her first ironman and was hot on Bek's heels for most of it. I overtook Leanda at about 60km. I just felt stronger and stronger on the bike. The sight of my brother at the top of Solarer Berg jumping up and down, screaming, 'Give it some, Christine!' was particularly uplifting. I'd never seen him so emotional. The last 10km is slightly downhill, and I steamed into T2. My time of 4hr 40min 28sec was a new world record for a bike split. Maths has never been my strong point, but I knew I must have been roughly on track to make history.

I felt pretty good for the first 10km of the marathon, too, but that was actually where I lost some ground to Bek and Cat. I knew I couldn't let up for a moment. Then from kilometres fifteen to twenty-five I started to feel like a plank of wood. That is when you just have to switch off the brain and go into autopilot. It wasn't until the final 5km that I really came out of it. By then I knew it was in the bag. People were shouting at me that I was on course to smash the record. With about 3km to go, you're presented with a range of hands to high-five, and you oblige. But I didn't want to celebrate until the finish line was in sight. As I said, maths has never been my strong point, but I knew my swim and bike times, and, roughly, what my transition times were, so I could tot it up. But the ironman athlete's mentality of one step at a time somehow doesn't allow the sum total to register fully.

It wasn't until I'd turned into Stadtpark to see the finish line that it hit me. There was the clock, and it read 8hr 31sec. I was flabbergasted. There were a few yards still to go, but I was going to break the world record by nearly a quarter of an hour! The noise was deafening, as Tina Turner blared loud over the cheering crowd: 'You're simply the best!' Four children followed me to the line trailing balloons. I waved and laughed and cried. A bouquet was thrust into my hand, and a Union Jack.

I reached for the tape 8hr 31min 59sec after we'd started. I'd improved Yvonne van Vlerken's mark by 13min 49sec. The elation was overwhelming. After the doubts and the shingles, I really felt I had achieved something remarkable. I dropped immediately to the floor to perform the Blazeman roll over the line and was hugged by Felix. Then came my mum and dad and brother, who were among about twenty friends and family at the finish. They give you a massive, three-litre glass of beer. I poured it over myself. Maybe it would help the shingles.

Bek crossed the finish line eight and a half minutes after I did. She, too, had beaten Yvonne's mark. She poured her beer over me as well. Cat came in nine minutes after that, breaking the nine-hour barrier in her first ironman. And Belinda came in fifth, having been hit by a car the week before.

It was a great day for the girls. We were pushing back boundaries in our sport. I'll take their word for it, but the mathematicians told me later that I had closed to within 7.5 per cent of the winning man's time – normally it is about 10 or 11 per cent. These were heady days! Anything seemed possible. We had raised the bar.

The WTC don't recognise the race at all. At Kona, when your year's results are listed as a form guide, there is no mention of Roth, or any of the other Challenge events. But everyone else in the triathlon world celebrated it. Breaking the record was so deeply satisfying, far more than I ever thought it would be. I had never taken much interest in times, but here was a tangible indication of how strong I had become and how strong women triathletes were becoming.

Before we get too carried away, records in ironman are arbitrary. It is not a controlled environment, as it is in an athletics stadium. You can be fitter and stronger, but there might be a hellish wind on the bike, so your bike leg is ten minutes slower. And people then speculate that you're not as good as you were. Wrong.

Times are not necessarily the best indicator of performance, but they are one of them. Is it more satisfying to break a world record than to win at Kona? No. I want to beat the best athletes in the world in the most important race of the year. That's what Kona requires of you. Doesn't matter how. I just want to beat the buggers. Once you've done that, you receive a gold medal that can never be taken away from you, whereas your world record is ephemeral and there precisely to be taken away. So winning is the most important thing. But second is the time.

The party continued long into the night. We stayed at the finish line, as always. It meant so much to share it with those closest to me. It was the first race my brother had ever been to, which was special.

Important people were there from all stages of my life. My cousin Tim made his usual appearance and cried his usual tears at the finish. This time he was joined by my other cousin, Rob; Billi was there, fresh from the summit of Everest; my Manchester University friends, Naomi (now pregnant), Laura and Rich; and Jules from, well, just down the road. Jules is my longest-standing friend. I'd stayed with her and her family in Bavaria as part of an exchange programme during my schooldays, when MC Hammer was all the rage and my hair was large. Little had I known I would be returning nearly twenty years later to break a world record! Jules and I have remained friends ever since – she lives in London now – and a few days after Roth I went to see her at her family home once more.

Roth had been a chance to see Tom, as well. He had spent a week with me in Boulder in April, but otherwise our relationship had consisted of endless Skyping, which was suboptimal but better than nothing, I suppose. Having him there was really special, and our relationship just grew stronger. We stayed in Europe after the race and embarked on a magical mystery tour of France and Germany for ten more days, taking in the Tour de France and the wedding of Gabriel, my friend from my teaching days in Boston. We rounded it all off by staying with Billi and celebrating her triumph on Everest. She lives in Garmisch-Partenkirchen, an Alpine town on the border with Austria. We had a lazy few days with her, during which we climbed the local mountain, named Wank. Cue a lot of comedy photos. But wait till you get to the top. You can eat, and even stay, in the mountain hut up there. It's called Wank-Haus.

Suitably refreshed, Tom and I headed for Munich airport and

went our separate ways, he to England, I to Boulder. That was it in terms of quality time together for the next few months. I knew more than ever that this was going to work, and that I wanted it to. I was in love with him by now, and because we were both confident the other felt the same way, there were no huge, teary goodbyes. It wasn't as if we were never going to see each other again. Leaving was sad, but I'm pretty pragmatic about these things. What can you do? You have to spend time away in our profession but if the will's there, you do what it takes to make it work. It helps, certainly, to have been single for so much of my twenties. I'm used to being on my own, and I know how to look after myself. I would have loved to spend more time with Tom, but I didn't need to. Knowing that he was simply there, though, put a spring in my step. I returned to Boulder ready to take on anything.

That meant tackling, finally, the situation with Simon. This was definitely not putting a spring in my step, so it had to end. The final split came at the running track. He knew that I hadn't been following his programme, so he'd guessed it was coming. In effect, our relationship had been over for a while, but bar a couple of inquests into why it was misfiring, we hadn't quite faced up to it.

'It isn't working,' I told him at a track session. 'I don't believe in the programme. It's too different from what I was doing before.'

He didn't take it lying down, nor did I imagine he would. 'You can't let go of Brett,' he retorted. 'You're not willing to try new things. There's no way it's going to work if you're not going to follow what I set you.'

I accepted that. It wasn't easy for him to coach me, when I came with such a rigid idea of how things should be done, instilled in me by so powerful a personality as Brett. After that, there was probably only one other person who could be my coach, and that was me. Julie was doing all right for herself as her own coach, so why shouldn't I?

In August, though, I started working in an informal way with Dave Scott – mostly strength and conditioning initially, but he set me a programme leading into Kona that year, and our relationship was to develop from there.

Julie was showing me how to do things in more ways than one. My next race was the long-course triathlon in Boulder. I found it strange preparing for a race at home on the course where I train. There was none of the travel and sense of anticipation that usually precedes the big day. On this particular big day, Julie was the better athlete. I came in second. It was a big disappointment, as always, not to win, but this was not quite Columbia. Julie is a top-class athlete, and losing is a very real possibility any time you toe the line with her. I hurt for a couple of days, but I suppose I took some consolation from the fact that it wasn't an ironman. This was becoming an unhealthy situation, I realised. The 'oh well, it wasn't an ironman' line of reasoning after any defeat was all very well, but where was I going to go if I ever lost one of those? I was now feeling as if the ironman was somehow my special race. Nothing could come between me and the ironman. But what if it ever did? How was I going to cope? It didn't bear thinking about.

Before heading back to Kona, I had one more race, the Timberman half-ironman in New Hampshire. I won it, but my run wasn't pretty. For a while, I had been carrying a niggle in my right hamstring. I didn't know it then, but it was a hamstring tendinopathy. I had told Brett about it when it had first developed in 2008. He made me wear rubber pants. He made me put green clay on it and wrap it in cling film. The pain would come and go, come and go, but now it was coming more than it was going. I'd lost the fluidity in my run and felt heavy and stiff. It hurt and was starting to plague me mentally. By the time Kona came along, seven weeks later, it was still troubling me.

* * *

One of my favourite moments is landing at Kona airport. That wave of warm air hits you on arrival. The smell of the bougainvilleas, the lei that is put round my neck by my Kona 'mom and dad' John and Linda, the smiles and the pre-race buzz lift the spirits. This is the island that has changed my life. I always feel as if I am coming home.

I savoured the week's build-up. Kona is a circus, but I was happy to expose myself to it now. I choose to run along Ali'i Drive, knowing that the attention I attract will give me a boost and add to the sense of occasion. But then I go straight back to the apartment and shut the door.

Behind that closed door, I was becoming increasingly concerned. My hamstring was so painful I was doubting whether I could run anywhere near my potential. An added dimension was the presence of Mirinda Carfrae for the first time. She had qualified by winning the Ironman 70.3 World Championships the year before. This was going to be her first full-length ironman – it was even her first marathon – so she was an unknown quantity. But what we all knew about was her running speed. If I was going to beat her, the damage would have to be done on the bike.

I sat with her at the pre-race press conference. Someone asked how I had improved since last year. I took the microphone and said: 'I'm stronger on the swim, stronger on the bike and stronger on the run.'

It was a bluff. True enough, maybe, for the swim and the bike, but my running was a major source of concern. This, though, was the most effective way of putting down a marker without inviting further scrutiny. Pick up the microphone, say something punchy, put the microphone back down again. I have never been a great one for 'smack talk', the art perfected by Chris McCormack, whereby athletes look for an edge through pre-race pronouncements, as a heavyweight boxer might. Here, though, was a rare example. It was relayed across the triathlon press in the build-up, creating a standard for myself to live up to and, hopefully, giving my competitors something to think about. I could see the benefit of that.

The big day dawned, and I was encouraged by an unusual steadiness in my bowels. This was the first time I had ever raced an ironman and not been plagued by gastrointestinal issues. In short, I didn't shit myself once, nor did I have to go in anybody's garden. I had a new pre-race meal – gone were the English muffins with cream cheese and honey; in came rice cereal with honey and nut butter. I drank a nice big cup of coffee as well, and didn't take caffeine tablets during the race. The key might have been not taking those tablets, but the upshot of it was that my constitution was settled on race day.

One of the special moments at Kona is sculling in the water just before the off. I turned to look towards the shore. It was shaping up to be a perfectly clear day. The dawn sun cast a beautiful light over the volcano. I was at peace, perfectly at peace.

And then the cannon fired. Cue carnage.

It turned out to be the best of my three swims to date at Kona. For much of it, I was alongside Normann Stadler. You can tell how well you're doing in the water by the athletes around you. I was surrounded by men. It later transpired that there were only seven girls ahead of me when I left the water in 54min 31sec, a two-minute improvement on the year before. So far so good.

On the bike, things got even better. By around the 30km mark I had the lead. This was early by the standards of my first two races at Kona. I was surprised at how easily it happened. I remember going past Tereza Macel, now one of Brett's athletes, after about 10km. She is a great athlete and had a couple of ironman wins under her belt that year. She didn't come with me, or even seem to try to. I felt so comfortable. My confidence grew with every kilometre. More to the point, my lead did too. I knew I had to put as much distance as possible between me and Rinny Carfrae, in particular, whose speed on foot was my chief concern.

The bike splits I was receiving boosted my confidence even more. I turned round at Hawi in great shape, spurred on by my family and friends who had taken up position there, as they had the year before. I was on course for a really fast bike split, but then I hit the Queen K. and a headwind that was particularly fierce. It meant that the wind had performed an abrupt turn since I'd last been on the Queen K. where I had felt a slight headwind going in the other direction. It had turned and intensified. And it was really hot now. We had a blast furnace to ride in for the last 50km of the bike. It is mentally tough to enter these conditions when you have been making such good progress. You have to drop your speed, and the road seems to stretch on for an eternity. But it's a road you know well, and you break it up into sections. The men are also a great help, if only as targets to pick off. I started to pass some pretty well-known triathletes on that stretch.

By the time I was setting out on the run, I had a big buffer on the nearest women. I was particularly grateful for that this year, because I had so little confidence in my hamstring. I hadn't felt it on the bike, but it had been ever-present in my mind. Now it took centre stage physically.

The dull pain kicked in almost immediately. It ebbed and flowed throughout the marathon. I was familiar with the pain now, though, having experienced it so often in training. The constant tug of the muscle intensified as the race wore on, but so did the realisation that I could run through it. By the halfway mark, I knew at least that my body was going to hold up. Because of my lead, this meant that, barring calamity, I was also going to win. Rinny was by now moving up through the field, but she had had nearly half an hour to make up on me over the run. She would have needed me to have broken down, and I had enough faith in my body and mind to know that this wasn't going to happen. Still, the landmarks on the course were taking an age to loom into view. Never had I had to dig so deep in a race as I did on that marathon. The last six or seven kilometres really did feel like a death march. My rhythm was shot to pieces. My legs were seizing up. This stage of an ironman is never easy, but I am good at making it look as if it is. This time, that feat was beyond me. It was clear from the look on my face and the awkward nature of my stride that I was in real pain.

I remember taking great strength from the memory of my grandfather Harry, who had died the year before aged 101. He was a man of such fortitude. I wanted to make him proud. The other thing that spurred me on was the message, which filtered through in the last few kilometres, that I was on schedule to beat the course record. At the time I didn't know what this was. I just knew that it was held by Paula Newby-Fraser, which meant it had probably stood for some time (seventeen years, as it turned out). That did give me an incentive to keep pushing at the end, even though the race had been won much earlier. I was fatiguing fast. My form had gone. It had been the hardest fight of any of my races – the hardest fight between my body and my mind.

Never had I been so relieved to see a finish line. It was a sight blurred by fatigue, blurred by tears. I approached it with laughter and relief tumbling out of me, as you might an oasis in the desert. Mike Reilly, the Voice of Ironman, whooped and hollered that I had broken the course record, as I reached out for the tape and with one last effort raised it high above my head. When I stepped back and lay down to perform my Blazeman roll over the line, I paused on the ground, exhausted. Jon Blais had never been far from my thoughts on that run. A few weeks earlier, his parents had given me the incredible honour of scattering his ashes in the New Hampshire countryside just before the Timberman half-ironman. If ever a tight hamstring needs a bit of perspective, there are so many tales of heroism against the odds that will render it laughable, and Jon's is one of them.

When I got to my feet, slowly, I looked around for my parents. A lei was hung round my neck and a wreath placed on my head. I continued to laugh and cry. I was wobbly with exhaustion, almost delirious. Finally, I saw Tom in the crowd and beckoned to him to come towards me. I really don't think I could have made it to him just then. Then I saw my parents approach from another angle, and I threw my arms round them and enjoyed the feeling of them holding me up. Tom hadn't been able to join us because he was behind a barrier, so next I went over and embraced him.

By the time Mike Reilly came over to interview me he had a wreck on his hands!

'Three years in a row!' he said. 'And a record we thought would never be shattered here in Kona, but it was, and you did it! Chrissie, it's beyond words!'

He was right about that. I just couldn't speak. The spasms of joy, relief and fatigue kept pulsing through me, the tears kept falling. I wanted to reply, but he had to stand there with his microphone for a while longer. Feeling practically drunk, I eventually put my arm round his shoulder and murmured the word *mahalo* into the microphone – Hawaiian for thank you.

When I had regained a measure of composure, I said: 'I never thought I would come here and break Paula's record. She's an absolute legend, and I feel kind of guilty to have taken the record away! This was one of the hardest things I've ever done, definitely the hardest ironman I've ever done. I had to really dig deep. I'm so proud!'

I thanked my friends and family for coming out to support me, and the crowd for spurring me on. I had finished in 8hr 54min 2sec, an improvement of just under a minute and a half on Paula's record. But I no longer held the marathon record at Kona, which I had set the year before. Rinny had shaved nearly a minute off that to take second place, having raced through the field on the run. It was a warning shot, in her first ironman. She had finished twenty minutes behind me, but if she hadn't left herself so much to do after the swim and bike it could have been interesting. Her run had been more than six minutes faster than mine, although at 3hr 3min mine had been my slowest marathon at Kona to date.

My strength returned quickly in the minutes that followed the race. After drug testing, the Wellington crew headed to the King Kam Hotel, where we broke open a few bottles of champagne. I devoured my obligatory three plates of chips. I jumped into the pool in my race gear; my mother jumped in after me in her clothes. We were drunk on champagne, drunk on euphoria.

After a shower and the press conference, it was back to the finish line, as always, at about 7.30 p.m., to cheer in the age-groupers until the gong sounded at midnight. It is tiring on the legs and makes for a long day, but adrenaline and caffeine get me through. Our sport is the only one I can think of where the elite take part alongside the amateurs, and it brings me such pleasure to honour that spirit and hand out medals to the age-groupers as they come in.

I never sleep well after an ironman. I was up at first light the next day to write my speech for the awards ceremony. And so the mayhem continued. There is never a spare moment in the hours after Kona, but I cherish every memory that I can take away from the scenes that flash past, particularly when they start to slow down in the days after the awards ceremony. Enjoying a long, lazy lunch with my friends and family; swimming out to the Cook Monument with Tom, Cat Morrison and her husband; touring the north of the island with John and Linda after everyone had gone – these were beautiful ways to spend the days that followed.

It was special, as well, to be able to share it with someone else. Tom and I went from Hawaii on a whistle-stop tour of America. We stopped at the Oakley headquarters, a huge silver monolith in Orange County, California, where they presented me with a special-edition watch containing nineteen diamonds. We went down to San Diego. We saw U2 in Phoenix. We returned to Boulder to pack up, then to the UK, then back to my old haunts in Nepal for an amazing three-week holiday, during which we trekked to Everest Base Camp, this time on the south side. It was wonderful to be with Tom in a country that meant so much to me.

It was a far happier way to spend the weeks following Kona than the stresses and struggles of previous years, and Tom was a large part of that. My third Ironman World Championship was a coming of age. I was my own boss now. The most important man in my life was my boyfriend, rather than my coach. With this race, I had finally walked free of Brett's shadow. I was confident in myself at last, knowing I could still dominate, even without him. It was a relief to be free of the politics of Team TBB, but I also realised that I had completed the picture Brett had had in mind for me. In Tom there was that person in my life to share things with. I hadn't spoken to Brett for a long time, and if I ever thought about him it was in a peaceful, affectionate way. I was striding out on my own two feet, and the further I walked away from him the more his teachings were being vindicated. I don't think I would ever have achieved what I had at that point without him, but, if going our separate ways had been hard, we both knew that it had to happen. I still needed reassurance, as most of us humans do, but I could seek that from other people. In terms of the overall strategy, I was in charge of my life now, and it was empowering.

Now it was time to take things to another level.

13

New Records and a Vicious Virus

The Surrey Hills is an area of outstanding natural beauty, so the signs say, and I couldn't agree more. A light sprinkling of snow on a January morning renders them even more picture-perfect. It also renders them lethal for cyclists.

It was a Saturday, the second day of the new year, bitterly cold. So many reasons not to go cycling in the hills. Then again, the prospect of another session on the turbo-trainer in a sweaty dungeon was not exactly appealing.

Since the start of 2008, whenever I have been in the UK I have rented a room in a beautiful big house in Putney. It is an ideal place to be. Owned by a wonderful lady called Liz, Hambro House is a home from home for athletes. Liz and her late husband, Rod, were heavily involved in running the Wandsworth Swimming Club, where their son was a star performer. When Rod was diagnosed with cancer a few years ago, they decided they would help support other athletes, so now Liz rents out the rooms in her sprawling house to anyone whose home is wherever they lay their Lycra. With Richmond Park, one of the best places to run in the world, a few steps one way, the Putney Leisure Centre swimming pool a few the other and her own generosity and warmth in the middle, Liz is certain of a steady flow of coming-and-going athletes. Her son and daughter may be away, but we bring a youthful energy to the house and a slightly disgusting smell of sweat. The whole place is turned over to our bizarre habits.

Liz's basement is where we set up our turbo-trainers, so that it is not dissimilar to Brett's dungeon in Leysin. After a month of cold weather, one of my fellow Hambro House-dwellers, Jonny Hotchkiss, and I had had enough of our confinement down there. The freeze was easing and the roads were clear, so we decided to wrap up warm and head for the hills for our next session. Tom came with us, as did another friend and fellow triathlete, Stu Anderson.

We headed south towards Dorking, then turned right onto the A25. Around Abinger, we turned off onto a B road, heading up Leith Hill. It was in the shade, and you could see the white frost glistening on the surface. I remember thinking, why are we on this road? Someone's going to have an accident here.

Sure enough, despite riding at a snail's pace, my back wheel caught some ice and suddenly went from under me. I slid into Stu's path, so that he fell on top of me, and I threw out my wrist to brace myself for the fall. Snap.

I knew immediately that it was broken, even though I was wearing a pair of big ski gloves. A car pulled up behind us. In it were a young family, who kindly drove me and Tom to the pub in Abinger Common. Jonny and Stu walked my bike there, which was about two miles. I was taken by ambulance to the Royal Surrey Hospital in Guildford. En route, they gave me gas and air to help deal with the pain, which was excruciating. My stomach churned at the sight of my wrist bone sticking out at an abnormal angle. At the hospital they yanked it back into place, after diagnosing impressive fractures in my radius, two metacarpals and a couple of fingers. Of my writing hand. Arm in a cast for six weeks. Happy New Year.

The pain I could endure. What concerned me most was the need to regain full mobility in my hand. My career was, if not quite at stake, certainly liable to be affected, should the treatment I received at this delicate stage not be up to scratch.

I needn't have worried. I was operated on there and then, with wires inserted into my wrist, and I settled down for a two-night stay.

Now, having won a fair few races, I am often asked for my advice on the various aspects of training and racing, and I willingly give it whenever I can. People should know, though, that if I come across as wise and all-knowing, it conceals the fact that I have often been guilty in the past of all the things I warn people against. One of my favourite subjects to hold forth about nowadays is how to deal with injury, but only after I had broken all the rules myself. I shall now describe how not to deal with injury; I shall now describe what I did in the aftermath of that crash in the Surrey Hills.

As soon as I came round from my op, with my right arm raised in a cast, I was trying to perform strength exercises in my hospital bed. The day after I was released from hospital I was down in the Putney dungeon on the turbo. I went running. I used the elliptical trainer. Within days, I was wrapping a plastic bag round my hand and going for a swim. One day I swam 4km with one arm. The bag leaked. My arm started swelling up, so that it was soon pushing against the inside of the cast. The pain was awful. Back to hospital. Off came the cast. My hand and wrist had blown up like a red balloon. The stitches had become infected. I was put on an antibiotic drip. Another few nights in a hospital bed. They took the wires out and gave me a new cast (this time waterproof), to be worn for another two weeks.

A week after the crash I had received an email from Brett. 'Just heard about your accident,' he said. 'Very very sorry to hear that you broke a few things. Take a tip. Don't rush it back. You got nothing to prove. A false start will cause you more drama than taking the month off now.'

Right, again. His words were actually a weight off my mind. One of the reasons I had pushed too hard too early in my convalescence was that I had thought this was what Brett would have recommended. In fact, the opposite was the case.

Only after my arm had been reset did I do what I should have done from the outset – relax, and realise that this injury was actually an opportunity to vary my training. Think about what you can do, rather than worry about what you can't. Swimming, I had to concede, was a bad idea with my wrist in a cast. Instead, I made regular appearances in the dungeon, using a towel to stop the sweat dripping down my arm. I worked furiously on my notoriously weak core, my hamstrings and glutes. The Swiss ball and I became best friends.

Talking of friends, this was an opportunity to see more of them than usual. There may be a temptation to dismiss such activity as frivolous, but I don't believe so. Often we athletes like to see ourselves as invincible, turning away from help because the idea of it challenges our claims to self-reliance. But when things are tough, particularly mentally (and injury has just as much of a psychological impact as a physical one), those rocks we call family and friends come into their own. Seeing them was a reminder that there is more to me than being an athlete. If that were all I saw myself as, my emotional and physical well-being would be determined only by my sporting performance, with debilitating consequences should that facility be taken away by injury or illness. But to see myself as, say, a daughter, girlfriend, Scrabble champion and *Masterchef* addict, as well as an athlete, is to leave me with other roles, so that my happiness and self-esteem can be maintained when the day job is compromised. It's a question of balance.

In mid-February, the cast came off. My arm was white, withered and hairy, but it was working again. That longed-for moment would have come sooner had I not rushed off to the pool so quickly with my leaky plastic bag, but I was fit to resume work just in time for some warm-weather training in Spain with Cat Morrison. We headed off to Águilas for around eight weeks. I have made a lot of friends in triathlon, but Cat is probably the closest of these. It was wonderful to spend some quality time with her away from the triathlon Mecca that is Boulder. We shared an apartment and went on rides through lemon and orange groves, often returning to base with our cycle jerseys laden with fruit. Cat is a superb cook, which was another benefit of spending time with her. She makes the best pizzas this side of Naples. Tom also came out for ten days and loved it. By the beginning of April, I was tanned and fit. All thoughts of icy roads and broken wrists might as well have been from another lifetime.

I flew out to Boulder in April for the new season. And it was to be new in a number of ways. First of all, after a semi-official relationship with him in the build-up to Kona the year before, I was now working with Dave Scott as my coach. Second, Tom and I were moving in together. We found an apartment in Gunbarrel, a suburb of Boulder, and so began a new phase of my life – cohabiting with a boyfriend.

I was very anxious. When I'd first met Tom, just over a year earlier, and been swept away by it all, I was fearful of losing control of my life and my independence. The idea of compromise, I realised, would sooner or later be introduced. Now the time had come. Our first year together had passed like a dream, but we had been living, for the most part, on different continents. This was jumping in at the deep end. Not only were we moving in together, we were doing so thousands of miles from home. It was a totally alien experience for me. And Tom was embarking on a new career as a professional triathlete, having had the operation that finally cleared up his knee injury. He was coming out to Boulder to be with me, yes, but also to train full-time. There was a lot at stake. I wasn't sure what would happen if it didn't work out. And then there were all the other concerns that I'd harboured when we first started seeing each other, but that had remained theoretical because we were living so far apart. These were about to become very real issues. All those questions of compromise that, I guess, are familiar to any couple, but were new to me. What would it be like going to the supermarket and having to choose for two? How would my beloved routines be affected? My obsession with control? I'm very set in my ways – could I continue to be? I was worried about dinner, and whether we would agree on what to eat. I was worried about bedtimes. Most of all, I was worried about my career. I was committed to Tom – I'd known that from the very start – but how would living with him affect my training?

Within a day or two, I knew I'd been worrying about nothing. We dovetailed perfectly. As readers will know by now, I can be feisty and obsessive; Tom is calm and considerate. Nothing is too much trouble for him – 'yes' features far more in his vocabulary than 'no'. Not only did our living together not impinge upon my training, or even my life, it actually enhanced it. I found his relaxed outlook rubbing off on me. The little things that I'd built up as issues turned out not to be issues at all. We went to bed at the same time; we ate the same things. He's a little tidier than I am (that's the army for you). I tend not to fold my clothes with a set square. Mine are thrown into a cupboard. Brett used to say that the state of your wardrobe, like the state of your bike, is a window into your soul – perhaps I still have work to do!

Our training meshed, as well. We both swam at Flatirons Athletic Club, and we did a lot of biking together. Or, rather, warming up on the bike. The minute any effort was introduced he was off down the road, and I laboured to catch him. Haven't managed it so far. Indeed, I now judge my fitness at any given time by the distance between me and him at the end of one of our intervals. On the bike, Tom followed my programme, pretty much, but because he's from a run background he had his own programme for running. We would see to it that our run sessions coincided with each other, but they would be independent.

My life in Boulder was now everything I would have wanted it to be. After the initial problems the previous year with Simon Lessing and the goldfish-bowl phenomenon, the set-up I had found for myself was really paying off. I had finally discovered, in Dave, the right coach to build on the work I had done with Brett. Dave is a legend of ironman, having won at Kona six times in the 1980s. As such, he is a very busy man. This was a problem for me early on, because I didn't feel I was getting enough of his time. But I came to accept that that was the way it was. Most of all, I just trusted him from the start.

After my experiences with Simon the year before, I was also wary of being coached by a former athlete, but Dave has long been out of the sport. He is still very competitive, like Simon. He cranks out hard swim sets in the pool, and he'll come back from a bike ride saying, 'I averaged 36kmph over four hours out there!' And I'll reply: 'Dave. I couldn't care less.' But the main problem with Simon was that he would join in with my training sessions, so it felt like a competition. Dave doesn't do that. He watches some of my sessions, but mostly it is a case of me reporting back to him about each one. And where Brett was authoritarian, telling you to do something and expecting you to do it without discussion, Dave is keen to explain the rationale behind everything. He comes from a sports-science background, and is a strong believer in strength and conditioning and the right nutrition.

He thought it important to address the weaknesses in my core, glutes and hamstrings. When I broke my wrist he agreed that I should have two Platelet Rich Plasma (PRP) injections to treat my chronic hamstring tendinopathy. This is a new technique, whereby healthy blood is taken from your arm and injected immediately into a damaged tendon, helping it to regenerate. The injections were followed by five days' total rest, then a programme of eccentric loading exercises, which means lengthening and shortening the tendon. I was really diligent with those during my convalescence and have been ever since. The hamstring pain that had plagued me for two years finally disappeared. My running started to improve significantly from that point on.

If Brett was the perfect man to whip me into shape and turn a nobody into a champion, Dave was the man to refine me. He adopted a reciprocal approach. I was free to choose when and where I raced, and he was happy to incorporate the parts of Brett's programme that I liked. He has since made changes gradually, almost without my noticing, so he is subtle. He knows I baulk at any change to my routine, and he has handled that very cleverly.

One morning in early May I came in from a run, and the red light was blinking on the answer machine. The message was from my mum, asking that I ring home. She sounded emotional, so I rang her immediately.

'Are you sitting down?' she said.

I wasn't. 'Yes,' I replied.

My mother then summoned her best posh accent and started reading from a letter. 'Dear Madam, The Prime Minister has asked me to inform you, in strict confidence . . .'

I started screaming. Then I fell to the floor in tears. Tom came rushing in. He hesitated as he tried to work out how serious things were. Laughter broke out, and then gave way to tears.

I was to be made an MBE – a Member of the Order of the British Empire. Or at least, the Prime Minister was going to recommend 'that Her Majesty may be graciously pleased to approve that you be appointed' as one, in the Birthday Honours List.

'Before doing so, the Prime Minister would be glad to know that this would be agreeable to you.' I laughed again. I'll say!

We were all crying. 'How proud would Nanna and Grandad have been,' was the first thing I said to Mum. Dad's parents, Harry and Romey, in particular, were staunch monarchists.

How proud was I. At last, what I was doing was to be recognised not just outside triathlon but outside sport. This was not quite the first time I had received recognition beyond triathlon. After my first win at Kona I had been named the Toughest Sportswoman of the Year at the Square Mile Awards, where I met and befriended James Cracknell. And after my third win, just a few months earlier, I had been named *Sunday Times* Sportswoman of the Year, which was a huge honour, beating off competition from the likes of Jessica Ennis and Victoria Pendleton. There was a feeling then that our sport might be on the verge of breaking into the British mainstream, and here was another step towards that goal.

I'd often been introduced as Chrissie Wellington, triple World Champion, sometimes even by myself, but I'd never really thought about what it meant. Now that the establishment was recognising me, it started to sink in. The Prime Minister had been made aware of what I had achieved, and soon the Queen would be. That meant I must have achieved something special.

The hardest part, for me anyway, was that I couldn't breathe a word of it to anyone until the list had been published. That was to be more than a month away on 12 June. By then my season had finally got under way, when I returned to Lawrence to win Kansas 70.3.

But, because of the broken arm, my first ironman of the season wasn't until Challenge Roth in the middle of July. The unique atmosphere in Bavaria, the support from the race organisers and my world record the year before made returning to this great event a no-brainer. I have described the atmosphere at Roth already – 2010 served merely to demonstrate that 2009 was not a one-off. The German passion for triathlon knows no bounds.

I hope I gave them something to celebrate in 2010. I smashed my own world record from the year before by nearly thirteen minutes, coming home in 8hr 19min 13 sec. My marathon was nearly nine minutes faster at 2hr 48min 54 sec. But it wasn't just the run – everything came together. I described it afterwards as my perfect race. That doesn't mean that there was no pain or discomfort; it simply means I overcame the pain and discomfort perfectly. And the finish time was significant. I'd broken my own world record by a lot, which was great, but I'd bettered the previous world record, Yvonne van Vlerken's mark over the same course in 2008, by nearly twenty-seven minutes. Bek Keat, whose time the year before had also beaten Yvonne's record, came in second again, but this time nearly thirty-three minutes behind me.

The real mark of progress, though, was the inroads I was making into the men. Against a top-class field, I came seventh overall. My time was less than 6 per cent slower than that of Rasmus Henning, the overall winner. The time is always useful in its own right, but Dave considers it, as Brett did, in relation to that of the lead man, as the true measure of my performance. This was as close as I had come to the lead man in a major ironman. It felt as if I had taken another significant leap forward.

However wonderful you feel after a race, you have to respect what your body has been through and observe an appropriate interval of rest, even if you feel ready to crack on within days. You should always err on the side of caution. You tend to balloon after an ironman. Everything becomes swollen and distended with fluid retention. Quads merge into knees, which merge into calves, which merge into feet. I look as if I'm wearing a Teletubby outfit. That goes down over the next few days, and the temptation is to think yourself recovered once it has. But there are deep-rooted changes to the chemistry of your body that take place during an ironman. You need longer to recover from these, and you may not be aware of when the process is complete – or not complete. Also, the sheer mental fatigue – the pressure beforehand, the nerves, the strength of will required during the race and the euphoria at the finish – should not be underestimated. These races take a hell of a lot out of you in so many ways, some of which may not be so obvious.

After Roth that year I took the usual few days' holiday, relaxing with Tom at the wonderful Sonnenalp resort on the border with Austria, by the end of which I had recovered from the more superficial scars of battle, the swelling and the physical fatigue. I flew back to America the following Saturday, six days after the ironman, but instead of flying to Boulder I flew straight to Chicago for some promotional work with one of my sponsors, Brooks. It was great fun, and brought me into contact with so many wonderful people, but it was not the most relaxing way to spend three days. All the more so given that Jesse, a Brooks sales manager, is a high-class marathon runner and suggested we go for a run on the Sunday, just seven days after Roth. Of course, I agreed. We ended up running for two hours.

I mention this because of what followed. I mention it because of all the agonising, soul-searching and reviewing that followed what followed.

I went into Kona in good form. In August I had won Timberman 70.3 in New Hampshire for the third year running, setting a new course record. But something was not quite right. Three weeks before Kona, I started to feel tired on the bike. In training, you're constantly treading that fine line between fitness and fatigue, so I thought I might just have crossed it and suffered a couple of dodgy sessions as a result. It didn't worry me unduly, but when I left for Hawaii ten days before the race I was still feeling a bit off. It was difficult to put my finger on what was wrong, other than that I just felt a little tired.

During race week this sluggishness on the bike continued, and now I was also overheating during my run sessions and suffering bad night sweats. I would wake up in the morning with the sheets wringing wet. That might not have been particularly noteworthy for a lot of people – this was Hawaii, after all, where it's ninety in the shade. But I tend to adapt well to the heat. This reaction was abnormal for me. I tried to focus on the positives, and shut out all thoughts of illness from my mind. I have often suffered from ailments in the build-up to a race, and come through them with the conviction that all will be OK.

Then, the day before the big day, I went for my usual 2km swim, followed by an hour-long spin on the bike. When I came back from the ride, my throat was sore. Something was definitely not right.

The Wellington crew were having their usual team barbecue that day, so I popped down to say hello. As far as possible, I tried to be myself, but in a quiet moment I told my mum that I wasn't feeling well. Later that afternoon, I went to rack my bike and saw Asker. My face was bright red, and I confided in him over my worsening condition.

Still trying to ignore the signs, I went out for my customary thirty-minute jog. When I came back, I was dripping with sweat and my throat was closing. I was concerned now, but continued with my race routine – tuna pasta and bed at 8 p.m. When I woke up to the alarm at 3.45 a.m. the next morning, covered in sweat, my throat closed up and my head pounding, I knew immediately that I wouldn't be racing.

Still, I had my pre-race breakfast, then called Tom and Ben. They knew something was up because I would never normally ring them on the morning of a race. I asked their advice, but in my heart the decision was made. When I called Dave, I told him that if I felt like this on a normal day I wouldn't train.

'Then you have your answer,' he replied. 'You'll have a great swim, a great first half of the bike. Then your body will give up on you.'

He was right. This is not the hundred-yard dash we're talking about here. This is not even the ironman in Roth. This is a brutal, brutal race. The heat, the humidity and the wind in Kona are relentless and make it the toughest race in our sport. It's not the Ironman World Championships for nothing. The damage you inflict on your body when you enter into it 100 per cent fit is quite enough; the damage you would inflict when only 50 per cent fit doesn't bear thinking about. At 5 a.m., with my head and heart in turmoil, I told Ben to announce my withdrawal.

It was the hardest decision I have ever had to make. The worst part was that I was not on my deathbed. I hadn't broken my leg. I could have started. But could I have finished? Never, ever give up, it says on my wristband, and, once under way, I would have given everything to get to the finish line. I might well have made it, as well. But at what cost? I could have put myself in a hole it would have taken months to emerge from. You have to keep things in perspective. I was not willing to take such a risk for one race, even if it was the World Championships, however much it hurt. It would have been dangerous.

It may not be politically correct, but there was another dynamic at work, too. I was unbeaten, and this would have been my tenth ironman. I do worry about the day I lose one of these races for the first time, but if and when it happens I want only one thing – to go down fully fit and able to fight to the very end. I never go into a race expecting to win, but I do go in expecting to fight. I couldn't have fought that day. I couldn't have done myself justice.

Cat had been ill that week, as well, since the Wednesday, but by the Saturday she was feeling better and chose to race. She pulled out halfway round and beat herself up over it. Should she have started at all? She didn't do her body any favours by racing, and when she gave in to the inevitable she gave her mind a battering as well. But there is no escape for the mind in that situation. She was damned if she did and damned if she didn't, just as I was. Dede Griesbauer raced fit and did finish, but well down on her expectations. What did she do? Beat herself up over it. The three of us were in despair the day after the race. We had all taken different paths but ended up at the same place.

The other thing that tore me apart was guilt that so many family and friends had travelled so far to watch me. I stayed in my apartment on race day. It was agonising, and would have been unbearable but for the steady stream of visitors. I cried and got angry, but no one let me wallow. We talked about anything but the race. We focused on the future. Tammy, my friend from Card Aid days, had come out, and we chatted about the foundation we want to start together.

Not for the first time, though, it was my brother, Matty, who offered the most telling reality check. I spoke to him that morning. 'Christine,' he said very firmly. 'No one's died.' This resonated all the more, because his best friend did die when he was seventeen. It has given Matty a more rounded perspective on life, and his simple words helped me enormously.

I followed the race intermittently online. It was a wonderful day for the British women, with three placed in the top ten. Julie Dibens finished third, while Rachel Joyce, my close friend from the swimming club at Birmingham University, came in fifth. Leanda Cave, the third Brit, was tenth.

But it was Mirinda Carfrae's day. I'd known she would be the girl to beat, and so it proved. She lowered her own record for the marathon at Kona and finished in under nine hours. She would have given me a real race, which made it all the more frustrating. Because I wanted a race; I wanted an 'iron war', the phrase they use to describe the epic race in 1989, when Mark Allen beat Dave, my coach, then the champion, by less than a minute. I wanted a race that forces me to finish absolutely crawling. Sometimes I think it's disrespectful that I'm OK after an ironman, that I dance at the finish line until well into the night. Did I really give it everything? During the race I feel I do, but I hadn't yet had to face that visceral desperation to dig to the depths that racing shoulder to shoulder with a competitor might inspire. I don't think you ever know just how much it is possible to give until someone pushes you to the limit. Rinny was shaping up to be that rival for me.

I kept a low profile in the days that followed. It wasn't my show; it was Rinny's. She had had a great race, and was a worthy winner. It was important not to detract from that. I spent time with my family, and as the days passed I came to terms with my no-show and started to deal with the practicalities of my next step. Back in Boulder, the results from my blood test came through – I was suffering from a vicious little cocktail of strep throat, pneumonia and West Nile virus. That told me what I needed to know – I had been right not to compete. I was suffering from a genuine illness. Every time you feel a niggle in the build-up to a big race, every time you feel the faintest flicker of ill health, the alarm bells ring. You monitor the situation minutely and obsessively until you're no longer sure whether the ailment is real or a figment of your imagination. I knew by race morning that my condition was genuine, but it was reassuring to see just how genuine. In the end, it took me two weeks and a course of antibiotics to recover.

More hurtful, though, were the rumours. Even before the gun went off, they were circulating. Chrissie's had a nervous breakdown; Chrissie's avoiding a drugs test; Chrissie's pregnant. The rumours hurt, because they undermine my credibility – I'm a warrior and a fighter, I race fair and I race clean. As a sensitive soul, the rumour-mongering hit me hard. How can people even think those things, I kept asking myself, let alone spread them as malicious gossip? Is everything I've worked so hard to achieve really so flimsy that it can be swept away at the first sign of a sore throat?

No. Of course not. The people who said those things don't even know me. Their opinions do not matter as much as those of the people who do, even if their tongues are free to wag. I fought the allegations that needed to be fought, and I laughed off the ridiculous ones. Pregnant?! We athletes are in bed by 8 p.m. If only!

The drugs allegations, though, were libellous, and we dealt with them seriously. For as long as anyone has cared to listen I have been loud and forthright on the issue of doping. All professional athletes should be subjected to the most rigorous of testing, if we are to ensure our sport stays as clean as possible. And it must. As soon as I won my first World Championship, I put myself forward for regular out-of-competition testing through UK Sport, and since then I have been included in the WTC's testing pool. I have to provide the World Anti-Doping Agency (WADA) with a one-hour slot in which they can turn up to test me every single day of the year. They can also appear any time outside this hour for a random test. This is supplemented with in-competition testing at most races. In 2010 I underwent eight blood tests and fifteen urine tests. I have also taken the step of publishing the results on my website. Far from avoiding drug-testing, I have submitted myself to the process without condition, and have been actively campaigning for improvements in testing across the ironman community. WADA know I'm clean; the gossip-mongers should just know better.

As for the nervous breakdown theory, it never even crossed my mind. Of course, there is pressure, and maybe there is more for me than for the other girls. I really am deadly serious about never wanting to lose an ironman! Yet every time I line up to race, the prospect of not winning is something I have to deal with. So it's tough. But it does surprise me, in the light of my record, that people should think I'm having a breakdown. I hope I've never given the impression that I'm about to have one over a race, because I really am not.

Tom returned to the UK for his cousin's wedding, so I flew to Boulder alone and began the process of healing. I was happy to be on my own – I enjoy the support of a network of friends and specialists out there. After a couple of weeks I started to feel better. My confidence returned as I put Kona behind me. I can throw my toys out of the pram with the best of them, but I am also quick to move on.

With my planned finale to the season up in smoke, I needed to find another race before the year was out. The options were ironman races in Mexico, Florida or Arizona. I chose Arizona. I had heard good things about it, and it was convenient from Boulder. Held towards the end of November, six weeks after Kona, the timing was right, too.

Even better was that Tom decided on an impulse to race there too. Until that point he had been competing over the half-ironman distance. He had never even run a marathon. But Tom, being Tom, didn't care about that. He had always intended to do an ironman one day, just not in 2010. When I decided, about four weeks before, to race at Arizona, he thought, why not?

He flew to Arizona from the UK, and we both arrived in Tempe, the venue for the race, on the same day. We had arranged a home stay with Craig Norquist and his wife, Laura. Craig is a medical doctor, an ironman athlete and an ultra-runner – which means he thinks nothing of running the equivalent of four marathons in a day. It was great to stay with him and Laura at their pad in Paradise Valley, where the houses are like shopping malls and the lawns, in the middle of a desert, are so perfectly landscaped.

I thought I would be more nervous than I was. I had a point to prove – I was fit, I wasn't having a breakdown, I wasn't pregnant. So there was apprehension, but my nerves were steady. Having Tom around helped. This was the first time we had stayed together in race week, but he was so relaxed, even though it was his first ironman, and his calmness rubbed off on me.

It is fair to say that I was more paranoid than normal about getting ill. Uh-oh, my throat's getting sore, my throat's getting sore. Is my throat getting sore? No, I think it's OK again. This hypersensitivity is quite normal before a race, but my levels were definitely raised, for obvious reasons. More than anything, though, I was just so excited about toeing the line again.

No last-minute withdrawal this time. I studied 'If' extra hard that morning. The poem had helped me more than ever in the weeks after Kona. Never had that line about Triumph and Disaster seemed so apt. Nor the one about dreaming but not making dreams my master. Nor the one about all men (and women!) doubting me. That poem speaks to us in so many ways, and the message is consistently true – that despite the ups and downs, dignity, balance and determination must remain our goal.

The lake was freezing, but I swam well. The bike, however, was tough. There was rain, there was hail, the winds were fierce and ever-changing, and I couldn't shake off Leanda and Rachel till about halfway.

By then I had also been overtaken by a familiar-looking human missile. Swimming is the one discipline where I have the advantage over Tom, but it didn't take him long to overturn that. About 20km into the bike, he came burning past me, shouting encouragement: 'Yes! Yes! Yes!' I knew then he was having a good race. As soon as I was onto the run, I started asking people how he was doing. Just knowing he was out there on the course gave me an unexpected sense of security and excitement. Part of me didn't want to see him again, because that meant he would be slowing up; part of me thought I would. He had never run a marathon. We just didn't know how he would fare. When I didn't catch him I was so elated and relieved. I knew by the end of my race how he had done. He had come third and broken the British record in a time of 8hr 11min 44sec. Far from struggling, he ran the fastest marathon of the day in 2hr 48min 11sec. His bike was third fastest. And all in his first ironman!

My race, meanwhile, was going really well, partly inspired by Tom's success, partly by the joy of being back doing what I love. Not that it was easy. The conditions were tough, and having not had a puncture all year my luck ran out about a mile from the end of the bike. Pop went my front tyre. As I was so close to T2, I decided to carry on and bump along on the rim for the last few minutes.

After a fine run of 2hr 52min, I came home in 8hr 36min 13sec. I had forgotten that there were two world records in ironman – the official 'branded' one, as recognised by the WTC, and the unofficial. In my mind, the world record was the one I had set a few months earlier at Challenge Roth, but somebody pointed out after I crossed the line in Tempe that I had just broken the Ironman (note the upper case) world record, set by Sandra Wollenhorst at Ironman Austria in 2008. By more than eleven minutes, it turned out.

I have never felt more relief after a race than I did after that one. A huge weight had been lifted. I was reported as saying that this was my Kona. I didn't say that. It wasn't Kona, and Kona hadn't been put to bed. It wouldn't be, unless I won it again some day. But I did say that that was the performance I would have liked to put on at Kona. Had I flopped, the doubts might have come crowding in, but to have given the best performance I could have hoped for under the circumstances – and to have broken a world record, to boot – meant I was back on track.

But the highlight of the day was to cross the finish line and be met by Tom, beaming from ear to ear. We embraced, and something did feel complete. Embraces at the end of an ironman are nothing new, but they are usually with loved ones or with people who share the bond of having just completed an ironman. I had never embraced anyone who qualified on both those counts. It was special.

A couple of days later, I received an email from Brett. He had seen the pictures of me and Tom at the finish line. 'This may be the final note and closure of a very special part of my coaching career,' he said. 'The last piece of the puzzle that I wanted to see complete from our first meeting has been delivered. I gained incredible satisfaction from your race at the weekend. No, not from the race performance – that didn't interest me – but to see you in full happiness in the arms of your man, looking up with all the admiration one can summon in a most happy and fulfilling time. That is what I will remember of 21

November 2010. I could tell the win was very special because your man of the moment was there sharing it with you. And therein lies my happiness. Chrissie Wellington is no longer the lone ranger. This was one of the magic moments. Priceless, just like the pics. Thank you for the journey. It has been a special time. Congratulations and best wishes for the future. Cheers, ex-boss.'

I told him not to be so melodramatic – this was not going to be the end of our relationship. Brett had taught me nearly everything I knew about triathlon, and I would carry this with me always. But he was right – I had never been prouder or happier to share the podium with the love of my life. It is a memory that will never fade. It is true that my season had not gone exactly as planned, but life was going very nicely. Then again, I'd broken two world records and won my tenth ironman out of ten, so 2010 really hadn't been that bad.

It held further treats in store. There was my investiture at Buckingham Palace as an MBE to look forward to, a week before Christmas, and a couple of days before that I was summoned to the University of Birmingham to receive an honorary doctorate. Yes, that's Dr Christine Wellington to you!

Returning to Birmingham turned out to be incredibly emotional. I gave a speech to hundreds of graduates under the ceiling of the Great Hall, and my parents were in the front row, crying. It took me back to when they had dropped me off there all those years ago, and Dad had told me to seize every opportunity and make a mark for all the right reasons. It took me back to when they came to watch me graduate three years later in 1998. Now we were here again. We had come full circle, and so much had happened in between.

The next day we gathered again at a hotel I had booked in St James's Park. My parents, Tom and I went out for dinner with my brother and his fiancée, Kelly. He had recently proposed to her, so there were so many reasons to celebrate. The following morning, my brother, my mum, my dad and I donned our gladdest rags and walked from the hotel to Buckingham Palace. The Queen must have been having the day off, because Prince Charles performed the honours. To be inside the country's most famous building was awesome, which I mean in its genuine sense – as in it inspired awe, as simple as that.

There was pomp and circumstance. And protocol – you had to walk a certain number of paces this way, and then a certain number that. Backwards. Everything had to be done on cue. I was terrified of a muppet moment. Surely I would trip over on these high heels I wasn't used to.

But everything went perfectly. I snatched a few words with Prince Charles.

'You have to be very fit to do what you do, don't you?' he said.

I confirmed this was true. When he asked me what was next, I told him it was to try to beat the men.

He pinned the MBE to my jacket. It was a fairy-tale way to end the year. To have my achievements recognised by the establishment, and to be surrounded by people who have done extraordinary things, was such a privilege. My parents and brother were so proud, and I kept thinking about my grandparents and how ecstatic they would have been.

When we left it was starting to snow. We headed to the pub. I had reserved an area, and friends from all stages of my life arrived to celebrate. Some had known me since childhood, some from school, university, and work. Some arrived with babies. We had all moved on, but we were all the same as we had ever been. Friends and family are the thread that runs throughout our lives, no matter where those lives take us. After my brush with royalty that morning, this was the only way to end the day.

14

The Heroes of Ironman

If you can't fly, run; if you can't run, walk;
if you can't walk, crawl.

Martin Luther King

Ironman inspires like no other sport. It transforms the lives of those who take it on; and those who take it on transform, in turn, the lives of others through the heroism of their deeds. The finish line at an ironman is a place awash with smiles and tears. The emotions evoked at the end of a race of that length are what help to bind our community so strongly together.

The pantheon of legends in ironman is well populated. Having come to the sport late, I knew little of their achievements, but now they are well known to me. Dave Scott and Mark Allen won six Ironman World Championships each in the 1980s and 1990s, the reign of the former ending with the start of the latter's in the epic race of 1989 – known ever since as the 'Iron War', when Mark and Dave duelled side by side for more than eight hours, Mark prevailing in the end by less than a minute. Paula Newby-Fraser, the 'Queen of Kona', won eight titles in the same era, including a record four in a row. Natascha Badmann won six in more recent times, including three in a row at the start of the millennium. There are others, of course; too many to mention, all of them legends, all of them huge inspirations.

But for these athletes, as for me and most of my peers, this is our job. One of the beauties of our sport is that we professionals get to race on the same stage as the amateurs, sharing the smiles, the grimaces, the highs, the lows, the tears and the joy, united by the same goal – to cross the hallowed finish line. We race together, suffer together and celebrate together.

Many of these athletes have contacted me to say that my achievements have helped to encourage them in their life journey, but, if that is so, it is not a one-way process. Because it is the recreational athletes who inspire me through the tough times, the everyday heroes who juggle training with a full-time job, a family and other commitments.

Among them are people whose achievements simply beggar belief. Could you imagine swimming, biking and running 140.6 miles, all the while pulling or pushing a son who can't walk? Or being a double amputee, and having to empty the blood and sweat from your prostheses during the marathon? Would it occur to you to enter an ironman having just been diagnosed with a terminal illness? And, despite everything, would you find it in yourself to devote still more of your time and energy to helping others?

Yes, incredible heroes abound in our sport, most of whom get nowhere near the podium. Here are just a few of my guiding lights, in no particular order, whose stories serve as the most moving tribute to the sport of ironman I can think of.

The Hoyts

In 1962, Rick Hoyt was born to his parents, Dick and Judy, with cerebral palsy. He was a quadriplegic. Dick and Judy refused to have him institutionalised, despite the advice of doctors. Rick has since lived as full a life as possible, able to communicate via a specially designed computer. He graduated with a degree in Special Education in 1993. His parents' refusal to accept the verdict of medical science has long since been vindicated, and that might be seen as quite enough of an inspiration in itself.

But in 1977 Rick persuaded his father to help him take part in a five-mile run to raise money for a lacrosse player who had been paralysed in an accident. He wanted to show this athlete that there was much he could look forward to, even if he was to be wheelchair-bound. Despite no background as a runner, Dick agreed to push his son round the course. That night, Rick told his dad that during the race he felt as if he weren't handicapped.

Dick and Rick have since completed more than a thousand races – including marathons, duathlons and triathlons (six of them ironmans). In 1992, they biked and ran 3,735 miles across the US in forty-five days.

In a triathlon, Dick attaches a bungee cord around his waist and pulls Rick along in a raft during the swim. He pedals a special two-seater bicycle for 112 miles. Then for the marathon he pushes Rick in a custom-made chair. 'The thing I would most like', Rick once said, 'is for my dad to sit in the chair, and I would push him for once.'

The Hoyt Foundation helps to support and inspire America's physically challenged youth. Their slogan is 'Yes You Can!'. Dick is now in his seventies and Rick his forties. They are still racing.

Jon Blais

In 2007, at my first Ironman World Championship, I saw Leanda Cave reach the finish line, lie down, stretch her arms out over her head and proceed to roll over it. I asked someone why she had done it, and they explained to me the story of Jon Blais, 'The Blazeman'.

Jon, a teacher of children with special needs, had died less than six months earlier, aged thirty-seven, of ALS. He had been diagnosed with the incurable condition in May 2005. Later that year, at Kona, he fulfilled a long-held dream to race in an ironman and in so doing became the first, and so far the only, person to complete an ironman with ALS. His worsening condition had meant that he had not been able to train for the race. His doctors had told him he would have to be rolled over the finish line. After sixteen and a half hours of agony, only half an hour before the cut-off time, Jon proved them wrong by finally reaching that line. Whereupon he rolled over it, in what is now known as 'Blazeman'-style.

I met Jon's parents, Bob and Mary Ann, in the evening of my first World Championship, and was so moved by his story that I followed Leanda and a few other professionals in becoming a patron of the Blazeman Foundation. We join a team of Blazeman Warriors around the world, committed to promoting awareness of the disease and raising funds for further research – 'So Others May Live', to quote the foundation's slogan.

I never met Jon, but it feels as if he is a friend, and The Blazeman is nothing if not an inspiration – to me and countless others. He called himself the ALS Warrior Poet, and this is his poem, 'Westward Bound':

Live . . .
More than your neighbors.
Unleash yourself upon the world and go places.
Go now.
Giggle, no, laugh.
No . . . stay out past dark,
And bark at the moon like the wild dog that you are.
Understand that this is not a dress rehearsal.
This is it . . . your life.
Face your fears and live your dreams.
Take it in.

Yes, every chance you get . . .
come close.
And, by all means, whatever you do . . .
Get it on film.

Jane Tomlinson

Having twice beaten breast cancer, Jane Tomlinson was told in 2000 that the disease had returned, this time in her bones and lungs. She was given six months to live.

In the end, she lived for another seven years and, while undergoing chemotherapy, raised nearly £2 million for charity through her participation in numerous endurance events. Among them were four marathons, three London Triathlons, two half-ironmans, a bike ride from John O'Groats to Land's End and another from Rome to Leeds.

In 2004 she completed Ironman Florida, becoming the first terminally ill person to try an ironman, let alone finish it. She said afterwards that that would be the last of her challenges, such was the pain and stress placed on her body. Then, in 2005, she ran the New York Marathon and, in 2006, she cycled across America. She finally lost her fight against cancer in 2007.

Jane's story resonates with me, because my grandmother survived breast cancer but eventually died from liver and bowel cancer. When Jane's husband, Mike, asked me to be a patron of the Jane Tomlinson Appeal, I didn't hesitate. She is a true British hero, and millions of pounds continue to be raised in her name through the Appeal and the Run For All races that she founded with Mike in the last year of her life.

Scott Rigsby

At my first World Championship in 2007, I saw someone pull off the unthinkable by finishing at Kona. That year, Scott Rigsby became the first double-leg amputee to complete an ironman. Scott came in barely a quarter of an hour before the cut-off time, at 16hr 43min. During the marathon he'd had to stop every few miles to empty blood and sweat from the inside of his prostheses. I had the privilege of putting a lei around his neck at the finish line, with tears welling up in my eyes. I was honoured to be able to do it again in 2011, when Scott finished at Kona for a second time.

In 1986, aged eighteen, Scott had been riding home from work with friends on the back of a pick-up truck in Georgia, when the truck was hit by an articulated lorry. He was dragged hundreds of yards beneath the trailer. He suffered third-degree burns up his back, his right leg was severed and his left was left barely intact. Nearly twenty years of pain and despair followed. After twelve years of operations and treatment, Scott decided to amputate what was left of his left leg. He suffered from depression and prescription-drug addiction. Then, in 2005, he had an epiphany and set himself the target of becoming an ironman. He has never looked back. Now he has set up his own foundation, and inspires people through public speaking and counselling.

I was there to witness the culmination of his mission to be an ironman, and I realised once again what power sport wields. Having just won the World Championship for the first time, I resolved there and then to use my new position well, to try to inspire, encourage and empower, just as people like Scott do.

Rudy Garcia Tolson

Scott Rigsby is the first double amputee to complete an ironman; and, in 2009 at Tempe, Arizona, Rudy Garcia Tolson became the first double-above-knee amputee to complete one. By then, at the age of twenty-one, Rudy had already won gold medals in the pool at the

Paralympics in Athens in 2004 (aged fifteen) and Beijing in 2008. He had raced at Kona in 2009, but missed the 5.30 p.m. cut-off time on the bike by eight minutes. He vowed to give it another shot and did so in Arizona six weeks later.

Rudy was born with numerous genetic defects, the worst of which were in his legs. He required fifteen operations as a child, before, aged five, deciding to have his legs removed altogether, so that he could get on with living on a pair of prosthetic limbs. He has become a sporting phenomenon and a hero to thousands, devoting a huge amount of time and energy to helping others, especially through the Challenged Athletes Foundation.

It is no wonder that Rudy struggled initially to make the cut-off time for the bike on an ironman. I cannot conceive of how anyone could ride 112 miles without any hamstrings or quads. In propelling his bike forwards, Rudy can recruit only his glutes. He can't stand up on the pedals or shift his weight around, which robs him of yet more strategies to ease the pain. He just has to sit there on a saddle for hours and hours, effectively clenching his buttocks.

I have met Rudy on numerous occasions, and have found his courage and determination wonderfully inspiring. He is a 'can do' person, who always finds a way of reaching his goal. His achievements at such a young age are astonishing and an example to us all.

Sister Madonna Buder

At the other end of the age spectrum is the lady they call the Iron Nun. Sister Madonna Buder started training at the age of forty-eight as a way of honing mind, body and spirit. Since then she has competed in more than 300 triathlons. At the age of fifty-five she took on her first ironman, and has now completed more than forty. 'I train religiously,' she says, by way of explanation.

Now in her eighties, she has kept pushing back her own world record as the oldest female to complete an ironman. Indeed, new age categories are continually being created for her. In 2005 it was the 75-to-79 category; in 2010 it was the 80-plus.

I met Sister Madonna properly at Ironman Arizona in 2010, and she was as kind, charming, energetic and passionate as I had imagined she would be. Truly, age is nothing but a number.

Jordan Rapp

Another person at Ironman Arizona that year was Jordan Rapp, a professional triathlete who was defending his title. But, since his victory the year before, he had come within a few minutes of death.

On a training ride in March 2010, a car pulled out in front of him. He hit it at high speed, flew through one rear passenger window and then out through the other, smashing both, and was left for dead on the highway. Along came a naval officer, Tom Sanchez, who, amid all the blood, reached into the gaping wound in Jordan's neck, felt something pulsing in there and, in a hit-and-hope fashion, applied pressure to it. He saved Jordan's life.

Jordan came round two days later and spent the next eighteen days in hospital, having severed two jugular veins, lost over two litres of blood and shattered his face, collarbone and shoulder. He wasn't able, physically or mentally, to resume proper training till that October. Yet, seven weeks later, there he was lining up for the defence of his title 'to show I'm back, still alive and healthy and strong'. He came fourth. He has registered a number of wins and podium finishes since, and is now a father. He epitomises the never-say-die spirit.

The Southwoods

Debbie and Tauny Southwood are the life and soul of the BRAT Club, where I was first introduced to triathlon. Debbie swam for Australia at the 1972 Munich Olympics as a sixteen year old, and still beats me out of the water. She was involved in a horrific bike crash in 2006, in which she fractured her pelvis and was left virtually immobile. Somehow, a mere seven months later, she not only started Ironman Switzerland but made the podium for her age group. In 2008 she earned a slot at Kona, where I had the privilege of racing with her on the hallowed lava fields.

All the more pressure, then, on Tauny, her husband. He is a global leader in the field of juvenile arthritis, a professor of paediatric rheumatology at the University of Birmingham and a consultant at Birmingham Children's Hospital. He is the chair of the BRAT club, helping to take it from a small group of passionate individuals to a 600-member organisation that inspires and supports athletes of all ages and abilities. He is a husband, a father of three, a doting grandfather and a wonderful friend to countless others, myself included.

As if all that were not enough to be getting on with, he has been set for years in the pursuit of his holy grail, a place at Kona. He is dedicated to his training programme (although four hours of sleep a night is somewhat suboptimal). He has broken bones and bled for his mission, but has never given up. And in 2011 he finally qualified by winning the 55-to-59 age group at Ironman St George, held in the desert of Utah, one of the most punishing races on the circuit. To be able to race with him at Kona in 2011 was incredibly special for me. His unadulterated joy at the finish line had me in tears once again.

Debbie and Tauny are special to me, but ironman is full of such heroes, who make the most of their lives and inspire others to make the most of theirs. In so doing, they bring a smile to all our faces. They make our sport what it is – the most inspiring of them all.

15

Rising from the Crashes

The year 2011 was always going to be a defining one. I was settled now as a professional athlete. There were no dramas over who should be my coach, no dramas over where I should live. My relationship with Tom was established, as was my wonderful network of friends and advisors in Boulder. I had just suffered the first major setback of my career and responded in as decisive a manner as possible. With all that behind me, the year ahead was a chance to explore just how far I could take things. No excuses, no dramas. Hopefully, no Muppet.

Did I say 'settled'? I spent a good chunk of the first few months of the year in an aeroplane. New Year was spent in France for Georgie's wedding. Then, having waited for the renewal of my US visa, I flew to California for the Endurance LIVE Awards in San Diego, where I won Performance of the Year for Roth. Then it was off to Tucson, Arizona, where I intended to spend the winter months training, until my first race of the year, Ironman South Africa in April. While there, I changed my mind and decided that South Africa was as good a place as any to winter, so I flew there in February, via the TCR (Triathlon, Cycling and Running) Show in the UK, where I won Female Elite Triathlete of the Year in the 220 Triathlon Awards.

* * *

I always enjoy it when I feel as if my life is coming full circle, when there is a symmetry and poignancy to it. Coming to South Africa was another example. Only this time it was as if there had been more than one revolution to this particular circle. I came to South Africa for the first time in 1999 as a young traveller just out of university; then I returned in 2002 as a civil servant in the UK Government for the World Summit on Sustainable Development; here I was in 2011, coming to train as a professional athlete. My life had brought me to South Africa three times and as three different people.

I had chosen to base myself in Stellenbosch. I'd been there in 1999 on a wine-tasting tour. For obvious reasons, I couldn't remember too much about the place from that time, but returning brought it all back – the whitewashed colonial buildings, the tree-lined avenues, the square, the café culture. It's a picture-perfect university town, about 50km inland from Cape Town, at the heart of South Africa's wine country.

I took an apartment in the Vilaroux complex, run by the wonderful Suzette and François Le Roux. There were a few of us training out there: Dion Harrison, a fellow inmate from Hambro House in Putney; Jan Frodeno, the Olympic champion; his girlfriend, Emma Snowsill, who also happened to be an Olympic champion; Tim Don; and Fraser Cartmell. I was never short of a training partner, and there was always someone on hand to have a coffee with at one of the many cafés just around the corner.

Another friend out there was an ultra-runner called Lizzy Hawker. I'd been introduced to her by Billi, albeit through email. Over two years we'd become friends in a pen-pal sort of way. She's an incredible person – intelligent (PhD in physical oceanography), passionate about the environment and one of Britain's best ultra-runners. She won the 100km World Championships in 2006; she ran from Everest Base Camp to Kathmandu in 2007 in world-record time; and in September 2011 she ran 153 miles in twenty-four hours, breaking the women's world record of eighteen years.

In February 2011, she was looking for somewhere to train, so I persuaded her to come to Stellenbosch. Finally, I met her, and so our friendship entered a new dimension – the face-to-face one! She was training for Comrades, an ultra-marathon of 87km between Durban and Pietermaritzburg. They love endurance sport in South Africa. Every day they show mountain biking, triathlon, ultra-running and ocean swimming on the TV. Comrades is the highlight of the year. It's the oldest and biggest ultra-distance race in the world, with tens of thousands of competitors. It's their equivalent of the London Marathon, except that it's twice the length. A marathon is nothing to a South African.

So this was a good a country to be training and racing in, and Stellenbosch one of the best bases within it. Everything is within easy reach. I could get wherever I needed to go on my bike. There are oak trees all over town, and legend has it that if you are hit on the head by an acorn it will bring you good luck. As race day approached, this was exactly what happened to me as I cycled along.

Even before the big race started, that luck was kicking in. I'd flown to Port Elizabeth, the race venue, on the previous Tuesday. On the Saturday, I racked my bike. Before I left, I noticed a group of people crowding round it. They seemed to be taking photos of the bike. That does happen sometimes, so I thought no more of it. Just as I was leaving, though, an age-grouper by the name of Franz came up to me.

'You do know there's a huge thorn sticking out of your front tyre, don't you?' he said.

Funnily enough, I didn't. I went across to my bike, nudging aside those people too busy taking photographs to alert me, and, sure enough, there it was, the size of my thumb, a whopping great thorn. I pulled it out. Hiss. The tourists were treated to a few more shots of me getting down and dirty, wrestling with a tube change. Thank heavens for Franz. I might have spotted the thorn the next morning before the race – I do always check my tyres – but, then again, knowing Muppet, I might not. I owed the man a Chenin Blanc.

It was a new bike, a Cannondale Slice, and I'd named it Jude, after the girl who had changed everything for me on my travels through Africa. Who knows, without Jude I might not have pursued a career in development, which means I might not have gone to Nepal, which means I might not have become so strong an endurance cyclist, which means I might not be where I am today. It was another reason why coming to South Africa felt significant. I was back in the land of Jude. After a couple of years' radio silence, I reconnected with her. Only by email, though – she lives in the middle of nowhere, north of Johannesburg, where she works in environmental education.

Jude (the bike) and I got off to a good start. Ironman South Africa is not known as a particularly fast course, so when I came home for the win in 8hr 33min 56sec I was euphoric. I'd improved my official world record by more than two minutes! Not bad for the first race of the season! Most pleasing was my marathon, which was the fastest of the day – of either sex. This was a serious achievement, considering the strength of the field. The men's winner, local boy Raynard Tissink, had come fifth at Kona six months earlier and here broke the course record. I came eighth overall.

My run was now consistently on a par with the men. I had been making dramatic progress. Finally fixing my hamstring was a huge part of it, but Dave had also started setting me treadmill sessions. This was something I had never done before, so I was initially averse to it. I'm still not entirely sure what the rationale behind it is, but that very fact alone shows that I trusted him. Although I had made no gains on the bike, which had been my strongest discipline, this improvement in my running had been so significant that I had to be excited by it. It meant I could now start to contemplate facing Mirinda Carfrae in a straight shoot-out on the marathon. The imperative to beat her on the bike was no longer quite so pressing.

I returned to the UK in high spirits. April was already shaping up to be a great month, and at the end of it I had The Wedding to look forward to. Yes, 29 April 2011, as for many British people, had been circled on the calendar for some time. My invitation to the big event had been sitting proudly on the mantelpiece. They'd even asked me to do a reading. I was so excited.

First, though, I went home to Norfolk and spent my days catching up with people. There was the BRAT Club's tenth anniversary ball to attend as well, where I presented Paul Robertshaw with an award. That was an emotional moment; after all he'd done for me – introducing me to the sport, selling me my first bike and finding me my first coach, Tim Weeks.

I was reunited with Tom, who had been in the UK the previous few months. He had taken a job with TYR as a sales manager. Although Ironman Arizona had gone well for him at the end of last year, talks with TYR were well advanced, and he decided to take the new job and try to combine it with his training. He loved the work, but it was full-time, and it quickly became obvious that it was incompatible with the lifestyle of a professional athlete. So, with regret on both sides, he tendered his resignation and we made plans to go to Boulder in early May.

But first there was The Wedding. We took a room in the Holiday Inn on the A1 just outside Barnet. While we were getting ready, we were able to watch, as a kind of warm-up, the televised coverage of some other wedding, which was taking place in London that day at Westminster Abbey.

But the main event was my brother's. Matty and Kelly were married in a lovely little church in Stanstead St Margarets in Hertfordshire. The reception was at Hatfield House. It was a truly wonderful day. To see my brother and his bride so happy brought me such joy. Matty looked a million dollars in the middle of it all, so confident and charismatic. And now with a gorgeous wife!

We lost ourselves in a bubble of family and celebrations, which carried on over to lunch the next day. It meant that Tom and I returned to Boulder on 1 May full of the joys and ready to take on anything.

May is usually when the weather in Boulder starts to warm up. Not so this year. There was torrential rain day after day from the moment we arrived.

After two weeks, this was still going strong. One Saturday, I was out on my long ride and only three or four minutes from home. I was in the time-trial position, with my arms on the bars. Unbeknown to me, the sleeve of my rain jacket had become caught on the armrest. When I lifted my arm to sit up on the bike, the sleeve jolted my handlebars, my bike flipped and I hit the deck. Hard. Muppet!

My hip was badly bruised, and I had broken a rib. My next race, Ironman 70.3 Kansas, was in four weeks' time.

I have written elsewhere on the subject of how a good, conscientious athlete should deal with injury. If I remember rightly, the gist of it is, above all else, rest.

Well, do as I say, not as I do. Here I was again, pushing the envelope. I was on the turbo-trainer the next day. That was relatively painless, other than getting on and off it. I needed Tom's help for that. But swimming was a different matter. For a week or so, I couldn't swim more than two lengths because of the pain. Still, I gave it a good go. Soon, I was putting myself through four kilometres' worth of pain in the pool. And running was hard. I did all my run training before Kansas on the elliptical. Despite the suboptimal preparation, the race went well. For the third year in a row I trotted down the Yellow Brick Road in first place.

Back in Boulder, it was time to focus on regaining full fitness for Challenge Roth in four weeks' time. No more stupid pratfalls. Not even I could keep having them. Surely.

A week later, I was heading out on an hour-long run on a trail close to our house. I like trail running, but there's no doubt it doesn't suit my accident-prone nature, and I prefer not having to look down at my feet the whole time. So much so that on this occasion I made a conscious decision: 'I'm fed up with watching my step,' I said to myself. 'I'm bloody well going to look up and enjoy the scenery.' Muppet!

Barely a few yards into my run, I tripped on a rock and went flying. Out came my hands to brace myself for impact. I had a nasty gash on one of my legs and surface wounds on the other and on my elbows. I decided to carry on and attracted some dodgy looks from other runners, what with the blood dripping from my elbows and down my legs. After a quick shower I went for a swim, but my wrist really started to hurt. The next day it hurt again in the pool, and when I went for a ride in the afternoon it was so painful I simply couldn't operate the bike.

We were about fifteen minutes into the ride – me, Tom, Dion, Matty Reed and his wife – and I had to stop. In tears, I told them I couldn't do it. I turned round and took myself off to hospital for an x-ray.

Tom said to Matty on the ride: 'Chrissie will go to hospital now and find out that she's broken her wrist. And, when I get home, she'll be on the turbo.'

That's exactly what happened. I had two little fractures in my right wrist, just where I'd broken it the year before. It didn't need a cast, but they gave me a splint. Riding outdoors was impossible for a week. Swimming was very painful. I wore a wrist guard while running.

But I never doubted I would race. By the time I left for Germany, the wrist was a lot better, although dragging my bike box was painful. It was the disruption to my preparation that worried me most. I had barely done any cycling outdoors since my first fall mid-May. Most of my running had been on the elliptical. There had been precious little swimming at all. And, as always at Roth, everyone was talking about world records. I was feeling the pressure. I couldn't see how I could improve on my race here the previous year, where I'd set the world record. That seemed to me like the perfect race, and here I was this time, secretly carrying a broken wrist, having had my preparation disrupted by that and the broken rib I'd picked up two months earlier. Oh, and, because of roadworks, the bike leg was to be 2km longer than usual. When people talked records this time, I just smiled and said I would do my best.

It was a particularly violent swim in the canal. At Roth the best age-groupers start with the pros, so there are a lot of competitors in what is a relatively narrow stretch of water. But I was pleased with my swim – Roth is a wetsuit race, so my wrist had some support from that, and I didn't feel it once. I came out of the water in first place. I wasn't so happy with my bike, but a split of 4hr 40min 39sec was enough to keep me twelve minutes ahead of Belinda Granger in second. In terms of world-record pace, though, I was three-and-a-half minutes down on the year before.

I really went for it on the marathon. The conditions were perfect – warm and dry – and I just pushed and pushed. I later asked Dave if he'd ever had a kind of out-of-body experience during his years as an ironman, when your legs almost feel as if they're not connected to your body. He replied that he had. That was what the last 3km were like for me. I was pushing so hard that in a strange way it felt easy. My legs were so fatigued that they just didn't hurt any more. It was the first time I'd felt like that. Crowd support does wonders for you in these situations, inspiring you on when all rational thought is telling you to slow down. In so doing, it moves you onto another level of consciousness – yes, like an out-of-body experience.

I turned into the finish arena amid pandemonium. When I looked at the clock, I saw why. It was reading 8hr 17min. By the time I'd run round to the finish line and reached for the tape it said, 8hr 18min 13sec. A new world record.

I stayed down longer than usual after I'd done my Blazeman roll over the line. I was too emotional to get up. I thought last year's race had been perfect. Here, I'd shaved off another minute from my own world record. It felt even better than smashing it had. What made it so special was that I'd had to fight for it. In view of my preparation and the concomitant doubts over whether I could improve, the euphoria was all the more intense.

My marathon split was 2hr 44min 35sec. It was the second fastest of the day, behind the men's winner, Andreas Raelert. And Andreas had just annihilated the men's world record. Having stood for fourteen years, it had been broken only the weekend before by Marino Vanhoenacker at Ironman Austria, where Tom had finished in an impressive fourth place, with a 2hr 44min 48sec marathon (thirteen seconds slower, Tommy!). Marino's mark of 7hr 45min 58sec wasn't destined to last long, though. Andreas won Roth in an incredible 7hr 41min 33sec. But my marathon split was less than four minutes slower than his. I was right in there among the best men. 'The fifth man is a woman' was one of the headlines the next day. I'd come fifth overall – my best performance at a major ironman.

Roth is one of my favourite races, but I feel such pressure there, more than anywhere else. Not only do I have to try to win, but I'm also expected to break the world record. People don't ask me whether I'm going to do it; my doing it is offered as a statement. The only question is by how much. I don't have that kind of pressure in Kona. There, it's a straight race against my fellow competitors.

Contrary to popular belief, I don't receive performance bonuses from my sponsors for world records. Brett thinks I'm financially incentivised to break records, and he doesn't approve of the way I push myself to the limit in these races. He feels I should do enough just to win, to save myself for the next fight. But the next one may never come. This is the only way I know how to do it. I give everything in training, and I give everything in every race. Even if it were for a penny, I would do it that way. I couldn't live with myself if I hadn't tried my hardest. And Dave is of the same mindset. He used to race like that himself. Do justice to the training you've put in is his mantra. It's not records I chase, it's self-improvement. And that cannot be done by taking it easy.

I was as overjoyed with my race at Roth as I have ever been. It brought home to me that there is no such thing as a perfect race. However perfectly you think something has gone, there is always room for more 'perfection'. What was clear, though, was that, muppet injuries notwithstanding, I was in the shape of my life.

So everything was set for Kona. I was much more sensible in the days following Roth than I had been the year before. Tom and I returned to the same hotel in Germany. This time we really did luxuriate – no long bike rides through the mountains, and then, when we returned to America, no two-hour workouts with a high-class marathon runner. With Kona three short months away, and acutely mindful of what had happened the year before, I was determined not to leave myself open to illness or fatigue. The injuries that had blighted my preparations for Roth had cleared up, and, as July turned to August and August to September, everything was in place. In August, I'd won Timberman 70.3 for the fourth year running. I was ready – and itching – to mount the mother of all assaults on that famously punishing course in the lava fields. This meant that, barring any mishaps before then or on the course itself, if anyone wanted to beat me they were going to have to produce something spectacular.

Barring any mishaps? I should have known better. Maybe I should make another joke here about Muppet, but no, I really don't feel inclined even now to make a joke about what happened next, so close did it come to ruling me out of Kona for a second year running.

It was a beautiful day in Boulder, Saturday 24 September, exactly two weeks before the race. Everything had been going so well; my spirits were high. Tom and I had been for a 5km swim in the morning. On the way back from the pool, I'd spoken to my mum and dad on the phone: 'Everything's great! We're just off for a ride. See you next week in Hawaii!'

There were five of us heading out on our bikes – me, Tom, Drew Scott (Dave's son, who was preparing for his first Kona), Curt Chesney and Sam Rix. We then met Tyler and Nikki Butterfield at the first set of lights, which swelled our number to seven.

Nikki and I were at the front, chatting away, taking the usual route out of Boulder. I know it like the back of my hand. Nikki and I were talking about her success in a recent race and the importance of bike-handling skills. I was musing about how crap mine were. I felt my weak cornering and descending had cost me time in Roth, where my bike split had been relatively disappointing.

As we were talking we approached a corner ourselves. It's one I've taken hundreds of times. There was a car at the junction, so we took it at a sensible speed. I was up on the hoods (sitting upright). It was a dry day. I turned to the left.

Suddenly, I was on the floor in agony. It happened too quickly for me to be able to impose much order on the feelings and thoughts that rushed through my mind or on the chain of events that had led to this crumpled, bloody mess on the road. My first thought was 'Kona'. Thereafter, they came thick and fast. Why am I on the floor? I'd taken out Drew's bike, and he'd come down hard, too. And then the pain kicked in. I cried out in agony and despair. I felt sure my elbow was fractured. My hip had taken a pounding and felt much the same way. My ankle had twisted awkwardly out of my now broken pedal. Cuts and grazes don't hurt initially, but I could see vicious wounds from my left ankle up my leg to the hip, and on my hands and elbow. My cycling shorts were torn and my shoes scuffed.

Within a few seconds I was surrounded by my biking partners and a group of onlookers. Tom had gone off ahead to 'use the facilities' and wasn't there. Somebody pointed out that my front tyre was flat. It wasn't pancake flat, and I had felt nothing on the long straight that preceded this corner, but that had to have been the cause for the crash. Taking this corner was a simple manoeuvre I'd executed countless times before and often much faster. Maybe someone with better handling skills could have righted the bike once it had started to slide, but I couldn't. It just happened too quickly.

A mother and daughter were passing by in their car and stopped to help. The mother, a lady called Heidi, was dressed in her pyjamas. A little earlier, her daughter, Karen, had swung by unexpectedly in her new car and persuaded Heidi to come for a ride.

'But I'm still in my pyjamas!'

'Doesn't matter! No one's going to see you! You'll be in the car!'

Little did Heidi know that not only would people see her in her pyjamas but she would end up in a book! Karen and Heidi were wonderful and drove me to hospital. Nikki escorted me, with Tom racing to meet us there once he'd returned to the scene to find out why nobody had caught up with him.

I was x-rayed extensively. Nothing was broken. 'Are you sure?' I asked the doctor. The pain was so intense, far worse than the injuries I'd suffered earlier in the year, both of which had been fractures. But the results were clear. I wept with relief and knew then that I was going to be racing at Kona, come what may. How I would do it, I had no idea.

I was in quite a mess. The abrasions, or 'road rash' as we cyclists call it, were really nasty. It wasn't just a graze, they'd said at the hospital. The top layer of skin had been taken off. It was the equivalent of a second- or third-degree burn. They applied anaesthetic to the wounds, which was excruciating, and then they scrubbed them, before wrapping them in bandages.

I rang my parents for the second time that day. 'You know how I said I was going for a ride . . . ?'

Their first thought must have been about another futile (and expensive) trip to Hawaii, but they never mentioned it. I was the one who brought it up.

'Don't worry,' I said. 'I'll be racing.'

'You just get yourself better,' said Dad. 'We can talk about that later.'

There was no way I was going to let my parents down this time, or any of the other friends and family who were making the trip. Not after last year. I was going to be on that start line, whatever it took.

The next day I didn't feel too bad. I walked to Dave's house to see Drew. The poor guy had broken the navicular bone in his wrist. He was racing in his first ironman in two weeks – at Kona, the scene of his father's greatest triumphs – and here he was, nursing an injury.

The day after that, though, was when it hit me like a truck. I woke up feeling very nauseous. I was going to go for a swim that morning. Tom took one look at me and told me to go back to bed. I did nothing that day, and my leg started to swell up and turn bright red. By the next morning there was a red vein-like line branching out from my knee to my groin, a sure sign of infection. I went to Flatirons for a swim and managed two lengths. It was excruciating. The sensation was the same as when my broken arm had become infected the year before – a deep, throbbing, pounding pain. I had to be lifted out of the pool, whereupon I sat by the side in tears. I couldn't walk, so they got me some crutches, and I hobbled inside to lie on a sofa. They covered me with a blanket because I was overcome with fever and chills, hot and cold. Eventually, Tom and Dave carried me out to the car. There were eleven days to go . . .

The antibiotics I was prescribed worked well. The infection had spread throughout my leg, but the next day I was well enough to do a two-hour session on the turbo. Over those few days, I was on a rollercoaster of fear and hope. There were times when I felt much better ('Tom, I'm fine! I'll be racing!') and others when I despaired ('Tom, my body's a wreck. How on earth . . . ?'). His reply was unfailingly supportive. My fitness hadn't gone anywhere; my strength hadn't gone anywhere. I'd done all the hard work. I should appreciate the extra rest. We would get me to that start line.

Tom was preparing for the biggest race of his life, his first Kona, and now he was having to look after me as well as himself. Preparing for any race is an emotionally tense time. You're on edge, and butterflies flutter in the pit of your stomach. For me to throw this spanner in the works made me feel insanely guilty. I'd taken Drew down with me physically; now there was the danger that my crash might affect Tom's race as well.

I was meant to fly to Kona the Wednesday after the crash, but my leg was pussy and swollen, and I couldn't move my elbow properly, so couldn't carry anything. I changed my flight to Friday, then again to Saturday – better to stay in Boulder near the army of wonderful professionals treating my various ailments than to head off to humid Hawaii. By Saturday, the infection had gone and I flew, but my wounds weren't healing. This was troubling everybody, and I received conflicting advice. To cover or not to cover? For the most part I opted for the former and kept it moist.

But the road rash was the least of my worries. The skin pain I could handle. It smarts like crazy when the sweat or the piss dribbles into the wounds, but it is a superficial pain. Far worse had been the night sweats and the fever of my infection, and the bruising to the hip and elbow. The hip, in particular, was becoming a problem because I was compensating for it with an altered gait, which was transferring discomfort to my right leg. For the most part though, I was able to run and bike. It was my swim training that was severely compromised.

As the plane came in to land at Kona Airport, I looked out over the volcano. I could see the Queen K. snaking its way through the lava fields and I felt the excitement rise up in me. For a split-second, I forgot my injuries and was moved by that naked instinct for the race. Even when I remembered my condition, I thought, 'I still have a week to get ready for this. Then bring it on!'

It was a beautiful day in Hawaii. Arriving felt just as special as it had ever done – that special smell, that unique feel about the place. John and Linda greeted me in the traditional fashion, placing a lei around my neck. Then it was back to theirs for a delicious ahi tuna steak, another tradition, with Tom.

At this point I felt very relaxed, but true to current form that changed very suddenly. My leg was starting to swell up again due to the flight and the road rash was causing me pain. That evening I was building my bike in the garage of the condominium. A journalist appeared at the door and asked if she could take my photograph. I was by then suffering a turn for the worse and felt as if my personal space was being invaded. I said no. She was decidedly unimpressed with my reply, but she left. Suddenly, everything seemed wrong, and I broke down in tears again. Somehow, for a moment, it felt as if the very fabric of my beloved Hawaii had become corrupted, as if even this perfect haven of positive energy was turning against me. The doubts and fears flared up again, the questions crowded in – how was I going to do this? I lost my temper with Tom for no reason and threw myself on the bed to cry. That was the way it was in the fortnight between my injury and the race – the days were peppered with wicked little about-turns in my state of mind.

Over the coming days people started arriving from the UK – my cousins, Rob and Tim with their partners, and on Monday my parents. Mum and Dad brought out some morale-boosting items. I had about thirty-five handwritten messages of support from the children at Feltwell Primary School. Georgie had driven to meet my parents at the Travelodge in Heathrow to hand over a cushion that she'd made for me. On the front it read, 'Go, Girl!', and on the back, 'road rash rocks'. And, of course, Mum had brought me a pot of Marmite.

Training-wise things were OK on the road, although my hip was still very painful and the raised levels of sweat in Hawaii made my flesh wounds sting horribly. My swim training, however, had been virtually non-existent. My elbow was by now feeling better, but there was no power in that arm.

On the Monday, I went for a 4km swim, my first hard session in the water since the crash. Towards the end my pectoral muscle was hurting badly, and it continued to deteriorate over the course of the day. I went for a ride that afternoon. It felt as if someone was stabbing me with a needle just above the left breast and into the underarm. Deep breathing was excruciating, as was riding on the hoods. Fortunately, that day Dr Mike Leahy arrived, whom I owe more than I could ever repay. He is an ironman athlete himself and has pioneered a technique called Active Release Therapy. Since the accident, one of the upper ribs, although not broken, had become misaligned. Mike treated it, and now started to work on what he said was a damaged pectoral muscle. I went to bed that night in huge discomfort. I couldn't lie on my left side anyway, because of the abrasions, but now I couldn't roll over at all.

The next day I was on the treadmill, which was fine as long as I didn't breathe too deeply. Then I went for a swim. I managed a kilometre, by which time I was crying into my goggles. The pain was unbearable. Tom lifted me out of the pool. I was convinced I'd broken my rib. Every breath hurt and I couldn't move my arm properly. I was in agony. That was to be my last swim before the race, which was now only four days away.

I called Mike, and he told me to go straight to hospital. He thought it was muscular, but he didn't want to keep treating it if it turned out to be a fracture. I drove to ER and was met there by John and Linda (I kept this latest development from anybody else, including my friends and family who had flown so far to watch me race). I was seen by Dr Richard McDowell, whose wife, Lesley, has won her age group at Kona eleven times. His first concern was actually my leg, which was still swollen from the flight.

'It shouldn't be like that,' he said. 'I need to test for a pulmonary embolism.'

I spent the next six hours in hospital, undergoing x-rays, CT scans and tests. I felt confident it wasn't a pulmonary embolism, and the CT scans and ECG came back clear. However, there had been significant damage done to my pec and intercostal muscles. I was not allowed to swim before the race – not that I would have been able to, even if I'd wanted. They also undid my bandages to check my wounds. John and Dr McDowell recoiled at the smell when the bandages were removed. My wounds were scraped clean, scrubbed and redressed. I was prescribed a new course of antibiotics.

The final few days were hard and beset by doubt. The road rash wasn't healing. I spent another hour in hospital on the Wednesday with Hawaii's leading wound specialist, who redressed my lesions once again. But road rash was the least of my worries. The pectoral injury was the biggest concern, followed by the hip. The elbow, however, was a lot better. I never doubted I would race, once the results of those first x-rays had made clear there was no break, and Mike reinforced that. Each day my condition was improving with his help and that of my acupuncturist, Allison. It was going to hurt, but by Saturday I would be able to race. To have medical professionals like that around me in the build-up was so important and a privilege that I appreciate is not available to most athletes at Kona. The added confidence their treatment and words inspired played a huge role in getting me to the start line, as did the endless support of Tom and Dave.

Would I be able to win? That was the question I was reluctant to confront. If I could just get through the swim and come out of it not doubled up in pain, then I reckoned I could contend, but there were so many unknowns. I hadn't been in the ocean at all. I wouldn't be swimming again until race day. I just had no idea how I was going to fare. And then there are all the other discomforts that unfold over an ironman at the best of times. Given my condition, how much more painful were they going to be? I just hoped that my mind would stay strong enough to cope. Because if it didn't it would be time to confront the biggest fear of all – the fear of losing an ironman.

Suffice it to say, I was the least confident I have ever been going into a race. At the press conference on the Thursday I played down my injuries as being little more than road rash, but the journalists picked up on a more apprehensive, less bullish air about me. They were right to. Still, I was determined to make the best of it and in a strange way it took some of the pressure off.

Friday was a good day. It has become a Wellington tradition to hold a lunchtime barbecue the day before the race at the complex of condominiums where my parents stay. I came down for twenty minutes or so. John and Linda had organised for a local spiritual leader to give a blessing and a welcome to everyone. Scott Rigsby was there, as were Mary Ann and Bob Blais, parents of Jon, so I had plenty of reminders to put into context the struggle I would face the next day. My spirits were high in the company of my friends and family. It brought home how differently I was feeling from the same time the year before. At the Wellington barbecue then I had been distracted, as the first clear signs of illness were taking hold. This time I felt almost at ease. I was going to give it everything the next day. Let the cards fall where they may.

Later that afternoon I racked my bike. There is always a degree of hoopla surrounding this process – journalists, the public and competitors crowd around the transition area, taking photos and inspecting bikes. The leading professional women are numbered from 101 onwards, according to ranking. Over the previous three years, I had grown accustomed to number 101. This year I was to wear 102. I set up next to the tiny little steed of Mirinda Carfrae, the new holder of bib 101. Again, it made me think back to the year before. There was a poignant photograph published in 2010 of my bike standing alone in transition after the others had gone. As I racked my bike this time – the bike I'd crashed nearly two weeks earlier, the bike I'd now given the name of Phoenix – I said to it, 'I really hope that tomorrow you're not left standing alone.'

By now, though, I was feeling confident. I was not without pain, but my spirit was on an upward flight. I felt the passion and determination coursing through me again.

I slept well that night and rose to perform my usual routine on race morning. I didn't have a shower because I didn't want to get my wounds any wetter than they had to be, and I applied antibiotic ointment to each one, but otherwise it was business as usual. I had decided to race with my wounds uncovered, other than the one on the hip, which would be rubbed by my race suit without some kind of protection. I had my breakfast of hot rice cereal and a mug of coffee. I read the countless emails of support I'd received. I read the cards I carry round as inspiration. I read 'If'. It would be a lie to say I was brimming with confidence – you always suffer doubt when you are not fully fit – but I was determined.

My biggest frustration was that I wasn't going to be able to do justice to the work I'd put in. I had been in the best shape of my life before the crash. I knew that in that shape, although no one is ever guaranteed victory, I was primed to break records. And yet now, with the injuries and preparation I'd had, I might not be able to give much more than 60 per cent, physically. I'd worked so hard that year, and the knowledge that I wouldn't be able to show just how much ate away at me. I was fearful that I might not even be able to show anything at all. And I was nervous, pure and simple, about the pain that I knew awaited me.

John took Tom and me down to the King Kam Hotel, where we went through body marking and the weigh-in. I was 136 pounds, which I felt was a little more than I should have been.

When I took to the water, the sun had yet to rise. It was with some trepidation that I waded in. This was the first time I'd ventured into seawater since the accident. To my relief, the cuts didn't hurt too badly My pec hurt, and there was hardly any power in my left arm, but I felt calm.

The ocean at dawn has always had this effect on me in Kona. The race has yet to start, but you have passed the point of no return. A tranquillity descends briefly as you step away from the craziness of life on the shore in race week and await the imminent fracas in the ocean when the canon fires – the calm between the storms.

I tried to find somewhere that gave me as much space as possible. It was important to minimise the chances of being hit on the elbow. I was resigned to my fate now. This was going to hurt and I was going to have a slow swim. In hindsight, I might have become too resigned and let it become a self-fulfilling prophecy. Dave had advised me to err on the side of caution in the water. But maybe I should have gone for my usual aggressive start; then again, maybe I would have broken down if I had. Who knows? Either way, I held back.

The first 200 yards of an ironman are key for establishing your position in the faster packs, but when the canon sounded I let those swimmers get away. You never know how fast your pack is swimming until you get out of the water, but I sensed that my pace was slower than usual. I was comfortable though. I felt nothing like the excruciating pain I'd experienced on Tuesday. I recognised the strokes and swimsuits of Cat Morrison and Jo Lawn nearby, so I was in good company, but I knew this wasn't a great swim. Once you're in a pack there's nothing you can do to bridge to another, which is why those first 200 yards are so crucial. I didn't panic. 'You're doing your best,' I kept telling myself, 'you're doing your best'. I was just thankful it wasn't hurting as much as I'd feared it would. My chances of at least finishing the race had improved dramatically.

I came out of the water in a time of sixty-one minutes, by far my slowest swim at Kona. But the sea had been choppy so all the swims were a bit slower. When I reached my bike I saw that Rinny's had gone, as had most of the others. It wasn't quite the lone bike of the year before, but it was clear that I was some way down. Then I heard I was nine minutes behind Julie Dibens, the leader, and four behind Rinny. Oh dear, it really hadn't been a very good swim at all. But my heart didn't drop, because you know it's a long day.

At the start of the bike at Kona you do an out and back before heading out onto the Queen K., so I was able to see for myself how far behind I was. People were already coming back as I was heading out. It was disconcerting to be so far down so early, but I kept thinking of Kipling. Just keep your head, keep your head. As always, the words of 'If' were written all over my water bottles. And I did keep my head. I surprise myself in race situations. In everyday life I am a worrier, but in a race I'm a lot calmer and more rational than people who know me might expect.

It turned out that I was in seventeenth place among the women. Soon, I was making my way through the field. Nothing too spectacular, but I kept up a steady pace. You are fed splits throughout the race, but they are unreliable and often inconsistent. Nevertheless, a clear dynamic was emerging. Julie was cycling like a bat out of hell.

She was streaking ahead of everyone. Karin Thuerig, who was behind me, was also making time. Karin is an Olympic time-trial medallist who had broken the women's record for the bike course the year before, so her speed was to be expected. So was Julie's, but her case was more interesting. Julie has been managing a foot condition for years. She had to retire from Olympic-distance triathlon because of it. They inserted a metal plate between two of her toes. With the extra mileage in ironman racing and training, her condition has deteriorated. Four weeks earlier, she'd had to drop out of the Ironman 70.3 World Championships in Las Vegas because of it. I'd been worrying about my injuries all week and marvelling at how fit and threatening everyone else had looked on the training beat in Kona. But it's easy to forget that, at this stage of the season, many of your competitors might not be as fit as they look. Julie and I had had a chat before we'd left Boulder the week before, confiding in each other about our respective injuries. When we left, she said: 'I'll see you on the Big Island. And, remember, I'll have my game face on.'

This was some game face. She'd stretched her lead over me to ten minutes in the first five miles of the bike. By the time she'd got to Hawi, she had fifteen minutes on me. Yet, the faster she went the less I worried. It was as if she had nothing to lose, a reflection, perhaps, of her concern that she might not be able to finish. Rinny was the one I had my eye on. Dave was also convinced that she remained the one to beat. I was gradually gaining on her and most of the other girls. My confidence was rapidly improving. I felt relatively comfortable. Niggles were developing all over – my hip ached, and a pain had developed on the inside of my knee, where I had banged a pre-existing calcification in the crash – but nothing was threatening to derail me yet. I tried to get up on the hoods and open up my hips and my back. I threw water over my head to cool down in the heat, which was now, by mid-morning, up past 80°F.

Suddenly, I noticed Rinny up ahead. I hadn't realised it was her until I saw the 101 on her back as we headed up to the turnaround at Hawi. I didn't hang about to chat. There was a headwind, which I always enjoy as it is the equivalent to a steeper hill, and I put my head down to push further ahead into it. Tom came past me on the way down from Hawi, which gave me a lift, and soon I could see for myself where the lead girls were. It was still some way ahead of me. Julie had extended her lead. Some ten minutes behind her were Rachel Joyce, my old friend from the swimming club at Birmingham Uni, and Caroline Steffen, now one of Brett's girls and a former professional cyclist. Caroline, in particular, was on the move and the only girl, other than Julie and Karin, who was cycling faster than me.

As you enter the town of Hawi, the terrain changes from stark lava field to something quite lush. You know you're getting there because palm trees start appearing. Then you turn a corner and confront the Wellington crew. I don't remember any faces, but I just sensed this wall of sound and banners along the side of the road. I headed back down into the lava fields with renewed vigour.

Karin caught me a few miles further on. We vied with each other for a bit, but she eventually pulled away. Meanwhile, the splits coming from Julie were astonishing. If they were to be believed, which it turned out they were, she was now getting on for twenty minutes ahead of me. She was racing at a near-suicidal pace. It didn't disconcert me. I am fully aware of how determined she is, but I knew she had run 3hr 27min at her last ironman, so even if she finished the race I reckoned I could give her the best part of half an hour and still hope to catch her, as long as my own run held up.

I rode alone along the rest of the Queen K. to Kona for a bike split of 4hr 56min 53sec. Not as fast as I would have wanted, but a race against the clock had long ago ceased to be relevant. This was now a race against the five girls ahead of me, and the one lurking a couple of places behind who was the only one who had run faster here than I had. Mind you, these days I reckoned my run was on a par with

Rinny's – but after the crash that might no longer hold.

One thing was for sure, injury or not, the days when I could expect to get off the bike with a comfortable lead at Kona were gone. Julie, Caroline and Karin had all come to the party in Hawaii the year before when I was unable to race, and these girls could ride. The dynamic had changed. I would have to get used to chasing.

I flew through transition and out on to the marathon. Right then I felt that winning this thing was a genuine possibility. Julie was nearly twenty-two minutes ahead of me; Rinny was nearly three-and-a-half minutes behind. I had to make hay, and I tore into the run. If I faded, so be it, but this was the time to make my play.

Physically, things were as good as I could have expected, but that was still a long way short of perfect. The abrasions hadn't been a problem. They'd stung whenever I'd had a pee on the bike, but otherwise they were fine. My hip, though, had been in constant pain. Now, as I belted out onto Ali'i Drive my hamstrings were seizing up as well.

Immediately, people were shouting encouragement at me. 'Chrissie, you look the strongest! The others are fading already!'

The out and back on Ali'i Drive, which constitutes the first ten miles of the marathon, is hard. It's very hot and humid, and there's no wind. If I could set out my stall here without overdoing it, that would give the others something to think about.

I saw my family at mile three and gave them a smile, but inside the pain was unbearable. There were several points in those first ten miles when I thought I wasn't going to make it. Do I quit? Do I quit? I had a demon on one shoulder and an angel on the other. 'Quit, quit, quit,' said one; 'No, it'll pass, it'll pass,' said the other. On my wristband, I had my motto: 'Never ever give up – and smile!' There wasn't so much of the latter this time, but neither was there any of the former. That Lance Armstrong quote was going round in my head as well: 'Pain is temporary; quitting lasts for ever.' I had those two voices arguing across my head, the angel and the demon, but the angel's was stronger.

Pain on a marathon is nothing new. In Roth that year, when I ran 2hr 44min, the first few miles had been hard. You know that there will be ebbs and flows, and you have to hold on to the knowledge that you have been there before and come through it. You can't latch onto the pain; somehow you must switch that part of your brain off and go into automatic pilot. I'm good at that, it's one of the keys to success, but, even so, this was the worst I'd ever known. You are going to hurt like hell, I said to myself, because this is just the start.

I caught Karin very early on. Then I heard from the spectators that Julie was walking. My first feeling, in all honesty, was sadness. All I wanted Julie to do was to finish, albeit shuffling along and just slow enough for me to catch her! I didn't want her to be going through the pain that I knew she was fearful of suffering and now clearly was. She's a good friend, and the news made me sad. But this is war, and you can't have too much sympathy for your competitors.

I turned around on Ali'i Drive to more reports of labouring athletes. On the way back I crossed Rinny, who was still on the way out. There was focus and determination in her face; her mouth was set in a hard line. I overtook Julie at an aid station a little further on. She'd stopped and conceded defeat. She had clocked a phenomenal 4hr 44min 14sec for the bike, which would have been a new women's record if she'd finished, but that foot just wasn't going to carry her through the marathon. A few miles further on, I overtook Rachel and offered a few words of encouragement. Now I was in third, with only Caroline and Leanda Cave ahead of me.

It ended up being the fastest first half of a marathon I've ever produced at Kona – 1hr 22min – and I'd stretched my lead over Rinny to five minutes. I passed Leanda at around the thirteen-mile point and continued along the Queen K. to the infamous Energy Lab, the island's renewable-energy centre, where we turn and head for home. The course is undulating here, and my pace slowed as the pain increased in the blistering heat, but I felt relatively strong, helped by a cooling breeze. Caroline was within my sights, and I knew my race was with Rinny now, who was gaining on me. At the entrance to the Energy Lab, I overhauled Caroline. At last, I had the lead.

From there, you head down the hill to the ocean and run along the shore, then turn round and begin the climb out of 'The Lab'. The heat is intense here and has been recorded at well over a hundred degrees. Energy is a precious commodity indeed, as you try to haul yourself back out onto the Queen K. On the way back I crossed the other lead girls. There was Rinny, looking strong, about a kilometre behind me – in other words, four minutes.

There is a stretch of roughly five miles along the Queen K. before you head down the hill into Kona and the finish line. I was fading badly for the last mile or so where the highway rises before the descent. It was not so much the physical energy, although my legs were seizing up again, it was the mental energy that I'd expended earlier in the run just to keep myself on course. Now I was hearing that Rinny was gaining fast. People were trying to tell me that she had made up a minute on me in the last mile. That's not possible at this stage of the race, I said to myself, just keep doing what you're doing. One foot in front of the other. It later turned out those reports had been exaggerated. When I made it over the brow of the hill, I had something like a three-minute lead over her with around three miles to go, about half of which was downhill. Unless I started walking, she wasn't going to catch me.

The familiar landmarks now tumbled past. You will the finish line to arrive, but you also don't want it to come because you want to savour every second. I let momentum carry me down the hill into the thick crowds, whose cheers sweep you along the final mile round town.

I was emotionally spent, virtually delirious. What have you done?

I kept asking myself. What have you done? I'd had an email from Matt Hawcroft, an old training partner from the BRAT club, before the race. If I could finish, he'd said, it would be amazing. If I could win, 'It would be epic. It would be beyond epic.'

That's what this was. I'd overcome more than I ever could have imagined. I rounded the corner onto Ali'i Drive for the last time. The crowds were screaming, there was the huge Banyan tree and the conch shells were sounding. The Hawaiians in their native dress were running ahead to welcome me home. This was like 2007 all over again. I was flabbergasted, baffled – this wasn't in the script, it was beyond my wildest dreams. I hadn't had such depth of feeling in 2008 and 2009 – not that those results had been expected, but both had been very real possibilities. Here I'd defied what even I had thought possible. I didn't know where a fourth win put me on the all-time list of triathletes, and I didn't care. I cared about the manner of the victory. I'd defied all the odds. It was worth a thousand ironman wins. People had questioned whether I would have the composure to win at Kona if things didn't go according to plan, whether I had the strength of spirit to fight if I ever found myself miles behind, rather than miles out in front. With this win I hope I showed them.

I approached the finishing tape, the usual bundle of smiles and tears, but there was an edge of delirium this time. I was at the end of my tether. I had nothing more to give. I reached for the tape and held it over my head, swaying with exhaustion. When I went to lie down so that I could perform my Blazeman roll over the line, nearby officials went to help me, thinking I was collapsing. They weren't far wrong, but I waved them off, and when I'd finished my roll I lay on my back sobbing and laughing. Eventually, those concerned officials helped me to my feet. Another Hawaiian in native dress came to place the winner's lei around my neck and the wreath on my head, just as Dad arrived to embrace me, followed swiftly by Mum. I kissed and hugged a perfect bundle of leaves and parents. Mum, Dad and my beloved crown, back in my arms again.

Then Tom arrived with a towel round his shoulders, fresh from his first Kona, which he'd finished in a brilliant eleventh place. When he held me, I wept freely and my empty legs nearly went from beneath me. If they had, he would have taken the strain. Dave was there, too. He and Tom knew what I'd been through. They'd carried me out of the club the week before when I'd been unable to walk, let alone cover 140.6 miles. Dave knew what that win meant; to share it with those two heroes meant more than I can say. And Drew, Dave's son, was out there on the course. He, too, had got up from that crash two weeks earlier and raced at Kona, despite the broken bone in his wrist. He has his father's determination, and his talent.

For the first time in my life, they put me on an intravenous drip after the race because I was so dehydrated. The medics were insistent and took me away to the medical tent, where I spent half an hour. They bandaged my wounds and weighed me. I was 128 pounds now – eight pounds lighter than I had been that morning. My pee looked like beetroot juice. I thought it was blood, but they assured me it was severe dehydration. So I headed to the swimming pool at the King Kam to meet the Wellington crew and replenish myself. Mum and Dad were in tears, my cousins Tim and Rob were in tears, I was in tears. This was where my story had begun, among loved ones. This is where it will always return.

It was the proudest moment of my career, the culmination of this unlikeliest of journeys I'd taken over the previous five years. I'd always said I'd wanted that 'iron war' – to be forced to take myself to the very brink and give everything I have to the sport I love. Rinny, Julie, Caroline and the girls had forced me to dig to unexplored depths, and for that I owe them so much.

But the other, more visceral war I'd fought was against the simple desire to give up. What a fight I'd waged with that! Physically, I'd probably been able to give 80 per cent, but mentally I gave every last morsel of the full 100. I wasn't fully fit for this race, yet I'd survived it on something other than physical aptitude. This was no technical masterclass. This was blood and grit, a war of attrition. My mind could have given up on me at so many stages, and I just would not let it. For that reason alone, this win, this most cathartic regaining of my crown, will stand as the ultimate accolade of my career.

Epilogue

Thirteen is an unlucky number for some, and so it nearly proved for me. Kona 2011 was my thirteenth ironman. I did indeed suffer some cruel luck two weeks before it. Then again, maybe coming off my bike that day was the stroke of luck I needed. I ended up having the race I'd always dreamed of, the race where I summoned up every last flicker of a fight from my body and soul. I discovered at last what it was to be taken to the brink.

Of course, it would be the height of vainglory for anyone to imagine they were indestructible – had my injuries been much worse, I wouldn't have been able to race – but it's all too easy, as well, to accept lying down as your only option, or even just standing still. No one should ever be afraid of failing; it's being afraid to give it your all in trying that I urge against. If there is one thing I have learned, particularly in my life as an athlete, it is that our limits may not be where we think they are. And, even when we think we've finally reached them, the next time we go there exploring we often find that they've moved again.

If you'd told me as a teenager preoccupied by notions of body image that within five years I would be representing the UK Government at a UN summit, I would never have believed you. If you had told me at the UN summit that within five years I would be a world champion I would have dismissed you out of hand. Even if you had told me at the finish line in Kona in 2007, that I would still be unbeaten over the ironman distance four years later with three more world titles and several world records under my belt, I would have looked at you askance. I still can't quite believe it now. I'm an ordinary girl from Norfolk, marked out by, if anything, an appetite for adventure and a will for self-improvement. These are qualities available to anyone who is of a mind to acquire them.

I have been through many changes in my life, never more so than in that first year as a professional athlete. It was hard, undoubtedly, but I reaped the rewards. I recently received an email from Brett after I'd told him I was writing this book, and his recollection brought back to me how far I have come since those first days as a rookie in Thailand in 2007:

'You were in such a hurry,' he said. 'I thought your desire to know now, your will to see the unseeable without paying your dues, was a bit rude. I knew you wouldn't hang around in triathlon beyond that year if you couldn't see a future for yourself in the sport. I think that set my mindset to give you the "full treatment". And if it broke you it did, but if you coped mentally I had no doubt that, physically, you were precocious. "Crash or crash through" was my catch phrase to myself, as I dealt out some very harsh realities. It was not easy from my end, but it was bloody hard from yours. I was brutal, and the fact you got through it amazed me. I haven't been as authoritarian since, nor have I had the desire to be.'

After Brett's crash course in how to become a champion, Dave has since finessed me to a stage where I now feel as strong as I ever have as an athlete. At the finish line in Kona 2011, my time was irrelevant, but I have since come to appreciate that, in the history of the World Championships, it was second only to the women's course record I'd set in 2009. And my marathon in 2011 was only

32sec slower than Rinny's, which was the fastest ever run by a woman at Kona.

The most recent lesson I've learned, though, is not to fall for these external measures of worth. Up until two weeks before the race, just before I had the crash, I might have felt differently. In five of my previous six ironman races I'd set a new world record, and the odd one out was the World Championships of 2009 when I'd set that new course record. In Kona 2011, I was intent on lowering it further. Things didn't turn out as planned. In the end, my time was nowhere near as fast as it could have been, but it was the best performance I have ever produced because it was the one that I finished emotionally and physically spent, with absolutely nothing more to give. That is the only measure that counts.

I have talked in the past about perfect races. I thought Roth 2010 was my perfect race. Then I thought Roth 2011 was. If Kona 2011 taught me one thing it was to look within for the real standard. You can never reach perfection. Your ambition should be directed towards your ability to overcome imperfection, and that is how I want to live my life. Trying to effect positive change has always been important to me, and that is not the same thing as chasing perfection.

Where will that process take me next? For now, I want to continue racing and eventually to test myself in other endurance challenges. But I will always want to be an ambassador for the sport I love. I want to represent the views of pros and age-groupers and to try to secure a higher profile for triathlon, better reflecting its status as one of the fastest-growing sports in the world.

More than that, though, is the desire to use well this privilege of being a world champion. It excites me to be in a position to make a difference. It excites me to see how sport can inspire people and change lives. I believe that the responsibilities of a professional sportsman or woman extend beyond their performance on the big stage. They have a role to play in shaping the health of their nations, spreading positive messages and doing their best to effect change. Not enough take that responsibility seriously. With it comes power, and you choose to use it or you waste it.

On a personal level, I want to spend more time with friends and family, and I would like to think that Tom and I will one day have more than just a bike box to call home and maybe more than just a couple of bikes to look after. Beyond that, motivational speaking and politics with a small 'p' are avenues that interest me, and if *Blue Peter* should ever be looking for a new presenter I will be first in the audition queue!

But how can I speculate on what the future holds, when the present is so astronomically removed from whatever expectations I might have had in my youth? I prefer to see my life as a tree, branching out in who knows what directions. There is never a destination, just the impulse to grow. My only policy throughout has been to keep an open mind and, whatever I may do, to give it my all. It still takes my breath away to think where that simple outlook on life has taken me, how many times I have managed to defy what I thought possible. I never set out to be a world champion – not many ordinary girls from Norfolk do – but neither have I ever wanted to be left wondering, 'What if . . . ?' To my amazement, at so many stages along the way, the limits that I thought I could see in the distance dissolved as I approached them. They turned out not to be real at all, but mere assumptions. And that has been the most exciting revelation of all.